Chinese-English Contrastive Grammar

Chinese-English Contrastive Grammar

An Introduction

David C. S. Li and Zoe Pei-sui Luk

HKU
PRESS
香港大學出版社

Hong Kong University Press
The University of Hong Kong
Pokfulam Road
Hong Kong
www.hkupress.org

ISBN 978-988-8390-85-4 (*Hardback*)
ISBN 978-988-8390-86-1 (*Paperback*)

British Library Cataloguing-in-Publication Data
A catalogue record for this book is available from the British Library.

10 9 8 7 6 5 4 3 2 1

Printed and bound by Hang Tai Printing Co., Ltd. in Hong Kong, China

Contents

Illustrations

Tables

Preface

This book is written primarily for Chinese readers who have at least some basic knowledge of English grammar, and who have attained a fairly high level of proficiency in English (roughly upper-intermediate or above). We believe this book will be a useful study companion for teachers and students specializing in a wide range of language-focused or language-related disciplines, including English, Chinese, linguistics, language information sciences, professional communication, language teaching, cultural studies, translation and interpreting, language pathology, and speech therapy. The main objective of this book is to familiarize our readers with a subset of the common difficulties encountered by Chinese learners and users of English, in Hong Kong and beyond, in ESL or EFL pronunciation and lexico-grammatical structures.[1] A second objective is to help our readers understand the ways in which the Chinese language has undergone structural changes as a result of Europeanization (especially anglicization) since the 1900s. Judging from the outcomes of such influences, some may be seen as beneficial while many more are demonstrably adverse. In scope, Europeanization is not at all limited to linguistic structures, but these structures also manifest in Chinese learners' and users' pragmatic competence and performance in their social interaction with others. Such socio-pragmatic competence (Kasper & Rose, 2002) is reflected in their choice of L1 pragma-linguistic resources when using L2, including 'pragmatic strategies such as directness and indirectness, routines, and a large range of linguistic forms which can intensify or soften communicative acts' (Kasper & Rose, 2002, p. 2). We will illustrate such interlanguage pragmatic (ILP) strategies with a couple of Chinese 'rules of speaking' when Chinese EAL learners and users are engaged in intercultural communication in English (e.g., preferring more Chinese pragma-linguistic strategies when realizing speech acts such as making requests or responding to compliments in English). We will also examine

---

1. Regarding the question, whether the status of English in Hong Kong is more appropriately characterized as a second language (ESL) or a foreign language (EFL), there is as yet no consensus among scholars (see Li, 2017, for an in-depth discussion). For our purpose in this book, we will use the term 'English as an additional language' (EAL) as a superordinate of ESL and EFL.

an apparently contrary case, namely EAL speakers' predilection for one linguistic subsystem in (especially American) English when interacting with others in Chinese or English, the adoption of an English(-sounding) first name.

The grammar of any language is a huge topic. And, given that Chinese and English are among the languages of wider communication with the largest numbers of first and/or second language learners and users in the world, to compare and contrast these two grammatical systems is an even more challenging task. In this book, we will follow Michel Paradis's characterization of language and grammar as follows:

> [Language] refers to the language system (phonology, morphology, syntax and semantics), often referred to as 'the grammar' or 'implicit linguistic competence' by contemporary linguists within the generative-grammar framework. Language is a necessary but not sufficient component of verbal communication. (Paradis, 2004, p. 240)

Thus, for our purpose, 'grammar' is used in a broad sense to include not only the morphology and syntactic structures (often referred to as 'morphosyntax') of a language but also its sound system (phonetics and phonology) and how these linguistic resources are used to make meaning when speakers/writers interact with others in context-specific situations (pragmatics). The scope of each of these research areas is huge. To make our task more manageable, the main focus of this book will be on lexico-grammatical deviations commonly found among Chinese EAL learners in the process of learning or using English (**Chapters 3–7**). This will be supplemented with a chapter on contrastive phonology between (Hong Kong) Cantonese and English (**Chapter 2**); a chapter that examines how, for over 100 years, Chinese grammar has been influenced by European languages (i.e., Europeanized) since the beginning of the twentieth century (**Chapter 8**); and a chapter on various socio-pragmatic problems, typically in intercultural communication contexts involving interaction between native and Chinese speakers of English (**Chapter 9**). As the non-standard lexico-grammatical and non-native pronunciation features (when using English) as well as socio-pragmatic choices (when using Chinese) arise from contact between English and Chinese via their speakers/writers, the problems identified in this book may be located in the contact zone of the grammars of these two languages (see Figure 0.1).

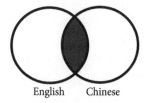

English   Chinese

Figure 0.1
The scope of Chinese-English contrastive grammar in this book

English and Chinese belong to totally unrelated language families, which is why the two languages have very little in common. A lack of similarities between English and Chinese helps explain the enormous learning difficulties on the part of Chinese learners of EAL.

English and Chinese belong to two typologically different language families, and the typological distance between them is huge. In the study of linguistic typology, languages are classified according to their structural features and functional affinities (i.e., similarities and differences), the goal being to describe and account for commonalities and diversity in the linguistic structures and functions of the world's languages. English is a Germanic language within the Indo-European family. Extending the kinship metaphor a little more, we may say that English has several cousins, of which the most prominent are German and Dutch. Also, practically all of the Scandinavian languages—Norwegian, Danish, and Swedish (but not Finnish)—are Germanic (see Crystal, 1997, for more details). The typological proximity between these languages helps explain why speakers of other Germanic languages tend to pick up English more easily, thanks to the systemic similarities in lexis and grammar between English and their native language. Similarly, English-speaking learners of French as an additional language will appreciate that many French words look like English words. The reason is that, for centuries, English has been heavily influenced by the French language. French, however, does not belong to the Germanic family; it is a prominent member within the Romance family, which includes other well-known European languages such as Spanish, Italian, and Portuguese (Crystal, 1997).

The two branches of Indo-European, Germanic and Romance, have many linguistic features in common. For instance, they all have a tense system, definite and indefinite articles, and they all distinguish between singular nouns and plural nouns. None of these features are shared by Chinese, which is a Sino-Tibetan language (Sinitic). Other Sino-Tibetan languages include Tibetan and Burmese (Tibeto-Burman) and Thai (the Tai division).[2]

The reason for going into some details of language typology here is that, for Chinese learners of English, many of the EAL learning difficulties may be accounted for by the notion of typological distance. In principle, the more linguistic features shared by the two languages in question, the easier it is for native speakers of either language to learn the other language. For instance, Ringbom (2007, p. 54) distinguishes between three levels of cross-linguistic similarity: (a) item level, (b) system level, and (c) overall level. Based on second language acquisition (SLA) data involving different language pairs, Ringbom concludes that cross-linguistic similarities such as 'item transfer' tend to facilitate language learning:

---

2. Although Japanese and Korean have borrowed and incorporated a large number of Chinese lexical items into their languages, they do not belong to the Sino-Tibetan family. It is widely believed that Korean and Japanese are Altaic languages. Such a belief would make them distant cousins of Turkish, Mongolian, and Manchu.

> Item transfer in comprehension is overwhelmingly positive: if cross-linguistic similarities between items can be perceived and established, comprehension is facilitated. Quick and effective item learning for comprehension is above all what distinguishes the learning of a related TL [target language] from learning an unrelated language. (Ringbom, 2007, p. 57)

Thus, for example, French learners of English will find in the tense system of French a convenient frame of reference when they try to make sense of the English tense system, and vice versa for English-speaking learners of French. Such convenience is not available to Chinese learners of English, however. Owing to tremendous typological differences between Chinese and English, the two languages have rather few linguistic features in common. These include subject-verb-object (SVO) basic word order, verb-particle constructions such as 'pick up' (拿起, *ná qǐ, naa4 hei2*) and 'put down' (放下, *fàng xià, fong3 haa6*), and double-object constructions like 'give me ten dollars' (給我十塊錢／畀十蚊我).[3] All of these seem to be relatively straightforward for Chinese learners and users of English, suggesting that positive transfer is taking place thanks to structural overlap between Chinese and English (Yip & Matthews, 2007).

Compared with structural similarities, however, there are many more structural disparities. One consequence is that native speakers of either language who want to learn the other language tend to come across enormous acquisitional problems. This is why Chinese learners of English tend to find it so hard to grasp, for example, the grammatical subsystems of tense and articles in English, among others (see Chapters 5 and 6; see also Li, 2017, for examples of common EAL errors). Similarly, many Westerners have tremendous difficulties mastering the tone system in Putonghua (Mandarin) or, worse still, Cantonese, mainly because tonal differences as the basis for differentiating lexical meanings are unknown in their languages (Li, Keung, Poon, & Xu, 2016).

Informed essentially by insights of research on contrastive analysis (CA), error analysis (EA), contrastive phonology (Cantonese and English), Europeanized grammatical features in Chinese, and intercultural pragmatics, this book highlights some of the salient acquisitional and communication problems encountered by Chinese learners when learning and using English (and, to a lesser extent, Chinese), with special reference to Hong Kong Chinese learners and users of English. Through systematic comparison and contrast between the relevant parts of (standard) English and (standard) Chinese/Cantonese grammar, it is hoped that the reader will better appreciate *why* certain anomalies occur and *how* to overcome them. A majority of the common learning difficulties discussed and exemplified in this book may be shown to be caused, at least in part, by adverse influence of the learner's mother tongue (i.e.,

---

3. *Gěi wǒ shí kuài qián, kap1 ngo5 sap6 faai3 cin4 / bei2 sap6 man1 ngo5.*

cross-linguistic influence or negative transfer), which in Hong Kong refers to spoken Cantonese (the vernacular) and Standard Written Chinese (SWC). Similar influence, more often adverse than conducive, may also be detected in the other direction, given that knowledge of English tends to impact negatively on Chinese speakers' or writers' native language due to 'adverse Europeanization' (非良性歐化, *fēi liángxìng ōu huā/ fei5 loeng4 sing3 au5 faa3*).

This book consists of nine chapters. At the end of each chapter there is a 'Further Reading' section pointing the way to accessible material on the main topics covered in the chapter and a list of questions or activities that are useful for reviewing the main points of the chapter. Suggested answers to these questions and activities may be found at the end of the book.

Regarding terminology, the term 'Putonghua' will be used when reference is made to the national spoken language in China. On the other hand, 'Mandarin' will be used to refer to (a) the biggest 'dialect' group in northern China (generally referred to as 北方方言, 'northern dialect', as opposed to other southern 'dialects'), or (b) the standard variety of spoken Chinese in Taiwan.

As the reader may have noticed, Chinese characters are transliterated into both Mandarin (Putonghua) and Cantonese: the former in pinyin, the latter in the romanization system devised by the Linguistic Society of Hong Kong (LSHK) called Jyutping (Tang et al., 2002). To cater for the needs of both readers who can read Chinese and others who may find romanization more convenient, each of the linguistic examples will be presented in Chinese characters, supplemented with inter-linear glosses, followed by the rendition of words at the morphemic level, plus an idiomatic translation of the example. As logographic Chinese characters may be read in either Mandarin or Cantonese, romanization in both pinyin and Jyutping will be provided (except for Cantonese-specific expressions). For highly technical, field-specific jargon in English, the Chinese equivalents will be provided but not the romanization. Finally, following common practice in applied linguistics research, an asterisk (*) placed at the beginning of an expression indicates that it deviates from the norms in Standard English, Cantonese, or SWC, while a question mark (?) at the beginning of a linguistic example signals that it is marginally acceptable.

This book grew out of our efforts in teaching an undergraduate course entitled Chinese-English Contrastive Grammar. We would like to thank our students for their feedback to an earlier draft of the manuscript prepared for that course. In the process of revising the manuscript for publication, we have also benefited from two anonymous reviewers' insightful, critical, and constructive comments, as well as useful input and instructive feedback from our colleagues Rebecca Chen, Regine Lai, and Christy Liu. Their kind assistance is hereby gratefully acknowledged. It goes without saying that, as co-authors, we alone are responsible for any inadequacies that remain.

Abbreviations

Adj	adjective
AmE	American English
ASP	aspect marker
BEI	passive marker 被 (*bèi*)
BrE	British English
CA	contrastive analysis
CL	classifier
CLI	cross-linguistic influence
DISP	disposal construction marker 把 (*baa2/bǎ*) or 將 (*zoeng1/jiāng*)
EA	error analysis
EAL	English as an additional language
EAP	English for academic purposes
EFL	English as a foreign language
English-L1	English as a first language
ESL	English as a second language
FL	foreign language
FN	first name (address system)
F.P.	final particle
GA	General American
HKE	Hong Kong English
IL	interlanguage
ILP	interlanguage pragmatics
IMPF	imperfective
IPA	International Phonetic Association
IVE	indigenized variety of English (cf. NVE)
L1	first language
L2	second language
LSHK	Linguistic Society of Hong Kong
MSC	Modern Standard Chinese
NVE	nativized variety of English (cf. IVE)

NOM	nominalizer 的 (*dik5/de*)/嘅 (*ge3*)
NP	noun phrase
NNS	non-native speaker
NS	native speaker
PERF	perfective
PL	plural suffix 們 (*-men*)
PP	prepositional phrase
RP	received pronunciation
S–P	subject–predicate structure
SLA	second language acquisition
SFP	sentence final particle
Q	question particle
SOV	subject-object-verb word order
SVO	subject-verb-object word order
SWC	Standard Written Chinese
T–C	Topic–Comment structure
TL	target language
TLN	title with last name (address system)
VP	verb phrase

1
Conversation Analysis, Error Analysis, and Cross-Linguistic Influence

Contrastive analysis (CA) and error analysis (EA)

Contrastive analysis (CA) is a language learning/teaching theory which promotes the systematic comparison and contrast between the grammars of two or more languages, with a view to better understanding the similarities and differences between those languages (James, 1980, 1998; Lado, 1957). CA was very popular in the 1950s and 1960s, when it was widely believed that such information could help explain language learners' learning difficulties and errors they make in the language-learning process. Mother-tongue influence, technically known as 'L1 interference' or 'negative transfer', was held to be a major source of learning difficulties (a more general and neutral term is 'cross-linguistic influence'; see Kellerman, 1995). The strong version of CA predicts that structural differences between languages will lead to learning difficulties and errors, while structural similarities will facilitate language learning or acquisition. Such a claim was later challenged after it was found that what CA predicts based on contrastive differences is not always valid. Quite the contrary, it was found that, whereas structural similarities may sometimes lead to errors, structural differences do not always give rise to learning difficulties. Notwithstanding these criticisms, many scholars still believe that mother-tongue or cross-linguistic influence (CLI) is very common and that more CA research is needed to better understand how systematic structural similarities and differences between languages may affect the relative ease with which second or foreign language learning takes place (Ringbom, 2007; cf. Ringbom, 1987).

In the late 1960s and early 1970s, CA gave way to error analysis (EA), another language learning/teaching theory which holds that learner errors are rule-governed and, as such, reflect the learner's underlying 'interlanguage' (IL) system (Selinker, 1972; cf. Richards, 1971, 1973, 1974). Language acquisition is thus postulated as a process that may be represented as a continuum, with the learner progressively approximating target language norms over a number of discrete stages. At each stage of the learning process, although the language output generated by the IL system is erroneous and thus substandard according to the norms of grammar, including pronunciation, research has shown that the learner's IL competence is just as rule-governed. For instance, many Chinese EAL learners have a tendency to pronounce words beginning with [n] (e.g., intending to say *no name*) systematically with [l] (e.g., pronounced and heard as *low lame*). We may say that such learners under-differentiate /n-/ and /l-/ at the syllable-initial position. While it deviates from Anglo-American norms of pronunciation, such a rule forms part of the learners' IL, which may or may not be overtaken by the normative pronunciation in the learning process.

Like CA, EA was later shown to be inadequate not only because focusing on errors ignored what the learner does know, but also because it overlooked the problem of avoidance (Schachter, 1974; Schachter & Celce-Murcia, 1977). That is, when the learners feel unsure about the correctness of certain grammatical structures or lexical items, they may consciously avoid using them in their language output. This is especially obvious when the learner's language output is assessed. Since learners' avoidance cannot be ruled out, the learners' underlying IL system may not be accessible to the researcher by conducting EA.

With regard to a systematic comparison and contrast between the grammars of two major languages in the world—Chinese and English—relatively little has been done, and yet it seems intuitively clear that many of the learning difficulties and errors commonly found among Chinese EAL learners may be accounted for at least in part by mother-tongue (or cross-linguistic) influence. This is the main reason why the authors decided to write this book: By analysing a list of non-standard anomalies commonly found among Chinese EAL learners in Hong Kong with reference to the relevant linguistic structures or functions (e.g., transitivity, passivization, tense and aspect, determiners, topic-prominence vs. subject-prominence), we hope to be able to shed some light on the extent to which such acquisitional problems are due to CLI. It should be noted, however, that CLI or transfer may not be the only cause of learner errors (Kellerman, 1995). As we will try to make clear in this book, many learning difficulties and non-standard grammatical features are triggered by some combination of both L1- and L2-related factors. Unfortunately, it is not always easy to isolate the two sets of factors unambiguously. Nevertheless, in our analysis of common errors, we will make a case for mother-tongue or CLI when the deviant/erroneous grammatical structure coincides, wholly or partly, with the correct, normative grammatical structure in the learners' L1 which, in the case of Hong Kong, corresponds with spoken (vernacular) Cantonese and Standard Written Chinese (SWC).

Error vs. mistake

Before moving on, we need to make an important distinction between two terms in SLA (second language acquisition) research: 'mistake' and 'error'. While the ordinary usages of these two terms are more or less synonymous, in SLA research they have rather different meanings. When a patterned deviation is characterized as a *mistake*, we mean that it is most likely a *performance* problem, an oversight which may be due to carelessness and/or fatigue. In other words, a mistake is deviation that the speaker/writer is capable of self-correcting if his or her attention is drawn to it explicitly. On the other hand, when a deviation is characterized as an *error*, we mean it is a *competence* problem, a rule-governed anomaly that reflects the learner's underlying substandard IL system. Unlike a mistake, therefore, an error is an anomaly which the learner cannot self-correct even if his or her attention is drawn to it explicitly, for he or she has no awareness of it being a problem.

Cross-linguistic influence: Positive transfer and negative transfer

Research in SLA has shown that knowledge of one or more previously acquired languages tends to have some influence on the learner's competence and performance in the target language. This is generally referred to as transference (also known as CLI). If the outcome of transference is positive (i.e., target language norms are acquired with no errors involved), this is known as 'positive transfer'. For instance, a sound knowledge of Chinese characters tends to enable Chinese learners of Japanese to be more successful in their learning of kanji (漢字) in Japanese, compared with European (e.g., French, German, or Spanish) learners who have no prior knowledge of written Chinese. In contrast, compared with Chinese learners, French learners of English tend to have an advantage thanks to the large number of cognates— words which are spelled identically or are similar in spelling, pronunciation, and/or meaning. Compare, for example, words like *courage, garage, international, history– histoire, hospital–hôpital*, and many other words ending with the same affix such as *combine–combiner, recycle–recycler* (verb); *civilisation, revolution–révolution* (noun). No such advantage is available to Chinese learners of English if they have no knowledge of French or any other European language.

Linguistically, transfer in the process of learning an additional language may be positive or negative. However, compared with negative transfer, positive transfer tends to be less visible. This is why the study of CLI as a branch of SLA research tends to focus on negative transfer. For instance, it has been shown that Chinese learners of English have a strong tendency to topicalize the subject in the sentence-initial position, even though the same person or thing is referred to by a subject pronoun in the following clause. Below are a few typical examples:

1. ? *According to* <u>*Tung Chee-Hwa,*</u> *he said that* $2 billion would be set aside for education reforms.
   (cf. According to Tung Chee-Hwa, $2 billion would be . . .)

2. ? *Based on the book, it describes* two ways to solve the problem.
    (cf. Based on the book, there are two ways to solve the problem.)
3. ? *In a reliable report, it says that* 300 cases have been reported to the police.
    (cf. In a reliable report, 300 cases have been . . .)

Strictly speaking, (1)–(3) are not so much ungrammatical as stylistically clumsy; they tend to give their listener/reader a poor impression of the speaker/writer. Since the underlined segments are co-referential (i.e., have the same referent by referring to the same person or thing), the topicalization is unnecessary (compare the normative version with unnecessary topicalization removed; see Chapter 7 for more details).

Similarly, in their corpus consisting of first- and second-year university students' EAL writing output, A. Y. W. Chan, Kwan, and Li (2003, p. 107) found that an independent clause is often misused as the subject of a sentence. For example:

4. **Snoopy is leaving* makes us all very happy.
5. **She was eager to quit* embarrassed her boss.
6. **He objected to your plan* was totally unreasonable.

That (4)–(6) are in part a result of mother-tongue influence is evidenced by their direct translation into Chinese in (4a)–(6a), where the corresponding underlined clauses are perfectly acceptable:

4. a. <u>史諾比要離開</u>讓我們非常高興。
        Shǐnuòbǐ yào líkāi ràng wǒmen fēicháng gāoxìng
        Snoopy will leave make us very happy
        'That Snoopy is leaving makes us very happy.'
5. a. <u>她堅決要辭職</u>讓老闆感到尷尬。
        tā jiānjué yào cízhí ràng lǎobǎn gǎndào gāngà
        she determined will resign make boss feel embarrassed
        'That she was determined to resign made her boss feel embarrassed.'
6. a. <u>他反對你的計劃</u>是完全不合理的。
        tā fǎnduì nǐde jìhuà shì wánquán bùhélǐ de
        he object your plan be completely unreasonable F.P.
        'That he objected to your plan is completely unreasonable.'

One way to help Chinese learners of English overcome such adverse influence or negative transfer is to raise their consciousness of such structural problems by going through self-correction procedures step by step (Li & Chan, 1999, 2001; cf. Chan, 2006c). Instruction to teachers and self-correction materials for learners showing how this consciousness-raising approach works with regard to 13 high-frequency errors may be retrieved from the following website (Li, Chan, & Kwan, 2002; see also Chan, 2006c): http://personal.cityu.edu.hk/~encrproj/error_types.htm.

English and Chinese: Between standard and local varieties

The terms 'English' and 'Chinese' (中文, *zhōngwèn/zung1 man4*) are ambiguous, for they give us the impression that we are dealing only with two languages. This false impression is no doubt reinforced by ordinary questions such as 'Do you speak English?' / '你講中文嗎？'[1] / '你識講中文嗎？'.[2] Yet students of English or Chinese will realize that there is a great deal of diversity behind the general labels 'English' and 'Chinese'. Consider the kinds of modifier that may be placed before them. It is well known, for example, that speakers of *British English*, *American English*, and *Australian English* have distinctive accents and often use different vocabulary items to refer to the same things. The following are some examples of lexical and spelling differences:

British English (BrE)   lorry / lift / petrol / storey / plough / cheque / grey / . . .

American English (AmE)   truck / elevator / gas / story / plow / check / gray / . . .

Contrastive examples such as these can easily be multiplied.[3] To a lesser extent, what is true of lexical and spelling differences may also be said of grammar. In any case, it is clear that grammatical norms are not identical across different English varieties. Thus in British English (BrE), a well-known grammatical rule stipulates that the present perfect tense should never be used in the presence of the words *ago*, *yesterday*, or any other time adverbials referring to the past. Similarly, in BrE, the word *already* collocates as a rule with the present perfect but not with the simple past. Thus the following sentences

He has eaten the cake yesterday.   He ate the cake already.

are considered ill-formed according to standard BrE grammar. However, as is noted by Milroy (1992, pp. 7–8), these rules are increasingly 'flouted' by native speakers of English in Great Britain, so that it is not uncommon to hear (though less often, read) sentences such as:

He's done it two days ago.   I've seen him last year.

---

1. *Nǐ jiǎng zhōngwèn má?/Nei5 gong3 zung1 man2 maa3?* ('Do you speak Chinese?').
2. *Nei5 sik1 gong2 zung1 man2 ma3?* ('Do you speak Chinese?').
3. Many more examples may be found, for example, in Hou (1992, pp. 132–138), who presents 10 systematic differences (BrE–AmE) as follows: (i) *-our/-or* (e.g., *colour/color*); (ii) *-re/-er* (e.g., *litre/liter*); (iii) past tense forms of verbs ending in *-el* or *-al* (e.g., *levelled/leveled*; *equalled/equaled*); (iv) *-ce/-se* (e.g., *defence/defense*); (v) *-ogue/-og* (e.g., *catalogue/catalog*); (vi) *-gramm/-gram* (e.g., *programme/program*); (vii) *-ette/-et* (e.g., *omelette/omelet*); (viii) *-xion/-ction* (e.g., *inflexion/inflection*); (ix) *-ae-* or *-oe-/-e* (e.g., *encyclopaedia/encyclopedia*; *manoeuvre/maneuver*); (x) *-ise/-ize* (e.g., *recognise/recognize*).

By contrast, the collocational restriction bearing on the adverb *already* and the simple past mentioned above is seldom followed in American English (AmE). Indeed, it is more common to hear Americans say 'I finished already' rather than 'I've already finished'. It is therefore not without reason that, according to one netizen, the Irish playwright George Bernard Shaw (1856–1950) was quoted as saying 'England and America are two countries separated by the same language'.[4]

The above examples have been drawn from countries where English is considered a standard language, suggesting that norms of grammatical correctness may not be the same across the continents. For our purpose in this book, we will follow Trudgill and Hannah's (1994) definition of Standard English as follows:

> Standard English [is] the variety of the English language which is normally employed in writing and normally spoken by 'educated' speakers of the language. It is also, of course, the variety of English that students of English as a Foreign or Second Language (EFL/ESL) are taught when receiving formal instruction. The term Standard English refers to grammar and vocabulary (dialect) but not to pronunciation (accent). (Trudgill & Hannah, 1994, p. 1; also cited in Widdowson, 2003, p. 44)

Following the spread of English as a world language as a result of worldwide influence of the US since the end of the Second World War, especially through the mass media, English has come to be used as a second or foreign language in many countries. In the former British colonies India and Singapore, for example, where English is one of the official languages, English is used as a lingua franca by many Indians and Singaporeans of distinct ethnic origins. Over time, English has developed its own norms distinct from Standard English in these countries at practically all levels—from pronunciation and vocabulary to grammar and the 'rules of speaking' (e.g., making a request, responding to a compliment; see Chapter 9). In the past, such deviations from Standard English were systematically dismissed as erroneous, substandard features which should be discouraged and corrected. Increasingly, however, partly in acknowledgement of the geographical and functional diffusion of such varieties of English as well as the tremendous number of speakers involved, many scholars feel that their legitimacy as indigenized or new varieties of English (IVEs/NVEs) should be recognized. Hence terms such as 'Indian English' and 'Singapore English' have gradually lost their derogatory connotations and are more and more widely accepted. One direct consequence of this development is that the word *English* has been pluralized as *Englishes*. For example, since the 1990s, a well-known

---

4. A similar saying has been attributed to different writers depending on the sources (mainly Oscar Wilde and George Bernard Shaw). The citation above was adapted from the website 'English Language & Usage Stack Exchange'. Retrieved from http://english.stackexchange.com/questions/74737/what-is-the-origin-of-the-phrase-two-nations-divided-by-a-common-language.

international journal, *World Englishes*, has been devoted to the description and study of IVEs as a result of contact with their 'parent language', English. One interesting question is whether or not there exists a Hong Kong variety of English (HKE), and if so, what its norms of reference are (see, e.g., Bolton, 2000, 2003; cf. Li, 2000, 2007).

The term *Chinese* (中文, *zhōngwén/zung1 man4*) is no less ambiguous. It is well known that, in mainland China, the accent changes from village to village, especially when villages are separated by natural boundaries such as mountains and big rivers. In general, the farther one travels away from one's native village or birthplace, the more progressively difficult oral communication becomes in one's own home dialect owing to tremendous differences in 方言 (*fāngyán/fong1 jin4*). Since many Hongkongers originate from different parts of the Mainland, they bring with them their unique accents which may not be comprehensible to native speakers of Cantonese in the territory. Indeed, communication difficulties were often dramatized, sometimes with exaggeration, in many local films produced in the 1960s, popularly known as 粵語長片 (*jyut6 jyu2 coeng4 pin2/Yuèyǔ chángpiàn*). What is generally known as Cantonese (廣東話, *guǎngdōnghuà/gwong2 dung1 waa2*) belongs to the 粵 (Yue) dialect group; it is one of many subdialects (e.g., 四邑, Szeyap; 台山, Toishan) spoken in the provinces Guangdong and Guangxi. There are altogether seven major dialect groups, each with considerable variation (for more details, see Chen, 1999; Norman, 1988; Ramsey, 1987). The tremendous interdialectal differences outlined above help explain the need for a national language, which used to be called 國語 (*guóyǔ/gwok3 jyu5*)—generally known in the Western world as Mandarin—and which was redesignated as 普通話 (*pǔtōnghuà/pou2 tong1 waa2*, meaning 'common language') in the 1950s. As the national language of New China, Putonghua is essentially based on the phonology of the variety spoken in Beijing, while exemplary literature written in 白話 (*báihuà/baak6 waa2*) since the turn of the twentieth century constitutes the model of its vocabulary and grammar (Chen, 1999, p. 24). However, the boundaries between different Chinese varieties, especially at the lexical level, are far from clear-cut.

Unlike the vernacular (i.e., the local spoken dialect or language variety), which presents enormous difficulties for intra-ethnic communication across different regions in mainland China, written Chinese characters have remained relatively stable since the Han dynasty (206 BCE–CE 220). Standard written Chinese, as it has come to be called, is among the most treasured heritages of Chinese civilization. There is a good reason for that. With the help of contextual information, much of the stock of Chinese characters can be understood by people from Heilongjiang to Hainan (province), or from Shanghai to Sichuan, despite the fact that they are pronounced very differently in the local Han Chinese dialects. This helps explain a popular belief that, in general, what cannot be communicated orally can be conveyed in print. In this sense, it is often claimed that SWC serves to unite the Han Chinese peoples throughout the world. In reality, however, this unifying function of Chinese characters is sometimes exaggerated, as it fails to take into account the significant differences in the two writing systems across the Strait of Taiwan since the promulgation of the simplified characters by the Chinese government in the mid-1950s (for more details, see Lee & Li, 2013; Li, 2006, 2017; Li & Lee, 2004).

Thus the answer to the question 'What is Chinese?' may be rather different depending on the locality. In the case of Hong Kong, the term Chinese may be further specified according to the spoken and written media. Whereas the vernacular is the variety known as Cantonese in the sense described above, the written medium may be described as SWC, which varies from place to place. For example, there exist considerable lexico-grammatical differences in the Chinese language of Taiwan, Hong Kong, and Singapore, as compared with the norms in mainland China.

For our purposes in this book, the term Chinese will be used in its broad sense to refer to Han Chinese varieties in general, covering Putonghua as well as regional dialects. Occasionally, reference will be made to its narrow sense, viz. Putonghua (Mandarin) and SWC. This will be clearly indicated. Although dialects or new varieties are no less important as carriers of their speakers' local/regional identities, in this book we will focus on the grammars of the two written varieties: Standard Chinese and Standard English (primarily BrE and AmE), with special reference to the use of English for Academic Purposes (EAP).

Synopsis of the book

The book is divided into nine chapters. **Chapter 1** outlines the background to research on CA and EA and how they relate to the key concepts of CLI and transference (positive transfer vs. negative transfer). **Chapter 2** gives an overview of the key features involved in Cantonese-English contrastive phonology, which helps account for some of the main pronunciation problems encountered by Cantonese learners of English. **Chapter 3** is devoted to transitivity, showing how the divergence of transitivity patterns in Chinese and English verbs may lead to frequent EAL errors concerning the non-standard use of verbs. **Chapter 4** examines the typical circumstances under which the English passive is used and why the passive in Chinese—typically using *the* passive marker 被 (*bèi*)—may or may not be appropriate. Such a contrastive difference, among others, helps explain frequent misuse of the English passive by Chinese EAL learners and users. **Chapter 5** explains the similarities and differences between two closely related concepts: tense and aspect. Standard English has both tense and aspect.[5] Since tense does not exist as a grammatical category in Standard Chinese or

---

5. For instance, consider the perfective aspect in simple past tense (e.g., *he came*), as opposed to the progressive aspect in past continuous tense (e.g., *he was coming*).

other Chinese dialects like Cantonese, Chinese EAL learners tend to experience a lot of tense-related problems and difficulties in the learning process. Aspect, being semantically akin to but conceptually distinct from tense, exists in both Chinese and English. We will illustrate the functions and meanings of aspect markers in Mandarin Chinese and demonstrate how knowledge of Chinese aspect may help account for some tense-related common errors among Chinese EAL learners and users.

Chapter 6 gives an overview of the contrastive usage differences associated with the use of determiners in Chinese and English. A noun phrase in English may include an article or a demonstrative pronoun, among other determiners. The typical functions of articles in English, and how they are embedded in a broader system of determiners, will be discussed and exemplified. Since articles do not exist as a grammatical category in Chinese, it is understandable that in general EAL learners find English articles difficult to master. Demonstratives exist in both Chinese and English, but they function somewhat differently. Apart from explaining the nature of the learning difficulties, the chapter will provide useful tips on how to avoid making common errors involving the misuse of articles. **Chapter 7** explains why, whereas English is syntactically characterized as a subject-prominent language, Chinese is more appropriately called a topic-prominent language. Topic-prominence in Chinese helps explain the tendency for Chinese EAL learners to compose English sentences using a topic-comment (T-C) structure, resulting in non-standard features. **Chapter 8** will examine language contact phenomena between Chinese and English since the 1900s and discuss some of the high-frequency problems associated with Europeanized linguistic features (歐化, or Europeanization) in Modern Written Chinese. In the last chapter, **Chapter 9**, we will exemplify some of the common socio-pragmatic problems that Chinese learners and users of English are likely to encounter in intercultural communication contexts, for example, when interacting with native speakers of English.

Questions and activities

1. What is meant by Standard Chinese and Standard English? Why do we need a standard variety? Which variety of Chinese/English was selected to be the standard? How were these varieties selected? By whom?

2. Is Cantonese a standard or non-standard variety? Does Cantonese have grammar? If so, what are some of the elements of Cantonese grammar that you have come across?

3. Which variety of English predominates in Hong Kong? Specify your answer with regard to the domains of government, education, business, law, and media (electronic and print).

4.   What is meant by 'mother-tongue influence'? How does it differ from transference? What other terms are used by SLA scholars to refer to the outcomes of transference? Can you illustrate your answer with one or two examples in your EAL language experience?

Further reading

Lado (1957) is a classic work written by the originator of the Contrastive Analysis Hypothesis. For a systematic introduction to CA, see James (1980). Littlewood (1984) provides an overview of various issues and key concepts in the field of SLA, including CA, EA, and IL that were briefly outlined and discussed above. More advanced students may wish to consult Richards (1971, 1973, 1974), who provides many instructive examples to illustrate CA, EA, and IL from a theoretical perspective. For EAL errors or mistakes commonly found among Chinese learners and useful strategies for correcting them, see practical works by Bunton (1989), Edge (1989), Newbrook (1991), Norrish (1983), Webster and Lam (1991), and Yiu (1992). A more recent, if more technical, introduction to the study of SLA is Gass and Selinker (2008). Seargeant (2012) and Seargeant and Swann (2012) are highly accessible introductory volumes on the historical background to the global spread of English as well as the critical (including ethical) issues arising. On linguistic variation within Greater China, including mainland China, Taiwan, and Hong Kong, see Li (2006, 2015).

2

Cantonese-English Contrastive Phonology

Background

Since the colonial era, English has been taught and learned in Hong Kong from preschool to tertiary level. Through education, Cantonese-dominant Hongkongers grow up and become bilingual in English. Whether English is learned under second-language (L2) or foreign-language (FL) conditions (Li, 2017), there are plenty of EAL learning difficulties to overcome, including non-native pronunciation features that may give rise to intelligibility problems or misunderstanding. For instance, English words that begin with the letter 'n', as in *no*, *name*, and *night*, tend to be pronounced with an 'l', making them sound like *low*, *lame*, and *light*. What is the status of such deviations from native (e.g., British, American, or Australian) English pronunciation? Should they be seen as 'errors' through teacher feedback until they get corrected (Li, 2000)? Or, should they be regarded as normal, as part of a new variety of English, 'Hong Kong English' (HKE)? There are no simple answers to these questions (see Li, 2007, for some of the critical issues involved).

In this chapter, apart from introducing the basics in articulatory phonetics and contrastive features of the phonological systems in Cantonese and English, we will draw on Tony Hung's (2002) empirical insights, with a view to elucidating the phonological system of HKE, as reflected in educated Chinese Hongkongers' English pronunciation. Where appropriate, we will also discuss some of the learning difficulties commonly encountered by learners of Cantonese from an English-L1 background.

Transcription vs. transliteration (romanization)

Since discussion in phonetics and phonology necessitates the use of written symbols to represent speech sounds in print, various systems of phonetic symbols have been proposed. The most commonly accepted system is known as the International Phonetic Alphabet (IPA) (International Phonetic Association, 2015), which will be used in this book. However, many of the IPA symbols are obscure to laypersons (many IPA symbols originate from Modern Greek letters). In addition, there are practical typographical difficulties involved when using phonetic symbols in writing or word processing on the keyboard. Largely for these practical reasons, an alternative romanization or transliteration system is often preferred, especially for language teaching purposes (e.g., *pìnyīn* in *pǔtōnghuà*). In a romanization or transliteration system, speech sounds of a given language are represented only by a combination of letters of the English alphabet. For instance, the Cantonese word *gweilo* is commonly used in English newspapers in Hong Kong in reference to 鬼佬 (*gwai2 lou2*, literally 'ghost guy'; more idiomatically 'foreign devil'). In the case of tone languages like Cantonese and Putonghua, sometimes additional tone markers known as 'diacritics' are added on top of the vowel (e.g., according to the Yale System, in a word like *gwái lóu*, the diacritic above the letters *a* and *o* symbolizes 'rising intonation').

There have been several competing transliteration systems to represent Cantonese in print. Until recently, the Yale System was the dominant system used in both Cantonese course books and academic discussions. In late 1993, the Linguistic Society of Hong Kong (LSHK) came up with its own transliteration system, called Jyutping, which has at least two advantages over the Yale System. First, the tone levels are indicated by numbers 1 to 6,[1] which is more user-friendly when word-processing (using a computer or mobile device) compared with marking tone contours using diacritics in Yale. Secondly, the LSHK system differs only minimally from IPA, which makes it easier to remember. Thus the Cantonese words 飲茶, 點心 and 韓語 are transliterated as *jam2 caa4*, *dim2 sam1*, and *hon4 jyu5*, respectively (for details of the LSHK Cantonese transliteration system, see Tang et al., 2002). It should be noted, however, that the same symbol does not necessarily represent the same sound in Jyutping and the IPA systems. For example, 'd' in the IPA system is a symbol for a voiced alveolar stop, while 'd' in the Jyutping system represents a (voiceless) unaspirated alveolar stop. In fact, this applies to other symbols such as 'b' and 'g', as Cantonese has no voiced stops (see below). In this chapter, all references to English pronunciation features are based on General American (GA, commonly heard in the US, e.g., on CNN), which is somewhat different from Received Pronunciation (RP, also known as 'The Queen's English' or 'BBC English' in the UK). The differences are mainly found in their vowel inventories (see, e.g., Rogers, 2000). We will use IPA throughout, supplemented with Jyutping in footnotes where appropriate, to better demonstrate the differences between the sound inventories between English and Cantonese.

Cantonese and English sound inventories: An overview

The phonemes of a language consist of vowels (元音) and consonants (輔音). Vowels are sounds that are produced by vibrating the vocal cords with little obstruction of the airstream at any point along the vocal tract. They are, therefore, usually loud. The

---

1. For instance, *si1* (詩), *si2* (史), *si3* (試), *si4* (時), *si5* (市), *si6* (事).

first sounds in words like *apple* and *eagle* are obvious examples. Consonants, on the other hand, usually involve some obstruction of the airstream during production. They may involve the vibration of the vocal cords. Because of the obstruction of the airstream, they are usually less loud than the vowels. Examples are the first sounds in the words *fit* and *pot*.

To people who have had no training in linguistics, it may seem difficult to describe what a speech sound is: How can one describe the difference between a [t] sound, as in *tap*, and a [k] sound, as in *cap*? In fact, speech sounds in any language, both consonants and vowels, can be described in systematic ways. Consonants are usually defined using three features: (i) place of articulation, (ii) manner of articulation, and (iii) voicing. Vowels can be described using another set of features: (i) height, (ii) backness, and (iii) roundedness.

Consonants

Place of articulation

The vocal tract consists of both the oral and nasal cavities. The vocal tract can be thought of as a flute: By placing fingers upon different holes on a flute, different sounds are produced. Different linguistic sounds are produced by obstructing the airstream at different locations of the vocal tract. Unlike playing the flute, however, in which case we would use our fingers, articulating speech sounds involves obstructing the airstream using different parts of the tongue and other muscles along the vocal tract. The place of articulation refers to the place where the obstruction occurs (i.e., the opening is the narrowest or closed). Figure 2.1 shows the different places of articulation that are involved in the production of sounds in Cantonese and English.

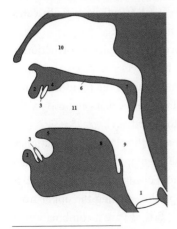

1. Vocal cords	7. Velum (soft palate)
2. Lips	8. Tongue (root)
3. Teeth	9. Pharynx
4. Alveolar ridge	10. Nasal cavity
5. Tongue (tip)	11. Oral cavity
6. Hard palate	

Figure 2.1
The vocal organs (adapted from 'place of articulation [active and passive]')[2]

The term 'bilabial' describes sounds that are produced by obstructing the airstream using the two lips (*bi* = 'two', *labial* = 'lips'). Examples of bilabial sounds are [m], [b], and [p]. 'Labio-dental' refers to sounds that are produced using the lower lip and the upper front teeth. Examples are [f] and [v]. 'Dental' or 'interdental' refers to the '*th*' sounds that are produced by putting the tongue in between the upper and the lower front teeth. Examples are [θ], as in *thank*, and [ð], as in *that*. Going into the oral cavity, the first place of articulation that we encounter is the alveolar ridge. It is the 'bump' located right behind the upper front teeth. Alveolar sounds such as [s] and [t] are produced by obstructing the airstream at the alveolar ridge with the tip of the tongue. Some sounds are produced slightly behind the alveolar ridge. They are referred to as post-alveolar sounds. Examples are [ʃ] as in *show* and [tʃ] as in *chin*. Further back is the hard palate. Sounds produced by narrowing the opening at the hard palate are called palatal sounds. An example is [j], as in *yes*. Velar sounds are those that are produced at the velum, which is behind the hard palate. Examples are [k] (e.g., *keep*) and [ŋ] (e.g., *wing*). Finally, sounds can be produced at the glottis, which is near the root of the tongue. In English and Cantonese, [h] is the only glottal sound, as in *house* and 好 [hou].[3]

Manner of articulation

It should be clear that using different places of articulation will result in different sounds. However, [m] and [p], for example, are both bilabial according to place of articulation, but they obviously sound different. How can we distinguish them? There is thus a need to specify the manner of articulation. Manner of articulation describes how the airstream is obstructed, such as whether it is partly or completely obstructed, and where the airstream passes through after leaving the lungs. There are six major manners of articulation: (i) stops (or plosives), (ii) fricatives, (iii) affricates, (iv) nasals, (v) approximants, and (vi) lateral approximants.

Stops (or plosives) (塞音) refer to sounds that involve a complete obstruction of the airstream. Take [p] as an example. One will not be able to produce [p] without closing the lips completely to block the air from coming out of the mouth. The lips will eventually open and allow the air to come out so that the speaker can produce the next sound in the word (consider the production of the word *pay*).

Fricatives are produced by creating a narrow opening at the place of articulation to allow the air to flow out of the oral cavity. Because the opening is too small, it creates a turbulence, which results in a high-frequency sound. For instance, [s] is a fricative produced at the alveolar ridge, and [f] is a fricative produced using the upper front teeth and the lower lip (i.e., labio-dental). Affricates (塞擦音) are a combination of a stop and a fricative, as evidenced in their IPA symbols. The first sound in *chin*, for

---

3. *hou2*

example, is produced by stopping the airstream at the alveolar ridge, and then releasing it through a small opening at the post-alveolar region (thus the IPA symbol [tʃ]).

Nasals are distinct from other manners of articulation, in that the air flows out primarily through the nasal cavity. That is why we have difficulty producing [m], [n], and [ŋ] when we have a stuffy nose, because air cannot flow through the nasal cavity.

The last manner of articulation is called approximants. Although approximants are classified as consonants, they are similar to vowels in that they involve little obstruction of the airstream and thus are comparatively louder than consonants produced by other manners of articulation. Examples are [j] (as in _yes_) and [w] (as in _win_). There is another kind of approximant known as lateral approximants. They are so named because the airstream flows on the sides of the tongue during their production. The only lateral approximant in English and Cantonese is [l] (as in _look_).

Voicing

The last feature that defines a consonant is voicing. A sound is voiced (濁音) when its production involves the vibration of the vocal cords. As mentioned above, all vowels are voiced. Consonants, on the other hand, can be either voiced or voiceless (清音).

Voicing can be illustrated using the sounds [s] and [z]. By putting our hands around our voice box (Adam's apple), and uttering the sound [z] until we are out of breath, our hand should be able to feel the vibration while hearing a hissing sound /zzzzzzz/. That sound, the voiced [z] sound from our voice box, is caused by the vibration of the vocal folds. Then, if the same procedure is followed to utter the sound [s], we should feel the difference: There should be no vibration in the voice box.

Theoretically speaking, one should also find the same difference in vibration between other voiced/voiceless pairs, such as [p] and [b]. However, because of their short duration, the difference is not easy to detect. One way of contrasting [p] and [b] is by putting them in between vowels, such as [apa] and [aba]. For [apa], one should feel a very brief period of time between the two vowels, during which there is no vibration of the vocal cords. In contrast, [aba] will produce continuous vibrations.

In Table 2.1 where American and British English consonants are shown, the IPA symbol on the left in each cell is voiceless, and the one on the right is voiced. Nasals, lateral approximants, and approximants are naturally voiced, so no such distinction is shown in the table for these categories. Table 2.2 shows the consonants that are present in Cantonese. Note that there is no voicing contrast in stops, fricatives, and affricates. Instead of voicing, Cantonese makes use of aspiration (e.g., [pʰa] 爬⁴ and [pa] 爸⁵ are two different words). Aspiration is indicated by the superscript 'h' after [p]. We will come back to this in the later sections.

---

4. _paa4_
5. _baa1_

Table 2.1

American/British English consonants

Manner of articulation	Place of articulation							
	Bilabial	Labio-dental	Dental	Alveolar	Post-alveolar	Palatal	Velar	Glottal
Stop/plosive	p b			t d			k g	
Affricate					tʃ dʒ			
Nasal	m			n			ŋ	
Fricative		f v	θ ð	s z	ʃ ʒ			h h
Approximant				ɹ		j	w	
Lateral Approximant				l				

Note: From *Handbook of the IPA*, by P. Ladefoged, 2009.

Table 2.2

Cantonese consonants

Manner of articulation	Place of articulation								
	Bilabial	Labio-dental	Dental	Alveolar	Post-alveolar	Palatal	Velar	Labio-velar	Glottal
Plosive	p pʰ		t tʰ				k kʰ	kʷ kʷʰ	
Affricate				ts tsʰ					
Nasal	m		n				ŋ		
Fricative		f		s					h
Approximant						j		w	
Lateral Approximant			l						

Note: From *Handbook of the IPA*, by E. Zee, 2009.

Vowels

Height

We now turn to another set of sounds: vowels. As mentioned, vowels can also be described with three features: height, backness, and roundedness. The first two features are used to indicate the location of the tongue. The vowel [i], as in *beat*, is a high vowel, because the tongue is raised when it is produced. The vowel [ɛ] (as in the word 姐 [dzɛ][6] in Cantonese or *bet* in English) is a mid-low vowel, because its production involves the lowering of both the tongue and the jaw. If one reads aloud [i] and [ɛ] repeatedly, one should feel the raising and lowering of the jaw.

---

6. *ze2*

Backness

As explained, [i] is a high vowel. It is also a front vowel when backness is concerned. When producing [i], the front part of the tongue is located in the front part of the oral cavity, somewhere right behind the alveolar ridge. On the other hand, [u], as in *boot*, is a back vowel with the same height (i.e., a high back vowel). If one reads aloud [i] and [u] repeatedly, one should feel that the tongue mass is moving back and forth.

Roundedness

Finally, vowels with the same height and backness may be perceived differently if they are different in roundedness. Consider the vowel [i]. It is produced by spreading the lips, as in the Cantonese word 衣 (/ji/).[7] In Cantonese, there is a rounded counterpart of [i], which is represented by [y]. It is the vowel found in the word 於 (/jy/).[8] Again, one can see that these two sounds only differ by roundedness by saying them aloud repeatedly. The inventories of vowels in (American) English and in Cantonese are listed in Figures 2.2 and 2.3 respectively. In these figures, each of the dots symbolizes the place of articulation of a vowel. If a symbol is placed on the left of the dot (e.g., [i], [e], and [ɑ]), the vowel is unrounded. But if a symbol is placed on the right of the dot (e.g., [u], [o], and [y]), the vowel is rounded. As shown in Figure 2.3, there are two high front vowels in Cantonese: unrounded [i] and rounded [y].

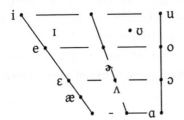

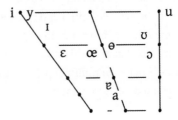

Figure 2.2
American English vowels. From *Handbook of the IPA*, by P. Ladefoged, 2009.

Figure 2.3
Cantonese vowels. From *Handbook of the IPA*, by E. Zee, 2009.

The vowels introduced so far are monophthongs (單元音). While producing these monophthongs, the tongue and the lips should remain in the same position, because there is no change in the quality of the vowel. Diphthongs (雙元音), on the other hand, involve 'a change in quality' (Ladefoged, 2001, p. 272). That is, the tongue and/ or the lips need to 'move' while producing the vowel. For example, the English word *buy* [baɪ] involves a diphthong, in which the tongue moves from a low back position

7. *ji1*
8. *jyu1*

to a high front position. An example of a Cantonese word that consists of a diphthong would be 包 [bao].[9]

Phonemes (音素) and allophones (同位音位)

Up to now, we have been concerned with the study of articulatory phonetics, which addresses the question of how specific speech sounds of a language are produced. Related to this is another question: How do we know whether a particular phoneme (vowel or consonant) is present in a language? The answer to this question involves a discovery procedure, which is crucial in the study of phonology.

When two speech sounds X and Y are said to be phonemes of a language Z, it means that they may be found in the pronunciation of individual words of language Z to differentiate between word meanings. This may be demonstrated through a discovery procedure known as 'minimal pair' (最小音對／最小對立體). According to Duanmu (2007, p. 10), a minimal pair 'is a pair of words that are identical in pronunciation except for one sound'. That is, any two words with distinctive meanings and which differ by only one segment of their phonetic shapes with regard to the *same position* will produce two phonemes. Thus, by comparing *bit* [bɪt] with *pit* [pɪt] (but not *bit* [bɪt] with *tip* [tɪp]), we can show that /b/ and /p/ belong to the stock of phonemes in English. This may be confirmed, for example, by other minimal pairs such as *tab* [tæb] and *tap* [tæp], which further suggest that the opposition between /b/ and /p/ in English may occur at the beginning as well as the end of a syllable (i.e., at both the syllable-initial and syllable-final positions). Further confirmation may be obtained by still other minimal pairs, such as *book* [bʊk] and *cook* [kʊk]; *rob* [rɑːb] and *rot* [rɑːt]; *pub* [pʌb] and *rub* [rʌb]; *cup* [kʌp] and *cut* [kʌt], etc. Through similar contrasts between minimal pairs in Cantonese, its phonemes may also be discovered and worked out accordingly.

Deviations of EAL from Standard English

Now we have seen the features used to describe consonants and vowels in any language. We can now discuss the deviations of EAL pronunciation with regard to the norms of native varieties of English using these features. The deviations can be classified into three categories of difficulty arising from:

(i)   the segmental differences between Cantonese and English,

(ii)   the differences in the restrictions of locations where a sound can occur in a syllable, and

(iii) the difference in syllable structure between Cantonese and English.

---

9. *baau1*

Segmental differences between Cantonese and English: Sounds that do not exist in Cantonese

There are differences and similarities between the speech sounds used in Cantonese and English. It has been argued that these differences can account for most of the deviations made by Cantonese EAL speakers while learning English, as well as pronunciation difficulties encountered by learners of Cantonese from an English-L1 background. We will discuss these differences in some detail, focusing on those that may give rise to intelligibility problems.

Voiced and voiceless consonants

One of the major differences between English and Cantonese is that English uses voicing *contrastively* (含對比性), but Cantonese does not. This means that, in English, if we only change the voicing property of a sound when it is used within a word, the meaning of the word will be changed. Consider a minimal pair like *sip* [sɪp] vs. *zip* [zɪp]. The only difference between these two words is the initial consonant: /s/ vs. /z/. Both /s/ and /z/ have the same place and manner of articulation; the only difference is voicing: /s/ is voiceless, while /z/ is voiced. This distinction is particularly difficult for native Cantonese speakers to perceive and produce, partly because voicing is not a distinctive feature in Cantonese consonants (i.e., in Cantonese, voicing is not used to distinguish between word meanings). Cantonese speakers often replace voiced consonants in English (i.e., /b, d, g, v, z, ʒ, dʒ/) with their voiceless counterparts, as in examples (1)–(5):

(1) /b/

e.g., modelling the pronunciation of *big* [bɪg] on Cantonese unaspirated plosive [p] (compare: 碧 [pɪk])[10]

(2) /d/

e.g., modelling the pronunciation of *Dick* [dɪk] on Cantonese unaspirated plosive [t] (compare: 的 [tɪk])[11]

(3) /g/

e.g., modelling the pronunciation of *got* [gɔt] on Cantonese unaspirated plosive [k] (compare: 葛 [kɔt])[12]

(4) /v/

e.g., modelling the pronunciation of *vogue* [voʊg] on Cantonese labiodental fricative [f] (compare: 福 [fʊk])[13]

---

10. *bik1*
11. *dik1*
12. *got3*
13. *fuk1*

(5)   /z/

e.g., modelling the pronunciation of *zip* [zɪp] on Cantonese alveolar fricative [s] (compare: 攝 [sɪp])[14]

For Cantonese speakers, the voiced post-alveolar fricative /ʒ/, as in the words *measure* (/ˈmeʒər/) and the lexical borrowing from French, *genre* (/ˈʒɑ̃ː.rə/), is not easy to produce. This sound is also found in the intervocalic position (e.g., between vowels) of a few other words borrowed from French (e.g., *garage, mirage, treasure*). The main challenge lies in the fact that it is voiced, which is probably the reason why a common pronunciation strategy among Cantonese speakers is to substitute the voiceless counterpart /ʃ/ for it, resulting in non-target-like pronunciation. This is empirically attested in Hung's (2002) study. For instance, instead of [ʒ], all 15 of the Cantonese-L1 subjects mispronounced the word *pleasure* (/ˈpleʒər/) with [ʃ] (p. 131).

Interaction between voicing and aspiration (送氣)

Phonologically, the English words *cot* /kɑːt/ and *got* /gɑːt/ only differ in one sound. The sounds /k/ and /g/ differ only in voicing: /k/ is a voiceless velar stop, while /g/ is a voiced velar stop. Their place and manner of articulation are the same (i.e., both are velar stops). Phonetically, however, these two sounds differ not only in voicing but also in aspiration. When pronouncing the word *cot*, if we place our palm in front of our mouth, we should be able to notice a puff of air rushing out. This additional puff of air is one defining characteristic of an aspirated sound. By contrast, there should be no detectable aspiration when pronouncing the word *got*.

The features, voicing and aspiration, are independent of each other. This is the reason why there are four possible combinations: (i) voiced aspirated, (ii) voiced unaspirated, (iii) voiceless aspirated, and (iv) voiceless unaspirated (see Table 2.3).

Table 2.3
Interaction between voicing and aspiration, as illustrated by the bilabial stops

		Voiced?	Aspirated?	Language	Example
[bʱ]	(voiced aspirated)	Yes	Yes	—	—
[b]	(voiced unaspirated)	Yes	No	English	*bill*
[pʰ]	(voiceless aspirated)	No	Yes	English	*pill*
				Cantonese	飄 (*piu5*)
[p]	(voiceless unaspirated)	No	No	English	*spill*
				Cantonese	錶 (*biu5*)

---

14. *sip3*

Although all of the sounds in Table 2.3 are *possible* sounds in human languages, in any single language we do not necessarily find all of the contrasts. In Cantonese, the aspiration contrast is present but not the voicing contrast. But in English, the opposite is true—only voicing is used contrastively, not aspiration. The reason is that, in English, 'voiceless aspirated' (as in *pill*) and 'voiceless unaspirated' (as in *spill*) are in complementary distribution, in that no minimal pairs may be found that consist of a contrast between 'aspirated' and 'unaspirated'. The contrastive difference between the distinctive feature of English stops on one hand, and Cantonese stops on the other, helps explain why, in the pronunciation of many Cantonese EAL learners, the voiced and voiceless stops tend to be treated as unaspirated and aspirated stops, respectively (Hung, 2002, p. 130). In fact, native Cantonese speakers often mistake the first sound in 爸 [pa]¹⁵ 'father' as [b] in English. As we will see below, this contrastive difference between Cantonese and English creates problems for both Cantonese-L1 speakers learning English and English-L1 speakers learning Cantonese.

Other missing consonants: /θ/, /ð/, /tʃ/, /dʒ/, /r/

As mentioned, the '*th*' sounds are said to be produced at the interdental position. There are two dental fricatives: one voiced (/ð/), as in several monosyllabic function words like *the* (/ð/), *that* (/ðæt/), and *these* (/ðiːz/); the other voiceless (/θ/), as in *thief* (/θiːf/), *thumb* (/θʌm/), and *enthusiasm* (/ɪnˈθjuːziæzəm/). There are variations in the way these sounds are produced, even within the so-called Standard Englishes. Whereas in AmE, speakers place the tongue tip in between their teeth (of the upper jaw and the lower jaw) when they say the *th* sound, in BrE (RP in particular), the '*th*' sound is not really produced at the interdental position. Rather, BrE speakers raise the tip of the tongue towards the back of the upper teeth when producing *th* sounds. Nonetheless, all *th* sounds in AmE and BrE alike are grouped collectively as interdental sounds, which for Cantonese speakers are not easy to learn. Apart from the fact that neither the voiced /ð/ nor the voiceless /θ/ is present in the Cantonese inventory of phonemes, both dental fricatives are rather difficult to produce from the articulatory point of view. This is why many Cantonese EAL learners tend to substitute other speech sounds for these interdental sounds, especially substituting the labio-dental fricative [f] for /θ/, and the voiceless unaspirated alveolar stop [t] for /ð/. Consequently, in their pronunciation, word pairs such as *thin–fin* and *those–dose* are often indistinguishable.

Both Cantonese and English have a pair of affricates. Similar to stops, the pair of Cantonese affricates is distinguished by aspiration, while the pair of affricates in English is differentiated by voicing. Apart from their difference in place of articulation

---

15. *baa*1

(alveolar in Cantonese vs. post-alveolar in English), the English affricates are further characterized by lip-rounding, a feature which is not shared by their Cantonese counterparts; instead, Cantonese affricates are characterized by lip-spreading. Cantonese EAL learners, especially beginners, may find it difficult to pronounce the sounds /tʃ/ and /dʒ/, and they often replace these sounds with /tsʰ/ and /ts/ respectively. In addition to lip-spreading, they may produce *jump* /dʒʌmp/ as 針 [tsɐm].[16]

Similarly, the 'r' (represented by an upside down /ɹ/ in IPA) is absent in Cantonese. Depending on its location in a word, it is realized in different forms. If it appears in the beginning of a syllable, as in *rest*, native Cantonese speakers may replace it with a [w]. Since /ɹ/ is produced with lip-rounding, this feature is maintained by Cantonese speakers as shown by the substitution of the glide [w], which also requires lip protrusion. Therefore, *rest* may be pronounced as *west*; *read* as *weed*; and *run* as *won*. According to Hung (2002, p. 136), the substitution of the glide [w] for [ɹ] is indeed attested in isolated word-reading data from educated Cantonese EAL learners, but such a tendency was found only among a small minority of the 15 subjects in his study.

When /ɹ/ occurs at the end of a syllable, it is either dropped[17] or replaced with a monophthong [ə] (e.g., pronouncing *pair* as [*pe] or in two syllables as [*ˈpeaː]), instead of the normative /peər/ pronounced with a diphthong and an [r]). Since syllable-final approximants in English are acoustically less salient and more difficult to perceive, they are more difficult to acquire.

Missing vowels

For the sake of convenience, we will examine monophthongs in two environments: open syllables (CV), and closed syllables (CVC). There are seven monophthongs in Cantonese (cf. Hung, 2002, pp. 122–127):

/a/: 沙	/ɛ/: 些	/i/: 詩	/ɔ/: 疏	/u/: 夫	/œ/: 鋸	/y/: 書
saa1	*se1*	*si1*	*so1*	*fu1*	*goe3*	*syu1*

This is remarkably similar to Hung's (2002, p. 127) data-driven analysis of the inventory of vowels in the EAL pronunciation of Cantonese-L1 learners, as follows:

---

16. *zam1*

17. Note that in BrE, [ɹ] that occurs in the syllable-final position is dropped unless the word is followed by a word that starts with a vowel. For example, the word *car* is produced without [r] when it is produced on its own, but when it is in a sentence like *The car is nice*, the [r] is produced, because it is followed by a vowel (i.e., [ɪ]).

Table 2.4

Inventory of vowels as shown in the educated Cantonese-L1 EAL learners

Vowel	Examples
[i]	*heat, hit*
[ɛ]	*bet, bat*
[u]	*hoot, hood*
[ɔ]	*cot, caught*
[ɑ]	*heart*
[ʌ]	*hut*
[ɜ]	*hurt*

Note: From 'Towards a Phonology of Hong Kong English', by T. Hung, 2002. In K. Bolton (Ed.), *Hong Kong English: Autonomy and creativity*, p. 127.

Table 2.5

Examples of Hong Kong EAL pronunciation, showing a loss of contrast in RP vowels

Words	HK EAL vowels	RP vowels
heed – hid, heat – hit	/i/	/iː/ – /ɪ/
head – had, bet – bat	/ɛ/	/e/ – /æ/
hoot – hood	/u/	/uː/ – /ʊ/
hawed – hod, caught – cot	/ɔ/	/ɔː/ – /ɒ/

Note: From 'Towards a Phonology of Hong Kong English', by T. Hung, 2002. In K. Bolton (Ed.), *Hong Kong English: Autonomy and creativity*, pp. 125–127.

According to Tables 2.4 and 2.5, educated Chinese speakers of English in Hong Kong tend to produce fewer monophthong vowel contrasts than do RP speakers. In the HKE vowel system, there is a 'lack of the tense/lax or long/short distinction, which more than anything else, accounts for the smaller number of vowel contrasts in HKE' (Hung, 2000, p. 125). Relative to the contrasts made in a number of RP monophthong vowels, we may speak of EAL speakers' under-differentiation of such vowels, as exemplified in the word pairs in Table 2.5.

The monophthongs in the Cantonese vowel inventory are relatively rich, and this seems to help Cantonese speakers produce more or less target-like vowel sounds in English. On the other hand, there are a few Cantonese vowels that are not shared in English. These missing sounds may lead to specific problems for learners of Cantonese from an English-L1 background. The high front rounded vowel /y/ (e.g., 書, [sy], 'book';[18] 住, [dzy], 'live'[19]) and the low mid-central rounded vowel /œ/ (e.g., 鋸,

---

18. *syu1*

19. *zyu6*

[koe], 'saw';[20] 腳, [koek], 'foot'[21]), for example, may be especially difficult for English speakers. Possible substitutions for these sounds include [u], [ɜ], and a diphthong like [iu].

There are three vowels which only occur in a closed syllable (CVC) in Cantonese:

ɐ 實   ɪ 激   ɵ 出
/sɐt/   /kɪk/   /tsʰɵt/[22]

There are some restrictions on what coda can follow these vowels. For instance, /ɐ/ can occur before any coda consonants, so it poses the least problem; /ɪ/, on the other hand, only allows the velar consonants (/ŋ/ and /k/) in the coda position. As for /ɵ/, it is also restricted, but in a different way. It only allows alveolar sounds (/t/ and /n/) to be in the coda position.

The vowel that generates the most problems for Cantonese speakers is the /ɪ/ vowel. As mentioned, its distribution is limited to syllables that contain a velar stop (/k/) or velar nasal (/ŋ/) in the coda position. English words do not conform to this Cantonese phonotactic rule, so words that contain the vowel [ɪ] but followed by a non-velar consonant coda are likely to be problematic for Cantonese EAL learners. As a result, they may replace [ɪ] with a vowel that can occur with a non-velar consonant, and that choice usually falls on [i], as in the following examples:

(6)   'sit'   /sɪt/   →   [sit]   (~ 'seat')
(7)   'mince' /mɪns/   →   [mins] (~ 'means')
(8)   'live'   /lɪv/   →   [liv]   (~ 'leave')

In effect, for such learners, word pairs like *chip–cheap* and *fit–feet* are phonetically indistinguishable. Non-target-like substitutions such as these may be accounted for by the absence of a similar functional contrast in Cantonese. As /i/ and /ɪ/ are contrastive in English (e.g., *chip* [tʃɪp], and *cheap* [tʃiːp]), it is not surprising that such mispronunciations may give rise to communication problems. Another problem has to do with the unstressed middle vowel 'schwa' [ə], which is not found in Cantonese. This is the case of a trisyllabic verb like *consider* (/kənˈsɪd.ər/). Many Cantonese EAL learners tend to assign the same amount of stress to all of the three syllables (i.e., [kɔːnˈsiːdɔː]), rather than pronouncing the first and last syllables with the unstressed schwa.

Native Cantonese speakers generally have little problem in producing the diphthongs in English, because Cantonese has some diphthongs that sound similar to their counterparts in English. However, in Cantonese a diphthong is never followed

---

20. *goe3*
21. *goek3*
22. *sat6, gik1, ceot1*

by a coda, whereas in English a diphthong is sometimes followed by a coda. This will be discussed in the next section.

Differences in the restrictions of sounds in onsets and codas

So far we have discussed problems encountered by Cantonese-L1 EAL learners due to the absence of some of the English sounds in the Cantonese sound inventory. Now we move on to discuss sounds that exist in both English and Cantonese but are nonetheless difficult for native speakers of Cantonese.

The lateral approximant /l/ exists in both Cantonese and English. The English lateral approximant /l/ can occur in the initial or medial position (i.e., the onset of a syllable, characterized as 'clear L'), as in the words *late* and *plate*, and in the syllable-final position (i.e., the coda of a syllable, known as 'dark L'), as in the words *cool* and *tail*. In Cantonese, however, the same sound can only occur in the onset position, as in the word 藍 /lam/.[23] Thus many Chinese EAL learners find it difficult to pronounce the dark L, which is non-existent in Cantonese or Putonghua. Often an epenthetic vowel (typically [ə]) is added to produce an extra syllable (i.e., [lə]). Another strategy employed by Cantonese-L1 EAL learners is to replace the syllable-final [l] with a [w]. This tendency is empirically supported in Hung's (2002) acoustic analysis, as shown in the average formant frequencies of the spectrogram for a word like *feel* (p. 134). Interestingly, according to the isolated word-reading data in Hung's (2002) study, the tendency to pronounce the syllable-final [l] with the velar approximant [w] does not apply when /l/ is preceded by a back vowel such as [ɔ] (e.g. *call*, [kɔː]) or [u] (e.g. *cool*, [kuː]). In this case, the [l] is simply deleted.

Onset: /n/ vs. /l/

In Cantonese, the alveolar nasal /n/ in the syllable-initial position can either be realized as [n] or the alveolar lateral sound [l]. When transferred into English, this free [n]/[l] variation in the syllable-initial position may lead to potential misunderstanding since these two sounds are phonemic in English (and therefore strictly non-interchangeable). Consider the following examples:

(9) 'knife' [naɪf] vs. 'life' [laɪf]
(10) 'night' [naɪt] vs. 'light' [laɪt]

Based on the phonological characteristics in Cantonese, it is predicted that Cantonese-L1 learners are likely to replace syllable-initial /n/ with [l] when speaking in English. This prediction is clearly borne out in Hung's (2002) empirical findings.

---

23. *laam4*

Interestingly, Hung (2002) found that the opposite direction of substitution (/l/ →
[n]) is also quite common in the English pronunciation of the 15 Cantonese-L1 EAL
students in his (2002) study, suggesting that both sounds are indeed treated like free
variants sometimes. Such a bidirectional substitution between /n/ and /l/ may also
be a result of hypercorrection, as when English words with /l/ in the syllable-initial
position are pronounced with [n]. Hung (2002, p. 135) found that, of the 29 words
showing a syllable-initial /n/ and /l/ (pronounced twice by each of the 15 subjects),
18 with initial /l/ were pronounced by some subjects with initial [n],[24] while 11 with
initial /n/ were pronounced by some subjects with initial [l].[25] What is interesting is
that if the rime contains a nasal (e.g. *line* and *lame*), initial /l/ tends to be pronounced
as [n] (i.e., *line* was mispronounced as 'nine' in 37% of all the tokens; *lame* was mispronounced as 'name' in 27% of all the tokens). Conversely, if the syllable begins with
the alveolar nasal /n/, the presence of a nasal in the rime decreases the possibility of
mispronunciation (i.e., *nine* was mispronounced as 'line' in only 7% of all the tokens;
name was mispronounced as 'lame' in barely 3% of all the tokens). In other words,
with a nasal in the rime, the likelihood of the syllable-initial /n/ being pronounced
as [l] is very low. These findings suggest that the variation between syllable-initial
/n/ and /l/ in Cantonese-L1 EAL learners' English pronunciation is not random but
appears to be partly conditioned by the phonological environment of the syllable.
One way to look into this issue more closely is to explore to what extent such a pattern
of variation is related to what Hung (2002) calls 'nasal harmony' (p. 135).

Coda: /n/ vs. /ŋ/

In the coda position, many Cantonese-L1 learners have a tendency to substitute
the alveolar nasal (/n/) for the velar nasal (/ŋ/) in their L1. For instance, the normative pronunciation of the disyllabic verb 翱翔 ('hover', [ŋou tsɜŋ])[26] and noun
銀行 ('bank', [ŋɐn hɔŋ]),[27] may be pronounced as [ou tsɜn] and [ɐn hɔn], respectively.
In both cases, the velar nasal [ŋ] in the onset position is dropped, whereas in the
coda position it is replaced with the alveolar nasal [n]. Such a tendency is likely to
be due to the fact that /n/ and /ŋ/ are treated by some Cantonese speakers as variants, and they use them interchangeably in the coda position. Similar to the [l]/[n]
confusion, the direction of substitution is two-way. That is, /n/ may also be replaced

---

24. These include: *line* (37%), *lame* (27%), *longing* (17%), *lead* (17%), *loose* (17%), *loud* (17%), *lower* (17%),
    lot (13%), *lake* (13%), *leafing* (10%), *long* (10%), *low* (10%), *leaf* (7%), *let* (7%), *leaving* (7%), *light* (7%),
    leave (3%), *lumber* (3%) (Hung 2002, p. 135).
25. These include: *night* (33%), *no* (23%), *naked* (20%), *number* (20%), *need* (13%), *not* (10%), *net* (10%),
    now (10%), *noose* (7%), *nine* (7%), *name* (3%) (Hung 2002, p. 135).
26. *ngou6 coeng4*
27. *ngan4 hong4*

by [ŋ], and /ŋ/ may be replaced by [n]. This tendency, which is often characterized as 'lazy pronunciation' (懶音, *laan5 jam1*, *lǎn yīn*), is getting increasingly common among younger Cantonese speakers, who in effect treat the velar and alveolar nasals as allophones in the coda position. For instance:

(11) 餅乾 /pɛŋ kɔn/ ('biscuit')
   a.   [pɛŋ kɔn] (regular pronunciation)
   b.   [pɛn kɔŋ] ('lazy pronunciation')

As shown in example (11), those Cantonese EAL learners who show intrapersonal variation in their pronunciation of 餅乾, as [pɛŋ kɔn] (11a) or [pɛn kɔŋ] (11b) may extend this pattern of variation to their English pronunciation. Since the two nasal sounds, /n/ and /ŋ/, are used contrastively in the coda position in English, replacing one sound with the other will deviate from the normative pronunciation. For example:

(12) 'hang' /hæŋ/ → [hæn]

It is not clear to what extent such a mispronunciation may be attributed to the practice of so-called lazy pronunciation in Cantonese. What is clear is that, if *hang* is mispronounced as [hæn], as in (12), it may conceivably lead to intelligibility problems, not only because there is no such word ([hæn]) in English, but perhaps more seriously, it may likely be heard as 'hand' rather than 'hang'.

Stops in the coda position

There is a fundamental difference between the English and Cantonese stops in the syllable-final position: Whereas the English stops are normally released (i.e., opening the closure at the place of articulation to let the air flow out of the mouth), as is the case with /t/ in the word *fat*, the Cantonese counterparts are not released, as is the case with /t/ in 發達 (/fat dat/,[28] 'get rich'). This contrast helps to explain some of the problems in pronunciation on the part of L2 learners of English or Cantonese. It is well known that Cantonese-dominant learners of English have a tendency not to release English voiceless stops. As for learners of Cantonese coming from an English-speaking background, at the initial stage of learning, they tend to carry over pronunciation rules from English and erroneously release the plosives occurring in the final position of a Cantonese syllable such as 發達 (/fat dat/, 'get rich') and 赤鱲角 (/tsɛk lap kɔk/,[29] 'Chek Lap Kok [Hong Kong International Airport]').

---

28. *faat3 daat6*
29. *cek3 laap6 gok3*

A logical consequence of releasing a coda is liaison (or linking), which happens if the next word begins with a vowel. As a result, the consonant is carried forward to the next syllable. For instance, the pronunciation pattern of *pick it up* should be [pɪkɪtʌp], so all of the three syllables are headed by a voiceless plosive, with no glottal stop in between. By contrast, liaison is uncommon in Cantonese (and Chinese varieties in general), since syllable-final plosives and nasals in Cantonese are not released. Consider a bisyllabic adjective like 不安 (*bat1 on1*, 'uneasy'): As the syllable-final /t/ is unreleased, it is not carried forward to the second syllable that begins with the vowel /ɒ/. This contrastive difference helps explain why many Cantonese-L1 EAL learners have a tendency not to release the syllable-final plosives of the words in a verb phrase like *pick it up*. Instead, a glottal stop is inserted at the boundaries between *pick* and *it*, and between *it* and *up*. Such a lack of awareness of liaison as a pronunciation feature in English is one of the many problems related to non-native accents among Chinese EAL learners.

The post-alveolar fricatives

The production of post-alveolar sounds in English could be problematic for Cantonese-L1 EAL learners. Although [ʃ] is a possible sound in Cantonese, it only occurs in very specific environments and is only produced by some speakers. For those [ʃ] speakers, the initial consonants of the words in (13) are all [ʃ], while for other speakers, they are [s]. This allophonic alternation only occurs if the alveolar fricative /s/ is followed by a high front rounded vowel /y/. Since [ʃ] is only available to some speakers as an allophone, many Cantonese speakers tend to replace the English /ʃ/ sound with [s].

(13)   書 / 雪 / 算
        [ʃy]   [ʃyt]   [ʃyn]
        syu1 *syut3* *syun3*

The matter is further complicated by the actual phonetic realization of the English /ʃ/. When producing the sound /ʃ/, native speakers of English typically protrude their lips simultaneously. This is not a necessary requirement for /ʃ/ in general but rather a language-specific feature in English (e.g., Japanese /ʃ/ is unrounded). As a result, many Cantonese-L1 EAL learners tend to replace the vowel immediately following /ʃ/ with a rounded vowel, as in examples (14) and (15):

(14)   'she'   /ʃi/   →   [*sy]
(15)   'shallow' /'ʃælou/ →   [*'sœlou]

Deviations that arise from the differences in syllable structure

Syllable structure in Cantonese and English

Unlike English, a language written with an alphabet, Chinese is written in non-alphabetic or logographic characters (漢字, *hànzì*, *hon3 zi6*). The written forms of most of the Chinese characters today may be traced to Shi Huang Di of the Qin dynasty (秦始皇帝, 221–206 BCE) over 2,000 years ago. The Qin emperor was the first to make an attempt to standardize the Chinese language, including the writing system. Since the Chinese writing system is logographic, the relationship between the written form and the pronunciation of a given character is often indirect, sometimes obscure. Low-frequency characters are easy to forget. This is reflected in the Chinese proverb 'pen ready to write, but don't know how to'.[30] This has implications for literacy acquisition, in that in general it takes more time for children to learn to read and write Chinese than to read and write an alphabetic language like English (McBride, 2016; for more in-depth discussion, see Li, 2017).

A Chinese character is normally pronounceable as a single syllable (音節). With few exceptions, most characters have one or more meanings.[31] As Duanmu (2007, p. 3) puts it, 'a character is basically a monosyllabic word written as one graphic unit'. The smallest unit of meaning is known as a morpheme. Given that almost all Chinese characters are monosyllabic and have a more or less well-defined meaning (i.e., morphemic), linguistically Chinese characters are also characterized as morpho-syllables.

The structure of a Cantonese syllable is much simpler than that of an English syllable. Take 飲茶 /jɐm tsʰa/[32] and 點心 /tɪm sɐm/.[33] There are four syllables in these two expressions. With the exception of [tsʰa], which has a consonant-vowel (CV) structure, each syllable carries the structure consonant-vowel-consonant (CVC). Empirical tests with other Cantonese syllables suggest that these three structural positions actually represent the maximal structure of a Cantonese syllable. In other words, no Cantonese syllable is found to contain an additional vowel or consonant position. There is thus one fundamental difference with regard to the systems of Cantonese and English consonants: Unlike English, Cantonese has no consonant clusters. This contrastive difference may help to explain why Chinese learners of English in Hong Kong tend to have difficulty pronouncing English words with consonant clusters properly, as in the case of *strengths* /stɹɛŋθs/. Its syllable structure, CCCVCCC, is probably the most complex in English.

---

30. 執筆忘字 (*zhí bǐ wàng zì*/*zap1 bat1 mong4 zi6*, literally 'hold pen forget character').
31. Consider a disyllabic word like 琵琶 (*pípá*/*pei4 paa4*): It is rare for 琵 or 琶 to be used in isolation; similarly, the first morpho-syllable of 蝴蝶 (*hú dié*/*wu4 dip2*) is seldom used on its own.
32. *jam2 caa4*
33. *dim2 sam1*

The syllable [tsʰa] in the above example has the structure CV (notice that [ts] is one single phonetic symbol representing the aspirated alveolar affricate, see Table 2.2). It can be shown that some other syllables carry the structure VC, as in 鴨 [ap], or just V, as in 亞 [a]. Hence there are four possible configurations or structures for a Cantonese syllable:

V   CV   VC   CVC

For the sake of convenience, the basic syllable structure in Cantonese has been summarized as

$(C_1) V (C_2)$

where the parentheses signal that the consonants on each side of the vowel (nucleus of the Cantonese syllable) are optional. As noted by Duanmu (2007, p. 15), the nucleus of a syllable is usually filled by a vowel; the part before the nucleus (C_1) is called the 'onset' (節首音) or initial (聲母),[34] the part after the nucleus (C_2) is known as the 'coda' (音節尾), while the nucleus and the coda together make up the 'rime' (also spelled 'rhyme', 韻母). As discussed above, some sounds can cause difficulties to Cantonese-L1 EAL learners because they occur in positions where the same sounds will occur in Cantonese. In the rest of this section, we further discuss how these differences in syllable structure between English and Cantonese give rise to EAL pronunciation difficulties.

Consonant clusters (輔音音叢／輔音連綴)

Two English consonants that are frequently embedded in consonant clusters are the two approximants /l/ and /ɹ/. In Cantonese, the lateral approximant /l/ occurs only in the syllable-initial position. On the other hand, the alveolar lateral /l/ in English may occur in the initial, medial, and final position of a syllable. The other English approximant /ɹ/ has a very similar distribution pattern. Since there are no consonant clusters in Cantonese (i.e., CC or CCC is not a possible sequence in the syllable structure of Cantonese), learners of English in Hong Kong, especially beginners, may experience some problem with /l/ and /ɹ/ when either of them forms part of a consonant cluster (Chan 2006a, 2006b, 2010). One commonly used strategy is to simplify the pronunciation by inserting an additional vowel—a process technically known as epenthesis—to the consonant preceding the English approximant. Accordingly, monosyllabic words like *crown* (/kraʊn/) and *clutch* (/klʌtʃ/) may be pronounced with two or three syllables as [*kɑˈrɑːn] and [*kɑˈlʌtʃy] (cf. Chan, 2006a, 2006b, 2010). By inserting

---

34. When there is no (C_1) to fill the onset position, the syllable in question is said to have 'zero onset'.

a vowel, the resulting pronunciation consists of syllables that resemble a Cantonese syllable structure CV.CVC or CV.CV.CV (the dots indicate syllable boundaries).

Another strategy is to delete one of the consonants in the cluster. For example, the word *frog* /fɹɒg/ is sometimes pronounced as *fog* [fog] by Cantonese-L1 EAL learners. Like epenthesis, deleting one of the consonants results in a CVC structure, which is a plausible structure in Cantonese.

In addition to a simpler syllable structure, Cantonese also has more restrictions as to what consonants can appear in the coda position of a syllable. In Cantonese, only stops /p, t, k/ and nasals /m, n, ŋ/ are allowed to occur in the coda position, as illustrated by the following morpho-syllables.

Coda position filled by a stop:			Coda position filled by a nasal:		
/p, t, k/			/m, n, ŋ/		
蝶 /dip/	dip6	'butterfly'	點 /dim/	dim2	'point'
跌 /dit/	dit3	'fall'	電 /din/	din6	'electricity'
敵 /dik/	dik6	'enemy'	訂 /diŋ/	ding6	'reserve'

On the other hand, in English, all consonants, except for the glottal fricative /h/ (喉擦音), may occur in the coda position. As a result, when Cantonese-L1 speakers encounter codas other than stops and nasals in English (e.g., /s/ as in *bus*), they tend to insert a vowel after it to make its syllable structure approximate the syllable structure in Cantonese (i.e., CV.CV, as in 巴士 [basi]).[35]

Diphthong + coda

Even though both English and Cantonese have diphthongs, in Cantonese a diphthong is not followed by a consonant. For instance, while /eɪ/ is found in both Cantonese (compare: 美 'beauty'; English: *may*, both pronounced as /meɪ/), there are no Cantonese morpho-syllables where /eɪ/ is followed by a consonant as coda. This is one possible reason why, for words like *claim*, *game* and *gain*, the target diphthong /eɪ/ is often reduced and replaced with /e/ (i.e., /kleɪm/ → [klem]; /geɪm/ → [gem]; /geɪn/ → [gen]). A similar problem occurs with other diphthongs below.

	Cantonese diphthong		RP diphthong		EAL pronunciation
(16)	/oʊ/ 奧 [ou]	~	'code' /koʊd/	→	[*kʰʊk]
(17)	/aʊ/ 拗 [au]	~	'count' /kaʊnt/	→	[*kʰaŋ]
(18)	/eɪ/ 你 [nei]	~	'came' /keɪm/	→	[*kʰɛm]
(19)	/ɔɪ/ 愛 [ɔi]	~	'coin' /kɔɪn/	→	[*kʰɔn]
(20)	/aɪ/ 哎 [ai]	~	'kind' /kaɪnd/	→	[*kʰan]

---

35. *baal si2*

Non-target-like substitutions, such as those in (16)–(20), are commonly heard among Cantonese-L1 learners of English. Another pattern of mispronunciation, often produced by elementary learners of English, consists of reanalysing English diphthongs such as (RP) *ear* (/ɪəʳ/), *air* (/eəʳ/), *more* /mɔːʳ/, and *poor* (/pɔːʳ/) as two monophthongs ([*ɪːaː], [*eːaː], [*mɔːaː], [*puːaː]). In addition, the word *lounge*, which contains a diphthong and whose target pronunciation is (/laʊndʒ/), is widely mispronounced by Cantonese speakers as [*lɔːntʃ], making it indistinguishable from another word with that pronunciation: *launch*. This pronunciation error is another salient example whereby a monophthong (/ɔː/) is used to substitute for a diphthong (/aʊ/).

Suprasegmental features

Word stress

Word stress in English is mostly unpredictable. There is no explicit rule that can predict which syllable within a word should be assigned the primary stress, although we could speak of a tendency. Trisyllabic English words which are morphologically related (i.e., sharing the same root) may not have the same stress pattern. This is the case of the words *summation* and *summative*: In the case of *summation*, the primary stress is placed on the second syllable [sʌ'**meɪ**ʃʌn], whereas the one for *summative* is placed on the initial syllable ['**sʌ**mətɪv]. In extreme cases, polysyllabic words formed by derivational morphology may assign the primary stress to the first, second, or third syllable. Compare:

an**a**lyze	**a**nalyst	an**a**lysis	ana**ly**tical
/'æn.əl.aɪz/	/'æn.ə.lɪst/	/ə'næl.ə.sɪs/	/ˌæn.ə'lɪt.ɪ.kəl/

Although there are a few word-stress rules in English (Halle, 1973), the acquisition of word stress, and stress assignment in general, is understandably challenging for Cantonese-L1 EAL learners (Chen, 2013; cf. Chen, 2015). In sum, the difficulties posed by English stress may be explained by both the absence of stress in Cantonese and the complications of stress placement in English.

Rhythm (節奏、韻律) *and intonation* (腔調)

Up to now, the focus of our discussion has been mainly on pronunciation at the word level. In this section, we will focus on connected speech. The most important differ-ence is that English is a 'stress-timed' language, while Cantonese is a 'syllable-timed' language. Syllable-timed means that every syllable is given roughly the same duration but not necessarily equal stress, as can be seen in Putonghua: 我學過法語 (*wǒ xué guò fǎyǔ*) and Cantonese: 我學過法文 (*ngo5 hok6 gwo3 faat3 man2*), both meaning 'I have learned French'. There is basically no reduction in vowel length or the intensity (volume or energy) with which each syllable is pronounced. In contrast, in English, the time given to each syllable varies: A stressed syllable is often given a longer duration than an unstressed syllable. This is understandable to the extent that most of the English words are polysyllabic, and so it would be very uneconomical and tiring if all the syllables in a word such as *communication* or *international* were pronounced with the same amount of linguistic effort. Thus in an utterance like *the match begins at seven*, stress is given on the underlined syllables. The real time assigned to the pronunciation of unstressed syllables is reduced considerably, sometimes imperceptibly. One way to get a feel for the stressed pattern is to clap our hands rhythmically while pronouncing the words aloud. This is particularly clear if each clap coincides with the stressed syllable.

The vowels of unstressed syllables are usually reduced to [ə], and they are often deleted in casual speech. For example, the word 'camera' /ˈkæ.mə.ɹə/ (three syllables) can be reduced to [ˈkʰæm.ɹə] (two syllables), but the unstressed syllable can never be pronounced with a full vowel: [*ˈkʰæ.mə.ɹɑ] or [*ˈkʰæ.mɑ.ɹə]. This property of the English phonology differs from that in Cantonese considerably because there is relatively little reduction in the pronunciation of Cantonese syllables.[36] Unlike English, the duration for each syllable in Cantonese does not depend on the stress assignment; rather, all syllables have roughly the same duration (with minor differences depending on the coda). Since the duration of each syllable is dependent on its stress assignment, English is characterized as stress-timed, while Cantonese is generally regarded as syllable-timed.

There is evidence that Cantonese-L1 EAL learners in Hong Kong tend to transfer the syllable-timed characteristic of Cantonese connected speech into English. This happens when each of the syllables in a polysyllabic word such as *international* is given the same amount of stress, *in-ter-na-tion-al*. How to help students overcome such a cross-linguistic influence in English connected speech is one pedagogical challenge for teachers of English.

Word stress vs. contrastive stress

It is useful to make a distinction between word stress (also known as 'word accent') and contrastive stress (Duanmu, 2007). When uttering a sentence like *the match begins at seven*, or a noun phrase such as *international conference*, stress is normally assigned to the underlined syllables as shown. Word stress is especially important for

---

36. Although infrequent and untypical, reduction does occur in Cantonese. For instance, 唔係呀嘛 [m haɪ a ma] (JyutPing: *m4 hai6 aa6 maa5*) is commonly reduced to 咪嘛 [maɪ ma] (Jyutping: *mai6 maa5*).

distinguishing between polysyllabic words which are spelt the same but which belong to different word classes, as in *import* (v.) and *import* (n.), *refuse* (v.) and *refuse* (n.). Since most Chinese syllables are morphemic, word stress is not so useful or relevant for analysing the pronunciation of morpho-syllables in Chinese, such as Mandarin and Cantonese.

Contrastive stress occurs when the speaker makes use of stress to bring out a contrast between the stressed unit and some other units that could have occurred in the syntactic position of the stressed unit. Thus in the utterance *Jim likes you*, the unmarked stress is the verb *likes*. But if the speaker wants to introduce a contrast between the subject *Jim* and other possible subjects (e.g., not John, nor George), the speaker could place the stress on *Jim* (i.e., *Jim likes you*, with the additional meaning: not others). Of course, similar contrasts may be applied to the verb *likes* or the object *you*—if the speaker wants to signal a contrast between 'likes' and some other verbs (e.g., not 'loves you', as you may think), or an object other than 'you' (e.g., not 'likes me', as you are imagining).

Duanmu (2007) explains that all languages make use of the Information-Stress Principle to mark contrastive stress. According to this principle, 'a word or phrase that carries more information than its neighbor(s) should be stressed' (p. 144). The reason is that 'contrasted words carry more information of interest and we give more stress to words that have more information and less stress to words that have less information' (p. 144).

In articulatory terms, how is stress produced or realized phonetically? Research in acoustic phonetics[37] shows that, whether it is word stress or contrastive stress, a syllable may be stressed by using one of three linguistic means: (i) a higher pitch level (comparable to a higher musical note), (ii) louder volume (larger amplitude), or (iii) vowel lengthening (longer duration), or any combination of these. For instance, to realize a contrastive stress such as *Jim* in *Jim likes you*, we may pronounce *Jim* (i) with a higher pitch, (ii) more loudly, or (iii) by lengthening the vowel [ɪ], or do any of these in any combination. According to our observation, compared with BrE and AmE speakers, educated speakers of English in Hong Kong tend to make more use of a higher pitch to produce or realize stress, while speakers of native varieties may make more use of the two other linguistic means.

Tones (聲調)

Tone and intonation are related but distinct concepts. Intonation refers to the speech contour of a unit larger than a word. Both Cantonese and English can make use of

---

37. Acoustic phonetics (聲學語音學) investigates speech sounds by measuring their frequency, duration, intensity, etc.

a number of intonation patterns to express a range of interpersonal meanings (e.g., surprise, irritation, doubt; Lock, 1996). In English, one obvious example is the intonation pattern used to realize a yes-no question, which may be characterized as 'rising towards the end' (e.g. 'Is it true?').

Unlike English, Cantonese does not make use of word stress, but it utilizes pitch for another purpose—tones. Like other Chinese dialects, Cantonese is a tone language, in that different pitch levels are used to differentiate lexical meanings. As is well known, Putonghua has four distinctive tones, while Cantonese has six: three level tones, two rising tones, and one falling tone. For example, the segmental in Cantonese /fu/ has six distinctive meanings depending on the tone level:

high level	high rising	mid level	low falling	low rising	low level
fu1 夫	*fu2* 虎	*fu3* 富	*fu4* 符	*fu5* 婦	*fu6* 父
('husband')	('tiger')	('rich')	('talisman')	('woman')	('father')

The Chinese characters here are stock examples only; we must bear in mind that for practically every tone level, a given morpho-syllable may have one or more homophones. Notice that the system used by Chinese phonologists is not quite the same. According to traditional Chinese phonology, Cantonese has 九聲 ('nine sounds'): six distinctive tone contours plus three 'entering tones' (入聲). An entering tone ends with a consonant (stop) in the syllable-final position. For example:

/sɪk1/ 色   /sɛk3/ 錫[38]   /sɪk6/ 食

Because of this feature in Cantonese, Cantonese-L1 speakers tend to assign tones to English words. A stressed syllable in a word is often given the high level tone (1), which has a high pitch level, whereas unstressed syllables are often given the low falling tone (4) or the low level tone (6). For example, a word like *national* is often pronounced by Cantonese EAL learners as [lɛk ʃɵn loʊ] (叻唇奴／叻唇勞).[39] As a result, the pitch contour of a word or a sentence may rise or fall rather abruptly, resulting in Cantonese-accented pronunciation.

English-L1 learners' problems pronouncing Cantonese sounds

The affricate sounds in English are /tʃ/ and /dʒ/, while those in Cantonese are /ts/ and /tsʰ/. Not only are their voicing and aspiration realizations different, but their respective place of articulation also differs slightly. Whereas the English affricates are in the post-alveolar region, the Cantonese counterparts are produced in the alveolar region. Although English consists of both alveolar sounds /t/ and /s/, and the sequence of /ts/

---

38. Notice that in *sɛk3*, there is a difference in vowel quality as well as tone.
39. *lek1 sheon4 nou4/lek1 sheon4 lou4*

is also phonotactically possible in words such as 'cats' [kæ**ts**], /ts/ remains a difficult sound for English speakers to produce when it occurs in the syllable-initial position in Cantonese. As a result, it is common for English speakers to replace the Cantonese aspirated affricate /tsʰ/ with /tʃ/ (e.g., pronouncing /tsʰa/, 茶, 'tea' as [*tʃa]). They also tend to substitute /dʒ/ or /z/ for the unaspirated affricate /ts/ in Cantonese. Thus the high-frequency word 紙 (/tsi/, 'paper') is often mispronounced by English speakers as [*dʒi] or [*zi].

Nasals in Cantonese, /m, n, ŋ/, have one distributional characteristic in common with stops in Cantonese /p, t, k/: They may occur in the final position of a Cantonese syllable, as shown in the brand name 任天堂 /jɐm tin tɔŋ/,[40] a Japanese company which specializes in computer games products. Such a distributional characteristic, however, is not shared between Cantonese and English nasals: Whereas all Cantonese nasals may occur in the syllable-initial position (e.g., the first-person singular pronoun 我 /ŋɔː/), the velar nasal /ŋ/ in English as a rule is not found in that position. Although /ŋ/ does occur as a syllable-initial consonant in Cantonese, there is considerable variation within the Hong Kong Cantonese community, in that some people treat /ŋ/ and the 'zero' phoneme in the syllable-initial position as variants, while others simply do not have /ŋ/ in their 'dialect'. For instance, depending on the individual, the first person pronoun 我 in Cantonese is pronounced either as [ŋɔː] or [ɔː]. For learners of Cantonese from an English-speaking background who are unaccustomed to the syllable-initial velar nasal, it is conceivable that they will have difficulty pronouncing Cantonese words like 我 [ŋɔː].

Hong Kong English: A new variety?

Up to now, we have characterized Cantonese EAL learners' non-native pronunciation features as deviations, with the implication that they are IL errors in need of teacher feedback and correction. Some scholars believe, however, that such deviations are motivated by the speakers' desire to assert their Hong Kong identity, which may be glossed as: 'I speak English with a Hong Kong accent because I want to be seen as a Hongkonger'. Regardless of whether English in Hong Kong is more appropriately analysed as a new variety (HKE), Hung (2002) believes the phonological system of English spoken by Cantonese-dominant Hongkongers should be investigated in its own terms. In particular, whether the purpose is to ascertain the relative autonomy of HKE, or to better understand how teachers can help them approximate the norms of 'native' pronunciation, there is a need for us to understand their EAL pronunciation

---

40. *jam6 tin1 tong4*

patterns and features using rigorous research methods. To describe the phonology or sound system of educated Chinese users of English in Hong Kong, Hung (2002) points out the need to investigate three dimensions or components, as follows:

1. An inventory of **phonemes**, or sound segments which contrast with each other;
2. Systematic variations in the **phonetic** realizations of these phonemes, i.e., **alternation**;
3. The **distribution** of individual segments in relation to other segments. (Hung 2002, p. 121, emphasis in original)

Whether such deviations from RP or Standard AmE pronunciation patterns are more appropriately seen as 'deficit' (therefore, IL 'errors' in need of correction) or mere differences indicative of the speakers' intended identity (HKE) continues to be debated. To the extent that English is not commonly used for intra-ethnic communication among Cantonese Hongkongers—unlike Chinese Singaporeans in this regard—it may not be as appropriate to characterize HKE as a new variety. This is also the reason why English in Hong Kong is variably seen as a second or foreign language (Li, 2017). More research is needed to better understand Cantonese-L1 EAL speakers' pronunciation features and EAL learners' pronunciation difficulties in the learning process.

Questions and activities

1. Name the place of articulation of the following consonants represented by IPA.
   (i) [b]
   (ii) [k]
   (iii) [ɹ]
   (iv) [θ]
   (v) [v]
2. Name the manner of articulation of the following consonants represented by IPA.
   (i) [f]
   (ii) [n]
   (iii) [j]
   (iv) [p]
   (v) [tʃ]
3. Compare the following words in English and Cantonese. How do they differ in pronunciation? Use as many of the features (e.g., place of articulation, voicing, and vowel height) as you can in your answer. You may use a dictionary to help you.

      (i)   鼉 (diu1) *deal*

      (ii)   風 (fung1) *phone*

      (iii)   先 (sin1) *sin*

      (iv)   鋪 (pou1) *poll*

      (v)   蒸糕 (zing1 gou1) *jingle*

4.   Explain why native Cantonese speakers tend to mispronounce the following words according to syllable structure.

      (i)   *program* → ['poʊkʷɛm]

      (ii)   *like* → [laɪ]

      (iii)   *game* → [kɛm]

      (iv)   *year* → [ia]

5.   The following is a transcription of an excerpt of the conversation between Jimmy Fallon (J), an American comedian, and Hilary Clinton (H). Assume you are one of them and read the lines aloud. Pay attention to word stress, intonation, and rhythm while you read. You can view the conversation at this link: https://www.youtube.com/watch?v=PiDFL8tgn0Q

J: . . . they don't just give this job, right? You really got to work for this job.

H: You really have to work.

J: And so I was just wondering this is the biggest job in the world, eh, it's almost like you're applying for this job.

H: Right.

J: And we're hiring you.

H: It's like a job interview.

J: It really is.

H: It goes on for months, but it is a job interview.

J: Well I was wondering if you'd like to do a job interview now.

H: Sure, sure.

J: Like you're applying for a job.

H: Absolutely. Absolutely.

J: The biggest job in the world, the president of the United States.

H: Okay. Alright.

J: Eh, hey Hilary, thank you for coming down.

H: My pleasure. Thanks for having me.

J: Eh, how'd you hear about the position?

H: Eh, fourth grade, social studies.

J: Why don't you tell us a bit about yourself?

H: Well, em, I think that I have the experience and qualifications, to tackle the range of challenges this job presents, like economy, national security, foreign policy, health care, education. I've done lot of work, and eh, I have references.

J: Why do you want this job?

H: 'Cos I really care about what happens to our country. It means a lot to me to make sure that we keep producing good opportunities for people, how everybody have a chance to live up to their God-given potential. And there's more we can do, and I want to try to make that happen for everybody.

Further reading

Chan and Li's (2000) study of Cantonese-English contrastive phonology is accessible and easy to follow, with many more examples of pronunciation difficulties commonly encountered by Cantonese EAL learners of English. Hung (2002) is a highly readable article introducing how to research the phonology of a language variety like HKE. To better understand the technical terminologies in the study of phonetics and phonology, visit the website of the IPA (2015) and the *Handbook of the IPA*, which is downloadable from https://www.internationalphoneticassociation.org/content/ipa-handbook-downloads.

3
Transitivity and Syntactic Structures

Argument structure

Argument structure is one of the most important domains in grammar that L2 learners need to master before they can form grammatical sentences in the target language. The study of argument structure, in turn, is premised on a good understanding of the concept of verb transitivity, because in many cases the verb determines what kinds of phrase should (not) be present. The following sentences were produced by students of the authors, and they all suffer from one problem of complementation or another:

(1) This essay discusses whether popular culture can enhance and motivate second language learners.
(2) The researcher proposed from the theoretical perspective.
(3) Students can easily access to different kinds of cultures.

In (1), *second language learners* cannot be the object of the verb *enhance*, because one can only enhance things such as *language learning* but not *second language learners*. The problem of (1) is thus the wrong choice of object. In both (2) and (3), the verbs *propose* and *access* require a noun phrase to follow them, but they are followed by the prepositional phrases *from the theoretical perspective* (2) and *to different kinds of cultures* (3) instead. These two kinds of error are common among second language learners of English. To help them deal with these problems, in the following, we explain when a direct object, and what kind, can be used with a verb to form a grammatical sentence.

Transitivity in English

In this chapter, we compare two major types of sentence structure, transitive and intransitive, and compare the ways they are used in English and Chinese. Before doing so, we need to know what the terms 'transitive' and 'intransitive' mean. Transitivity is often seen as a property of a verb, of which the information is stored in the lexicon

(Chomsky, 1981; Jackendoff, 1990). Transitive verbs require a noun phrase as an argument to follow the verb directly (Hartman & Stork, 1972; Kleiser, 2008; Richards, Platt, & Weber 1985; Robins, 1964). Consider (4)–(6):

(4)   Peter broke the vase.
(5)   Susan bought a bicycle.
(6)   Mary scolded her son.

We can see from (4) to (6) that the verbs *break, buy,* and *scold* are all followed directly by a noun phrase: *the vase, a bicycle,* and *her son.* We therefore call these verbs 'transitive verbs' and the following noun phrases 'objects'. If the noun phrases are removed, these sentences would become unacceptable under most circumstances, as in (7) to (9):

(7)   *Peter broke. (to mean: Peter broke something)
(8)   *Susan bought.
(9)   *Mary scold.

Some verbs, however, do not require any noun phrases to follow them. Look at examples (10)–(12):

(10) Peter ran.
(11) She laughed.
(12) Helen fell.

In each of these examples, no noun phrase is required after the verb to make the sentence complete. In fact, if we add a noun phrase after the verb in (11) and (12), the sentence will become unacceptable,[1] as shown in (13) and (14). We therefore call these verbs 'intransitive verbs' (Carnie, 2006; Kleiser, 2008).

(13) *She laughed me.
(14) *Helen fell the ground.

Although noun phrases often cannot be added as complements after intransitive verbs, prepositional phrases and adverbial phrases may be added, as illustrated in (15)–(17):

(15) Peter ran to the store.
(16) She laughed at me.
(17) Helen fell suddenly.

---

1. For Example (10), some noun phrases can follow *run.* For instance, one can say *Peter ran a mile.* Even in this case, however, *run* is not considered a transitive verb, because one cannot change it into a passive sentence, such as *A mile was run by Peter.*

In (15) and (16), *to the store* and *at me* are prepositional phrases, because they are led or introduced by a preposition, *to* or *at*. Because they are not noun phrases, we do not call them objects. Some English verbs can be both transitive and intransitive depending on how they are used, as shown in (18) and (19):

(18) Mary ate <u>an apple</u>.
(19) Mary ate.

We can see that the object *an apple* in (18) can be omitted, as in (19), although the meaning may be slightly different from (18). Now compare *eat* with the verb *break*. We have shown above that *break* is a transitive verb. Like *eat*, *break* can be an intransitive verb but not in the same way as *eat*, as shown in (18) and (19). Look at (4) and (7), reproduced below, and (20):

(4) Peter broke the vase.
(7) *Peter broke.
(20) The vase broke.

We have seen that (4) is grammatical, but (7) is not. However, if we select the object in (4) to be the subject, as in (20), the sentence becomes acceptable. Thus the difference between *eat* and *break* is that, in the case of *eat*, no change to the subject is required regardless of whether the verb is used transitively (18) or intransitively (19), whereas in the case of *break*, the subject is a doer (i.e., *Peter*) when *break* is used transitively, and is an object (i.e., *the vase*) when the verb is used intransitively. We will discuss this below using the concept of 'semantic roles'.

One of the problems L2 learners of English face is to remember which verbs are transitive and which are intransitive, and learners' ability to do so is often influenced by their first language. Chan (2004), for example, showed that Hong Kong secondary students tend to use *care* as a transitive verb, as in *We should always more care old men's health* (p. 65), of which the corresponding verb in Chinese is a transitive verb. Unfortunately, there is no universal rule about whether a given verb is transitive or intransitive. In other words, a transitive verb in, say, Chinese, does not necessarily mean that the corresponding verb is also transitive in English (see below).

There is, however, a cross-linguistic trend that, the more semantically transitive[2] an event is, the more likely it will be described with a transitive construction (Hopper & Thompson, 1980; Tsunoda, 1985). For example, across languages, it is more likely for the act of killing somebody to be described transitively than is the act of liking

---

2. Hopper and Thompson (1980) proposed 10 parameters that measure transitivity semantically. Examples of these parameters are kinesis, punctuality, and volitionality. For example, *John killed Mary* is semantically more transitive than *John likes beer* because the act of killing is an action (kinesis), whereas liking is a state; killing is punctual, whereas liking is stative; and killing is often volitional, whereas liking is often not.

somebody, because the act of killing is semantically more transitive in the sense that it involves a transfer of force from one participant to a second participant, causing the second participant to change its state (from being alive to being dead). The act of liking, on the other hand, does not involve any transfer of forces from one participant to a second participant, and the second participant is usually not affected by the act of liking. In English, since transitivity of a verb is often opaque, the best way is to look up a good dictionary when unsure whether a verb is characteristically used transitively or intransitively, or both.

Transitivity in Chinese

Let us turn to transitivity in Chinese. We noted above that transitivity is related to whether a verb requires an argument to follow it. The same definition may be applied to Chinese. Look at (21)–(23):

(21) 張 三 打 破 了 花 瓶。
Zhāngsān   dǎ   pò   le   huāpíng
Zhangsan   hit   broken   ASP   vase
'Zhangsan broke the vase.'

(22) 李 四 買 了 一 輛 腳 踏 車。
Lǐsì   mǎi   le   yī   liàng   jiǎotàchē
Lisi   buy   ASP   one   CL   bicycle
'Lisi bought a bicycle.'

(23) 她 罵 我 的 兒 子。
Tā   mà   wǒ   de   érzi
She   scold   my   NOM   son
'She scolded my son.'

We can see from these examples that these verbs (打破, *dǎ pò*, 'break'; 買, *mǎi*, 'buy'; and 罵, *mà*, 'scold') allow a noun phrase to follow them. It should be noted that 了 (le) is a perfective marker and is part of the verb phrase. However, the situation is more complicated in Chinese than in English. In English, subject-verb agreement, word order, and case marking (e.g., the use of *him* instead of *he* tells us the phrase serves as an object in the sentence) give information on whether a verb is transitive or not. In Chinese, however, identifying transitive and intransitive verbs is not as straightforward as in English, for three reasons.

First, Chinese allows for a null argument. A null argument is understood to be present but not included or pronounced. In other words, a language allows null arguments if the language allows the subject, the object, or both to be omitted from a sentence. To illustrate how Chinese allows null arguments, we may use the same test as we did for (7)–(9) to test whether the sentences in (21)–(23) become unacceptable without the object in Chinese. We can see that, except for (23), the sentences are acceptable without an object, for example, as a response to a question like (24):

(24) 甲：那 個 花 瓶 呢？
　　　Nà　gè　huāpíng　ne
　　　That　CL　vase　　Q
　　A:　'(what happened to) that vase?'
　　乙：張 三 打 破 了。
　　　Zhāngsān　dǎ　pò　　le
　　　Zhangsan　hit　broken　ASP
　　B:　'Zhangsan broke (it).'

One may argue that the object can be omitted because both interlocutors know that they are talking about the vase. In fact, omission of an argument is very common in Chinese but less so in English. If we compare the equivalent conversation in English in (25), we can see that the pronoun *it* is still needed after *broke*. The reason is that a null argument is not usually allowed in English.

(25) A:　What happened to the vase?
　　B:　Peter broke i̲t̲.

That Chinese allows a null argument thus poses a problem in identifying transitive and intransitive verbs in Chinese. Because arguments can be omitted, it is sometimes difficult to decide whether a verb is transitive or not.

Second, Chinese does not have as many prepositions as English does. Consider the examples in (26) and (27):

(26) 靜 香 會 去 學 校。
　　　Jìngxiāng　huì　qù　xuéxiào
　　　Jingxiang　will　go　school
　　　'Jing xiang will go to school.'
(27) 靜 香 會 去 三 個 小 時。
　　　Jìngxiāng　huì　qù　sān　gè　xiǎoshí
　　　Jingxiang　will　go　three　CL　hour
　　　'Jing xiang will go for three hours.'

In (26), it appears that 去 (*qù*, 'go') is a transitive verb, because 學校 (*xuéxiào*, 'school') follows the verb directly. However, if we compare it with (27), we can see that 學校 (*xuéxiào*, 'school') may not be a direct object. 學校 (*xuéxiào*, 'school') is a location where 靜香 (*Jìngxiāng*) went, but 三個小時 (*sāngè xiǎoshí*, 'three hours') in (27) is the duration over which 靜香 (*Jìngxiāng*) will be going. Both of them appear directly after the verb. This is different from (24), for example, since 花瓶 (*huāpíng*, 'vase') is the thing that was broken, any noun phrase occupying the same position must be a thing that was broken. The equivalents in English in (28) and (29) below include the prepositions *to* and *for* respectively. In other words, given that Chinese verbs and prepositions are often indistinguishable, the latter are often referred to as co-verbs in Chinese, which is another reason why it is relatively more difficult to decide whether a verb is transitive in Chinese than it is in English.

(28)   Peter went to school.

(29)   Peter went for three hours.

Third, compared with English, topicalization is more salient or commonly used in Chinese. Topicalization will be covered in more detail in Chapter 7 (subject-prominence versus topic-prominence), but we will briefly explain it here to show how it causes difficulty in identifying transitive verbs in Chinese. We will briefly illustrate how the identification of transitive verbs in a Chinese sentence may not be as obvious due to topicalization.

When a phrase (e.g., a non-subject noun phrase (NP)) is moved to the beginning of a sentence because the speaker/writer wants to focus on the phrase, that phrase is topicalized. In other words, it is the topic of the sentence from the speaker's or writer's point of view. Example (30) is a post on Facebook, in which a Mr Huang (黃先生) was invited to donate money to a charity organization:

(30)   多 謝 黃 先 生 的 邀 請，<u>善 事</u> 一 定 要 做 !
       Duōxiè huáng xiānshēng de   yāoqǐng   shànshì   yīdìng yào   zuò
       Thank Huang mister   NOM invitation charity work must   need do
       'Many thanks to Mr Huang for his invitation. Charity work must be done.'

We can see that 善事 (*shànshì*, 'charity work') should be an object of 做 (*zuò*, 'do'). That is, the canonical (i.e., normal) order should be 一定要做善事[3] ('must do charity'), but because the speaker wants to emphasize charity work, as opposed to other deeds, it is moved to the beginning of the sentence. Topicalization, together with null arguments, makes it technically more difficult for us to determine the transitivity of a Chinese verb. Consider sentences (31)–(33), which are possible utterances said by the same speaker in the same situation. Note the position of 藥 in particular.

(31)   我 吃 了 藥 。
       Wǒ chī le   yào
       I   eat ASP   medicine
       'I took medicine.'

---

3.   Mandarin: *yīdìng yào zuò shànshì*; Cantonese: *jat1 ding6 jiu3 zou6 sin6 si6.*

(32) 藥 我 吃 了。

    Yào   *wǒ*   *chī*   *le*

    Medicine I   eat   ASP

    'As for medicine, I took (it).'

(33) 藥 吃 了。

    Yào   *chī*   *le*

    Medicine eat   ASP

    'As for medicine, (I) took (it).'

Example (31) is a canonical word order in Chinese, in which 我 (*wǒ*) 'I' is the actor and the subject, and 藥 (*yào*) 'medicine' is the thing affected, hence the object. In (32), the object *yào* 'medicine' is topicalized (i.e., moved to the front or utterance-initial position). This gives the meaning equivalent to 'I have taken medicine and not something else'. In (33), the argument *wǒ* 'I' is removed. This is acceptable in Chinese, because, as discussed earlier, Chinese allows null arguments. The resulting sentence in (33) now contains only one noun phrase *yào* 'medicine' and a verb phrase *chīle* (吃了) 'took', and this makes the sentence look like an intransitive sentence. So should we say *chī* (吃) 'take' is functioning like an intransitive verb?

Semantic roles

We have said that *eat* and *break* can be either transitive or intransitive, but they are different. In this section, we introduce the concept of semantic role, which is useful for explaining the syntactic difference between *eat* and *break*. Consider the sentences with *eat* and *break* again (reproduced below):

(18) Mary ate an apple.

(19) Mary ate.

(4) Peter broke the vase.

(20) The vase broke.

The sentences in (18) and (19) have the same subject, *Mary*. Because *Mary* is a person who initiates an action, we call *Mary* the 'Agent'. It is important to distinguish between the terms 'subject' and 'Agent'. 'Subject' is a role determined by the sentence structure. For example, Standard English grammar stipulates that an *-s* should be added to the verb if (i) the subject is *he*, *she*, or *it* (or any singular noun or noun phrase), and (ii) the sentence is in present tense, as in (34):

(34) He cleans his cars every day.

The third-person singular morpheme (語素) *-s* on the verb suggests that *he*, and not *his cars*, is the subject of the sentence. The position of the noun phrase in the sentence also suggests that it is a subject. In English, the subject of a sentence usually occurs in a pre-verbal position (i.e., before the verb). The Agent, in contrast, is a different concept. It is not determined by the sentence structure but by the meaning of the sentence. The Agent and other semantic roles are 'semantic relations between predicates and arguments' (Frawley, 1992, p. 201). That is why we call them semantic (i.e., related to meaning) roles.

Returning to the *break* example in (4), the subject of the transitive verb *break* is also an Agent. However, when it is used as an intransitive verb, as in (20), the subject is no longer an Agent. In (20), *the vase* is not an Agent, because it is not an actor initiating an action. Instead, it is the thing affected by the action. If someone or something is affected by an action, we call it a Patient. The difference between *break* and *eat* is summarized in (35a) and (35b). We call the *break*-type verbs unaccusative verbs, whereas the *eat*-type verbs are unergative verbs (Levin & Rappaport Hovav, 1995).

(35a)

	Subject	Verb	Object
Transitive	*Mary*	*ate*	*an apple.*
Semantic role	Agent		Patient
Intransitive (unergative)	*Mary*	*ate.*	(Φ)
Semantic role	Agent		

(35b)

	Subject	Verb	Object
Transitive	*Peter*	*broke*	*the vase.*
Semantic role	Agent		Patient
Intransitive (unaccusative)	*The vase*	*broke.*	(Φ)
Semantic role	Patient		

Similarly, a Patient is conceptually different from an object. Like the subject, the object is a syntactic element. We determine the object from its structure. Typically, in English, the object is the noun phrase in the post-verbal position (i.e., after the verb). The Patient, in contrast, is a semantic role determined by the meaning of the sentence. To further illustrate, consider sentences (36) and (37):

(36) Bill killed Chris.

(37) Chris was killed by Bill.

In (36) and (37), which NP is the subject/object, respectively? From the point of view of semantic roles, which NP serves as the Agent/Patient, respectively? The answers to these questions are elucidated in (38). See if you can work out the answers before continuing reading.

(38)

	Subject	Verb	Object	Oblique
Active	*Bill*	*killed*	*Chris.*	
Semantic role	Agent		Patient	
Passive	*Chris*	*was killed*	(Φ)	*by Bill.*
Semantic role	Patient			

There are many other semantic roles. They are summarized in Table 3.1 (adapted from Saeed, 2003, pp. 149–151).

Table 3.1
Different semantic roles, their definitions, and examples

Semantic roles	Definition	Examples[4]
Agent	An entity that initiates an action or an event, which usually causes changes in another entity	*Peter broke the vase.* *Bill killed Chris.*
Patient	An entity that undergoes changes in an event	*Peter broke the vase.* *Bill killed Chris.*
Theme	An entity that changes in location in an event, or whose location is described	*Bill sent the books to Mary.* *The ball rolled into the river.* *The books are now at Mary's house.*
Percept	An entity which is perceived or experienced	*John likes Mary.* *Chris angered Steve.*
Experiencer	An entity that experiences a change in emotion	*John likes Mary.* *Chris angered Steve.*
Location	A place where an event takes place	*Peter lives in Thailand.* *I bought it at the flea market.*
Source	A place or person from which an entity originates	*I got this ring from my grandmother.* *She borrowed this book from the library.* *We heard about the accident from his family.* (metaphorically)

(continued on p. 49)

---

4. Semantic roles are not always as typical as the examples in Table 3.1. Some linguists argue that a noun phrase in a sentence can fulfil more than one semantic role (Jackendoff, 1990). For example, in the sentence *Pete threw the ball*, *Pete* can be an Agent and a source.

Table 3.1 (continued)

Semantic roles	Definition	Examples
Goal	A place or person to which an entity moves	*Jill walks to <u>school</u> every day.* *Bill sent the books to <u>Mary</u>.* *Jill told <u>her kids</u> a story.* (metaphorically)
Instrument	An entity that is used as a tool	*Peter goes to school by <u>bus</u>.* *Sarah broke the coconut with <u>a hammer</u>.*
Beneficiary	A person who benefits from an action or event	*Keith washed the car for <u>his father</u>.* *I cooked <u>her</u> a dinner.*

Note: Adapted from *Semantics* (2nd ed.), by J. I. Saeed, 2003, pp. 149–151.

Some common errors by Chinese learners of English

As we saw at the beginning of this chapter, there are two major types of error commonly made by Chinese learners of English: (i) selecting the wrong subject/object, and (ii) omitting an argument. Some verbs in English are particularly difficult for learners who speak Chinese or Cantonese as their first language. For example, the verb *concern* is often misused. *Concern* is often taught to mean 關心 (Li & Chan, 2001; cf. Li et al., 2002, http://personal.cityu.edu.hk/~encrproj/error_types.htm). In Chinese, we often say something like (39). Some Chinese learners of English would produce (40) as an English equivalent of (39):

(39) 我 關 心 她 的 健 康 狀 況。
    Wǒ guānxīn   tā   de   jiànkāng zhuàngkuàng
    I   care.about her NOM health   condition
    'I care about her health condition.'

(40) *I concern her health.

However, the correct sentence should be (41). We can now explain the difference between 關心 and *concern* by semantic roles. In Chinese, 關心 takes the Experiencer (i.e., the person who feels worried) as the subject, and the Percept (i.e., the thing or person that causes worries) as the object. In contrast, English *concern* takes the Percept as the subject and the Experiencer as the object. The resulting sentence in fact sounds more like Example (42):

(41) Her health concerns me.

(42) 她 的 健 康 狀 況 使 我 憂 慮。
    Tā   de   jiànkāng zhuàngkuàng shǐ   wǒ   yōulǜ
    her NOM health   condition   make I   worried
    'Her health condition worries me.'

The second type of error is omitting an object. As we have seen, Chinese allows null arguments. Given a rich context, such as when the subject or the object has been previously mentioned in the discourse, the object, or the subject, or both, can be omitted. More advanced learners in general do not omit the subject, but the problem of omitting the object is still rather common among intermediate learners. For example, Yuan (1997) reported that even very advanced L2 learners who speak Chinese as their first language tend to accept the second sentence in (43), where the object of *repair* is missing:

(39)   Mary's bike has gone wrong. Tomorrow I am going to repair for her.

According to Standard English grammar, the pronoun object 'it' should be added after the verb *repair* (i.e., '. . . to repair it for her'). Learners of English should understand that arguments in an English sentence cannot be omitted like in Chinese. Even if it is clear from the context what is being referred to in a conversation, a pronoun, if not the full noun phrase, should be used.

How to avoid errors regarding transitivity

Confusion of verb transitivity is a problem confronted by many L2 learners of English which often persists throughout their learning process. For example, Chan (2004) interviewed 16 lower-intermediate and 26 upper-intermediate learners of English in Hong Kong, and found that 75% of the lower-intermediate and 46% of the upper-intermediate participants made errors in verb transitivity. It was also the most common error for both groups of participants.

We believe a better understanding of semantic roles will help learners to become more aware of the normative syntactic structures of English and Chinese, and, at the same time, make them more conscious of the roles which are likely to occur in the subject or object positions. This in turn will strengthen their ability to form grammatical sentences in accordance with the norms in Standard English.

If in doubt, learners are also encouraged to check the dictionary regarding how a given verb should be used. For example, if one looks up the verb *concern* in *Longman Dictionary of Contemporary English* (n.d.), one will find that one of the explanations is 'to make someone feel worried or upset'. One can insert the subject and the object into the appropriate positions in the explanation, such as [*her health*] *makes* [*me*] *feel worried or upset* (and not *I make her health feel worried or upset*). This in turn will make it clear that *her health* should be the subject (and *me* the object) of the verb *concern*.

In this chapter, we have looked at syntactic structures associated with transitivity in English and Chinese. We have shown that transitive and intransitive verbs are relatively easier to identify in English than in Chinese. The lack of a common set of criteria to identify transitive and intransitive verbs in Chinese and English may be a source of learning difficulties encountered by Chinese learners of English when using English, often resulting in errors involving the wrong choice of transitivity pattern. These errors include (1) adding a noun phrase directly after an intransitive English verb, (2) omitting a noun phrase in the object position of a transitive verb, and (3) assigning the wrong semantic roles in the subject/object position of a verb. It is hoped that, by introducing how sentences can be analysed syntactically (sentence structures) and semantically (semantic roles), learners of English will find it easier to make grammatical judgements about sentences in both English and Chinese.

Questions and activities

1. Decide whether the following verbs in English are (a) transitive verbs, (b) intransitive verbs, or (c) both. Make a sentence with each of these verbs to justify your answer.
   i. borrow
   ii. wash
   iii. walk
   iv. trust
   v. melt
   vi. hang
   vii. smile
   viii. escape

2. Decide whether the following verbs in Chinese are (a) transitive verbs, (b) intransitive verbs, or (c) both. Make a sentence with each of these verbs to justify your answer.
   i. 踢
   ii. 委託
   iii. 進去
   iv. 死
   v. 開始
   vi. 微笑

3. You may have noticed when doing Exercise 2 that 死 can appear in a sentence like 他死了父親. Do you feel comfortable calling 死 a transitive verb? Why (not)?

4. Identify the semantic roles of the underlined noun phrases.
   i. Brenda cried at her mother's funeral.
   ii. The painter put his paintings into a large bag.
   iii. I heard a loud noise and the glass door shattered.
   iv. Paul caught a rat in the kitchen.
   v. Fred saw a man with a telescope. (Be careful! There are two interpretations.)
   vi. Susan hates carrots.

5.   Apart from *concern,* can you think of another verb in Chinese and a corresponding verb in English that have the same meaning but select different semantic roles as their subjects?

Further reading

Levin (1993) is a classic study that examines over 3,000 English verbs and shows how a verb's syntactic behaviour is related to its meaning. Hale and Keyser (2013) also provide a detailed discussion of three cases of transitivity alternation in English. Readers who are interested in the issue of transitivity in Chinese can find a more in-depth discussion in Zhao (1982).

4
Passive Voice

What is the passive?

In this chapter, we will discuss what the passive is and how it is used in English and Chinese. To begin with, consider (1)–(3):

> (1)   *I am graduated from the Education University of Hong Kong.
> (2)   *She has been suffered from cancer for the past two years.
> (3)   *The accident was happened five years ago.

In all of these sentences, the auxiliary verb *be* (i.e., *am graduated, has been suffered, was happened*) should be deleted. The correct versions thus are (4)–(6):

> (4)   I graduated from the Education University of Hong Kong.
> (5)   She has suffered from cancer for the past two years.
> (6)   The accident happened five years ago.

The question that arises is: Why is it ungrammatical to passivize the verbs in (4)–(6)? This has to do with the properties of the verb.

Transitivity and passive voice in English

Before discussing the issues regarding the passive, it is necessary to understand what a passive sentence is. The passive construction is often misunderstood to be a construction that takes an undergoer as the subject (Liberman, 2009; Pullum, 2011). In fact, the passive is a syntactic phenomenon (Haspelmath, 1990). In English, a typical passive sentence[1] has the auxiliary *be* and the past participle of a verb. Therefore, *He died* is not a passive sentence, whereas *He was killed* is.

In Chapter 3, we discussed transitive and intransitive verbs. To recapitulate, transitive verbs require a direct object, and intransitive verbs do not allow a direct

---

1.   There is also the *get*-passive in English (e.g., *the car got stolen*).

object. These are closely related to the passive construction in English.[2] Consider (7) and (8):

(7)   Peter broke the vase.

(8)   The vase was broken (by Peter).

We can see that (7) is a basic active (as opposed to passive) sentence with the verb *break*, which is a transitive verb, in this case because it is followed by a noun phrase *the vase*. Example (8) is a passive sentence, as evidenced by the presence of an auxiliary *be* before the main verb, which is in the past participle form *broken*. The difference between (7) and (8) is that the object in (7)—*the vase*—becomes the subject in (8).

In other words, a passive sentence can be seen as a product of 'transformation' from an active sentence. It thus follows that, if there is no direct object in the active counterpart, the corresponding passive sentence (via transformation or otherwise) will not be feasible. This is illustrated in (9) and (10):

(9)   Mary laughed [ ].

(10)   *[ ] was laughed.

Laugh is an intransitive verb. When it is used in an active sentence, the result is *Mary laughed*, as in (9). In other words, after the verb *laugh*, there is no noun phrase following it. We saw in (7) and (8) that the passive is formed via moving the object in the active sentence to the subject position (i.e., the beginning of a sentence). However, there is no object in (9). The resulting sentence in (10) lacks a subject and is thus ungrammatical.

Returning to the sentences in (1)–(3), the verbs *graduate*, *suffer*, and *happen* are intransitive verbs. They all take either a Theme or a Patient as the subject, as shown in (11)–(13).

(11) | the person who completes the study programme in a school | *graduates*
       [Theme]
(12) | the person who is sick | *suffers* [Theme/Patient]
(13) | an event | *happens* [Theme]

Because these verbs are intransitive, we do not need to, and in fact we cannot, transform these active sentences into passive sentences. Verbs that can take a Theme or a Patient as their only argument are called ergative or unaccusative verbs, and they

---

2. In some languages, it is also possible to passivize intransitive verbs. For example, in Japanese, one can say 息子に死なれた *musuko ni shin-are-ta* [(lit.) I was died by my son], in which the verb *shinu* 'die' is used with the passive morpheme *-are*. The sentence means 'my son died on me'.

are more susceptible to over-passivization than are other intransitive verbs such as *walk* and *run*, which take an Actor/Agent as the only argument. Yip (1995) argues that learners might have interpreted these verbs as 'underlyingly transitive' (p. 137).

Although a passive sentence involves a transitive verb,[3] it should be noted that not all transitive verbs can be passivized. For example, one can say *he resembles his father*, but not **his father is resembled by him*. The explanation is beyond the scope of this book.

The passive in Chinese

According to Li and Thompson (1981), the term 'passive' in Mandarin Chinese is often used to refer to sentences containing the word 被 (*bèi*). In syntactic structures, Chinese is similar to English, in that only transitive verbs can occur in passive sentences. This is illustrated in (14)–(17).

(14) 張 三 殺 了 李 四。
      Zhāngsān   shā   le   lǐsì
      Zhangsan   kill   ASP   Lisi
      'Zhangsan killed Lisi.'

(15) 李 四 被 殺 了。
      Lǐsì   bèi   shā   le
      Lisi   BEI   kill   ASP
      'Lisi was killed.'

(16) 李 四 死 了。
      Lǐsì   sǐ   le
      Lisi   die   ASP
      'Lisi died.'

(17) *[ ] 被 死 了。
            bèi   sǐ   le
            BEI   die   ASP
      '[ ] was died.'

We can see in (15) that 殺 (*shā*, 'kill') can occur in a passive sentence, because it is a transitive verb, as shown in (14). On the other hand, 死 (*sǐ*, 'die') cannot occur in a passive sentence, as shown in (17), because it is an intransitive verb, and there is no object that can be moved to the subject position of the passive sentence.[4]

---

3. Some passive sentences involve an intransitive and a prepositional phrase (e.g., *the bed has been slept in*).

4. In recent years, there has been a tendency to use *bèi* with intransitive verbs such as 自殺 (*zìshā*, 'commit suicide'), 辭職 (*cízhí*, 'quit a job'), etc.

Differences in using the English and Chinese passive

Using the English passive

According to Thompson (1987), the use of the passive is mainly for two reasons (p. 497):

A: If the agent is not to be mentioned, use the passive.

B: If the agent is to be mentioned, then use the passive only when the non-agent is more closely related than the agent either

B1:   to the 'theme' of the 'paragraph', or

B2:   to the participant in the immediately preceding clause.

To elaborate, the passive is used (i) because the Actor (Agent) is unknown or unidentifiable (corresponding to A above), or the Actor is either irrelevant or unimportant to the hearer (corresponding to B1), and (ii) the discourse drives the use of the Patient to be in the subject position (corresponding to B2). We will illustrate these in the following.

The reader might have experience shopping online, and might have seen emails like the one in (18):

(18)   Your item has been shipped.

The use of the passive is motivated by the fact that the person who shipped the item is not important to the receiver of the email. In fact, it would be strange if the company sends you an email like (19), because the most important message is the whereabouts of the item and not who took it to the post office:

(19)   Michael has shipped your item.

The use of the passive in (18) is therefore justified because the person who shipped the item is not important, at least to the receiver of the email, and thus this information should not be included. On the contrary, if information about the 'shipper' is included, as in (19), the receiver of the message might find it confusing and wonder why it is relevant.

Now consider another case involving the use of a passive sentence. Compare the two paragraphs in (20) and (21). Example (20) is an excerpt from the novel *Harry Potter and the Sorcerer's Stone* (Rowling, 1998), and (21) is a slightly modified version:

(20) Albus Dumbledore didn't seem to realize that he had just arrived in a street where everything from his name to his boots was unwelcome. He was busy rummaging in his cloak, looking for something. But he did seem to realize <u>he was being watched</u>, because he looked up suddenly at the cat, which was still staring at him from the other end of the street.

(21) Albus Dumbledore didn't seem to realize that he had just arrived in a street where everything from his name to his boots was unwelcome. He was busy rummaging in his cloak, looking for something. But he did seem to realize (<u>the cat/something/someone</u>) was <u>watching him</u>, because he looked up suddenly at the cat, which was still staring at him from the other end of the street.

Although (21) is possible, the reader will probably agree that the original excerpt in (20) sounds better. The reason is that the whole paragraph is talking about Albus Dumbledore. If we imagine the situation as if we are watching a movie, our eyes are on Dumbledore from the beginning of the paragraph. If an active sentence is used and *the cat* is mentioned, as in (21), our focus would have to shift to the cat, and then back to Dumbledore (because the cat was watching <u>him</u>), and then back to the cat again (because he looked up at <u>the cat</u>). This shift of focus would cause an abrupt transition of attention from Dumbledore to the cat.

Consider another example of the English passive. The excerpt in (22) is a narrative about how olive oil is made:

(22) 'the fresh fruit <u>is collected</u> into a weighting hopper along with some leaves and twigs, but these <u>can easily be removed</u> later. A machine like this can collect as many olives in an hour as it would take the traditional farmer to collect in an entire day. When the harvest reaches the production plant the fruit <u>is washed</u> to remove leaves and twigs in the collection process. The more stubborn twigs and branches that remained <u>are filtered</u> out using a grill, which only allows the fruit to pass through'

The use of the passive in (22) can be explained by both reasons discussed above: (i) the excerpt is about olive oil production, focusing on the main ingredients—olives—and so the doer(s) in the process is(are) unimportant information, and (ii) the excerpt has been following the 'fate' of the olives: the olives, together with the leaves and twigs, are collected, and then the leaves and twigs are removed and filtered, and the olives are washed. By using the passive in this excerpt, the reader will not need to attend to other entities that are seen to be 'peripheral' in the process. The excerpt would look very different if the passive sentences were changed into active ones. The reader might want to do it as an exercise.

Using the Chinese passive

Unlike English, the Chinese passive is traditionally used to express adversity (i.e., unfavourable situations) (Li & Thompson, 1981). Consider (23) and (24).

(23) 我 的 錢 包 被 人 偷 走 了。
  Wǒ de qiánbāo bèi rén tōu zǒu le
  I NOM wallet BEI people steal away ASP
  'My wallet was stolen by someone.'

(24) 他 的 褲 子 被 狗 咬 破 了。
  Tā de kùzi bèi gǒu yǎo pò le
  He NOM pants BEI dog bit torn ASP
  'His pants had a hole bitten in them by a/the dog.'

Examples (23) and (24) are typical unfavourable events from the subject's point of view. Interestingly, when a neutral verb is used, the adversity meaning is still at play. Examples (25) and (26) are adapted from Li and Thompson (1981, p. 496).

(25) 張 三 被 人 看 見 了。
  Zhāngsān bèi rén kànjiàn le
  Zhangsan BEI people see ASP
  'Zhangsan was seen by someone.'

(26) 我 們 的 話 被 聽 到 了。
  Wǒmen de huà   bèi tīngdào le
  We NOM conversation BEI hear ASP
  'Our conversation was overheard.'

In (25), although it is not clear under what circumstances Zhangsan was seen, we can be sure that Zhangsan did not want to be seen. In other words, this is an unfavourable situation for Zhangsan. It is also clear in (26) that the speaker was not happy about the fact that their conversation was overheard.

Usage of the Chinese and English passive: Contrastive differences

Whereas the Chinese passive is often used to express adversity, there is no such tendency in English. The mismatch in function in the use of the passive between Chinese and English explains why many passive sentences in English cannot be translated into Chinese using the passive. Consider the examples in (27)–(32):

(27) The bridge was built in 1908.

(28)   *這 條 橋 於 1908 年 被 建 成。
       Zhè tiáo qiáo   yú   1980 nián bèi   jiàn   chéng
       this CL   bridge in   year BEI   build complete
       'The bridge was built in 1908.'

(29)   這 條 橋 於 1908 年 建 成。
       Zhè tiáo qiáo   yú   1980 nián jiàn   chéng
       this CL   bridge in   year build complete
       'The bridge was built in 1908.'

(30)   The bill has been paid.

(31)   *這 賬 單 已 經 被 繳 付 了。
       Zhè zhàng dān jǐjīng bèi   jiǎofù le
       This CL   bill   already BEI   paid   ASP
       'The bill has been paid.'

(32)   這 賬 單 已 經 繳 付 了。
       Zhè zhàng dān jǐjīng jiǎofù le
       This CL   bill   already paid   ASP
       'The bill has been paid.'

We can see that (27) and (30) are legitimate passive sentences in English. However, their directly translated passive counterparts in Chinese in (28) and (31) are unacceptable. When 被 (*bèi*) is removed, as in (29) and (32), they become acceptable.

These examples show clearly that the passive in English functions differently from that in Chinese. In Chinese, if the object of a verb is to be the focus of the sentence, one only needs to place it at the beginning of the sentence. This is called topicalization, which has been briefly discussed in Chapter 3 (see also Chapter 7). The freedom to topicalize almost any noun phrase in Chinese allows Chinese to avoid using the passive in most cases, and the use of the passive in Chinese (i.e., the *bèi*-passive) is traditionally reserved for expressing adversity, even though under the influence of the English passive, the *bèi*-passive is getting more and more widespread (for more details, see Chapter 8, Europeanization).

The non-adversity use of the passive 被 (*bèi*) construction in Chinese is increasingly popular (Li & Thompson, 1981). For example, many native speakers would find (33) quite acceptable.

(33)   他 的 工 作 表 現 被 老 闆 賞 識。
       Tā   de   gōngzuò biǎoxiàn   bèi   lǎobǎn shǎngshí
       He   NOM work   performance BEI   boss   recognize
       'His performance at work was recognized by the boss.'

In addition to 被 (*bèi*), words such as 獲 (*huò*), 受到 (*shòudào*), or 得到 (*dédào*) have passive meaning, which can be used in favourable situations. Example (33) can thus be rephrased as (34):

(34) 他 的 工 作 表 現 獲／受 到／得 到 老 闆 賞 識。
     Tā de   gōngzuò biǎoxiàn   huò/shòudào/dedào lǎobǎn shǎngshí
     He NOM work   performance receive   boss   recognize
     'His performance at work was recognized by the boss.'

To summarize, the use of the passive in English is often driven by the demotion or backgrounding of the Actor/Agent or the promotion or foregrounding of the Patient/Theme. That is, in English the passive is used because the Patient/Theme is more relevant to the conversation or in a written text than the Actor/Agent is. In contrast, the passive in Chinese is often used to express adversity, although the use of the formal passive using the passive marker 被 (*bèi*) to refer to neutral or even favourable situations is getting more and more common. If there is a need to focus on an object of an active sentence in Chinese, the object will be placed in the topic position of the sentence (i.e., the beginning of the sentence) without using any marker, such as *bèi*.

As mentioned, the difficulty Chinese learners of English have with the passive in English is partly related to topicalization. In fact, it is also related to other syntactic properties of the Chinese language, including the serial verb construction and the *ba*-construction (把字句).

Over-passivization and how to avoid it

Over-passivization, which refers to passivization of intransitive verbs, is a type of error often made by Chinese learners of English (Yip, 1995). In fact, over-passivization is a common error among English learners of different L1 backgrounds (Zobl, 1989). In general, learners tend to over-passivize a certain type of intransitive verb called 'unaccusative verbs'. Unaccusative verbs take a Theme or a Patient as the subject. Examples are *suffer*, *happen*, and *disappear* (see examples 1–3 above). On the other hand, learners are less likely to over-passivize 'unergative verbs'—verbs that take a doer as the subject—such as *walk*, *laugh*, and *play*. In fact, all the examples given at the beginning of this chapter involve unaccusative verbs.

Since the passive is closely related to transitivity, it is important for learners to understand the syntactic patterns in which a given verb occurs, that is, whether a verb is a transitive or intransitive verb, and what arguments it takes as the subject and the object. Learners should also understand that the subject of a sentence is not necessarily a doer or initiator of an action or event, as in the case of unaccusative verbs. Looking up the transitivity pattern of a verb in a good, reliable dictionary is a good practice.

Questions and activities

1. Decide which of the following verbs can be passivized. Make a sentence with each of the verbs that you think can be passivized. Explain the meaning of the sentence (N.B.: a verb can have many senses. Sometimes it can be passivized in one sense, but not in others).

    i.   think
    ii. call
    iii. slip
    iv. notice
    v.   walk
    vi. give

2. For the following verbs, decide how many arguments (e.g., subject, direct object, indirect object) it can accommodate. Then describe the semantic role of the arguments as in Examples (11)–(13). You may use a dictionary. Finally, if they have two arguments, form a passive sentence with the verb. Are they good passive sentences? Why or why not?

    i.   suit
    ii. frighten
    iii. flatter
    iv. vanish
    v.   lack

3. Go to google.com. Search for 被 (*bèi*), and look at the first 20 entries where it is used as a passive marker (ignore irrelevant entries such as 綿被). How many of them are associated with adverse meanings?

4. Translate the following English text into Chinese. When translating, bear in mind the differences between Chinese and English discussed in this chapter.

    > The World Health Organization recommended Tuesday that nations regulate electronic cigarettes and ban them from use indoors until the exhaled vapor is proven not to harm bystanders. It also called for a ban on sales to minors of the popular nicotine-vapor products, and to either forbid or keep to a minimum any advertising, promotion or sponsorship.
    >
    > The Geneva-based agency said the "apparently booming" $3 billion global market for more than 400 brands of e-cigarettes means appropriate regulation is needed. Regulation "is a necessary precondition for establishing a scientific basis on which to judge the effects of their use, and for ensuring that adequate research is conducted and the public health is protected and people made aware of the potential risks and benefits," the report said.
    >
    > (Adapted from NBC News. Retrieved from http://www.nbcnews.com/health/health-news/who-urges-stiff-regulation-e-cigarettes-n189176.)

5.   Look for two signs, one in English and one in Chinese (e.g., on campus, near your home, etc.) in which the passive is used. Can you explain why the passive is used in each of the two cases?

Further reading

Brinton and Brinton (2010) discuss the syntactic structure of the passive construction in English, and provides many examples of transitive verbs that cannot appear in a passive sentence. Li and Thompson (1981) include an in-depth discussion of the variations in the use of the passive construction in Chinese. For more advanced readers, Shi (1997) offers an informative overview of various syntactic features associated with the Chinese passive.

5
Tense and Aspect

Introduction

Tense and aspect are two linguistic domains that are often treated as if they are the same. In fact, they highlight different time-related meanings of an event. For example, there are subtle semantic differences between (1) and (2):

(1)   I *did* my homework.   (past tense)
(2)   I *have done* my homework.   (present perfect tense)

Although the process is the same (i.e., 'do my homework'), notice that (1), with simple past tense *did*, is expressed as an action in the past which is unrelated to the present. By contrast, in (2), with present perfect tense *have done*, while the speaker similarly considers the action ('doing homework') is completed as of now, the result of that action (i.e., completed homework) continues to be relevant to the present (e.g., the speaker makes a case to his mother that he now has the right to play computer games). In this chapter, we will explain what tense and aspect are, how they are expressed in English and Chinese, and the common errors made by Chinese learners of English.

Tense and aspect in English

Before we explain what tense (時態) and aspect (時貌) are, let us consider the sentences in (3) and (4). Example (3) is adapted from a novel, and (4) is a modified version of (3).

(3)   The man was running so hard and it must have been cold because smoke and foam were spewing from his mouth in puffs as it had from the horses before. (van Dijk, 2006, p. 569)
(4)   The man ran so hard and it must have been cold because smoke and foam spewed from his mouth in puffs as it had from the horses before.

Both sentences describe a man-running situation. The event described in both sentences happened in the past, as indicated by the past form of the verb *be* (i.e., *was/ were*) in (3), and the use of past tense forms (e.g., *ran*) in (4).

But there is another obvious difference between (3) and (4). Example (3) uses present participles such as *running* and *spewing*, whereas (4) uses the past tense forms *ran*, *spewed*, etc. The 'tense' in (3) is often called 'past continuous tense', but in linguistics, the 'continuous' part is referred to as **aspect**. That is, Example (3) is in past tense, and it has 'progressive' aspect. Example (4), on the other hand, is in past tense but has 'perfective' aspect.

Tense indicates *when* an event happens/happened (Comrie, 1976): whether it happened in the past, is happening now, or will happen in the future. Strictly speaking, English has only three tenses: past, present, and future.[1] One does not have a choice of which tense to use when describing an event, because if the event happened in the past, one is bound to use the past tense form, as shown in (5) and (6).

> (5)   I <u>was</u> born in 1993, when my mother <u>was</u> 30 years old.
>
> (6)   I <u>was</u> cleaning the floor when you <u>called</u> (last night/two months ago).

In contrast, aspect represents how the speaker views an event (Brinton & Brinton, 2010; Radden, 2007): whether he or she sees an event as a complete whole, or one that is ongoing or developing. The situation described in (3), where the progressive is used, is more vivid and may give the reader a sense that he or she has gone back in time, looking at the event happening or unfolding in front of his or her eyes, as illustrated in Figure 5.1. The bar in grey symbolizes the length or duration of the event. With an imperfective (progressive) viewpoint, the event is viewed from within. In other words, the event is seen as having an internal time frame. In contrast, (4) may give the reader a sense of viewing that same event from the outside, as illustrated in Figure 5.2. The event is viewed externally as if it were a black dot, with no attention to the 'inside' of the event. The event is not seen as having an internal time frame. We call the viewpoint in (3) 'imperfective' (or, specifically, progressive), and the viewpoint in (4) 'perfective'. It should be noted that, regardless of the viewpoint (i.e., perfective or imperfective) one takes, it does not change the fact that the event happened in the past and past tense must be used.

---

1.   Some linguists argue that there is no future tense in English. We are not going to elaborate on this because it is beyond the scope of this book.

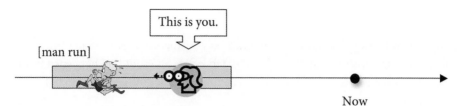

Figure 5.1
The progressive (imperfective) viewpoint in a past event

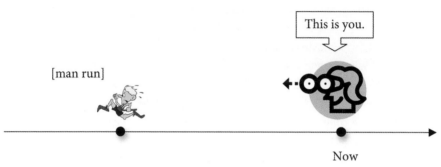

Figure 5.2
The perfective viewpoint in a past event

As long as the man-running event happened in the past, both (3) and (4) are grammatical sentences. The only difference between the two versions is how the writer presents the event to the reader. The writer/speaker thus has relatively more freedom in choosing an aspect than in choosing a tense.

There is a recurrent past situation where both the progressive and perfective viewpoints must be used (see, e.g., (7)). When two events are referred to, one serving as the 'background' to the other 'foregrounded' event, the background event must be expressed using the progressive aspect (e.g., *was cleaning*), while the foregrounded event has to be in perfective aspect (e.g., *called*). Compare (7)–(9):

(7) John was reading when Mary entered.
(8) Sue was going to the library when she met Tim.
(9) We were watching TV when the telephone rang.

Such a type of situation has been characterized as 'incidence schema':

PERF + IMPF (foreground + background; main foreground event cutting into background event) (Sasse, 2002, p. 228; cf. Li, 2011, p. 46)

It is important to make a clear distinction between tense and aspect when English and Chinese are compared, because Chinese (and Cantonese), unlike English, does not have tense markers; it only has aspect markers.

Aspect in Cantonese and Mandarin Chinese

Native speakers of Cantonese, when asked how pastness is expressed in Cantonese/ Chinese, often answer that 咗／了 (*zo2/le*) indicates an event that happened in the past. However, this is a common misconception. Consider the sentences in (10)–(12) below:

(10) 我 尋 晚 睇 咗 一 齣 電 影／我 昨 晚 看 了 一 部 電 影。

Ngo5	cam4	maan5	tai2	**zo2**	jat1	ceot1	din6 jing2
Wŏ	zuó	wăn	kàn	**le**	yī	bù	diànyĭng
I	last	night	watch	ASP	a	CL	movie

'I saw a movie last night.'

(11) I saw a movie yesterday.

(12) 你 尋 晚 打 比 我 嗰 陣 我 抹 緊 地／
你 打 電 話 給 我 的 時 候 我 在 擦 地 板。

Nei5 cam4	night	maan5 daa2	bei2 ngo5	go2 zan2		ngo5 maat3	gan2 dei6

Nei5	cam4	maan5	daa2	bei2	ngo5	go2	zan2	ngo5	maat3	gan2	dei6
You	last	night	call	give	I	CL	moment	I	clean	ASP	floor
Nĭ	dă	diànhuà	gĕi	wŏ	de		shíhòu	wŏ zài	cā		dìbăn
You	call	phone	give	I	NOM		moment	I ASP	clean		floor

'I was cleaning the floor when you called.'

In (10), 咗／了 (*zo2/le*) appears after the verb 睇／看. The time of the event is yesterday, and it may lead us to think that 咗 (*zo2*) functions as a past tense marker like *saw* in (11). However, if we compare (12) and (6), we will have a different conclusion. In (12), the time of the event is still yesterday, but no 咗／了 (*zo2/le*) is used. The past tense forms *was* and *called* in the corresponding English sentence (6) have no equivalents in (12).

On the other hand, 咗／了 (*zo2/le*) can be used in non-past events (i.e., present or future). Consider the sentence in (13).

(13) 下個星期五我已經去咗 (了) 英國啦。

Haa6	go3	sing1kei4ng5	ngo5	ji5ging1	heoi3	zo2	jing1gwok3	laa3
Xià	gè	xīngqīwŭ	wŏ	yĭjīng	qù	le	yīngguó	le
Next	CL	Friday	I	already	go	ASP	England	SFP

'I will have gone to England next Friday.'

The sentence in (13) describes an event (going to England) in the future (next Friday). If 咗／了 (*zo2/le*) was a past tense marker corresponding to the regular past -*ed* in English, we would not expect 咗／了 (*zo2/le*) to appear in (13), because it is an event in the future. However, (13) is perfectly acceptable. This further shows that 咗／了 (*zo2/le*) is not a past tense marker. In fact, 咗／了 (*zo2/le*) is a perfective marker which is used to indicate the completion of an event in relation to a point in time (e.g., next Friday). The completion point can be in the past, as in (10), or in the future, as in (13).

Chinese thus has no tense markers. Consider (12) again. Although the events (me cleaning the floor and you calling) happened in the past, there is no marker such as -*ed* that signifies this past tense meaning. Rather, *ngo5 maat3 gan2 dei6/wǒ zài cā dì bǎn* 'I am/was cleaning the floor' are both compatible with situations happening at present, in the future, or in the past as in (12).

A friend of one of the authors, who is a native speaker of English, once asked how Chinese speakers know whether they are talking about a past event or not if Chinese does not have past tense markers such as -*ed*. Although sometimes clarification is necessary, in general Chinese native speakers have little problem understanding when an event happens/happened while interacting in Cantonese/Chinese. We have other linguistic devices, such as phrases of time serving as adverbials (*yesterday*, *last Monday*, etc.). Even without these adverbial phrases, often we can deduce time-sensitive information from the context at large. For example, in (14), despite a lack of tense marking, we can still easily infer that the two persons are talking about things that happened in the past:

(14) 甲：我星期日去咗海洋公園慶祝母親節。你呢？

Ngo5	*sing1 kei4 jat6*		*heoi3*	*zo2*	*hoi2 joeng4 gung1 jyun2*
I	Sunday		go	ASP	Ocean Park

hing3 zuk1	*mou5 can1 zit3.*	*Nei5*	*ne1*
celebrate	Mother's Day.	You	Q

A: 'I went to Ocean Park to celebrate Mother's Day on Sunday. What about you?'

乙：我朝早飲茶，下午睇戲，夜晚就煮飯俾畀媽媽食。

Ngo5	*ziu1 zou2*	*jam2 caa4,*	*haa6 ng5*	*tai2*	*hei3*
I	morning	yum-cha	afternoon	watch	movie

je6 maan5	*zau6*	*zyu2*	*faan6*	*bei2*	*maa4 maa1*	*sik6*
evening	then	cook	rice	give	mother	eat

B: 'I had yum-cha in the morning, saw a movie in the afternoon, and cooked dinner for my mother in the evening.'

In fact, the utterance by B in (14) can also be an answer to the question 'What are your plans next Sunday?', and in this case, the events will happen in the future.

Past tense in English and perfective marker in Cantonese/Mandarin Chinese

Although the past tense marking function in English (i.e., regular past -*ed* and irregular past) and the perfective marker in Cantonese/Chinese 咗／了 (*zo2/le*) are conceptually distinct, functionally they overlap in meaning to some extent. The reason is that the past tense form in English also has perfective as part of its meaning. In other words, English past marking has two functions: indicating an event that happened in the past, and viewing the event externally. For example, (15) would be unacceptable if the man is still running a marathon at the time of speech.

(15)   The man ran a marathon.

The logical next question to ask is whether a past tense marker can be imperfective. That is, can we view an event that happened in the past as if it has not yet ended? The answer is yes. In Example (6), the verb form *was cleaning* is progressive (i.e., imperfective). In other words, we can 'pretend' that we are in the past and look at the event as it unfolds from within (as shown in Figure 5.1). In many languages, such as Spanish and French, there are two kinds of past tense, perfective and imperfective.

Perfective and perfect

In English, perfect 'tense' refers to the form *to have + past participle*, as shown in (16).

(16)   I have sent her an email about the exam.

Perfect 'tense' seems to be very similar to simple past tense in that both denote a completed event, but they have rather subtle differences. Compare (16) and (17).

(17)   I sent her an email about the exam.

Out of context, it is difficult to tell which utterance is 'correct' or more appropriate. In fact, either of them can be correct, depending on the speaker's focus. The use of *have* in (16) suggests that the sentence is in the present tense ('present perfect'). It might seem odd at first to use the present tense when the event is obviously completed, but the use of the present perfect in fact indicates the relevance of the event to the present time. Example (16) can be rephrased as (18):

(18)   I am currently in the state of having completed the action of sending her an email about the exam.

This 'state' of current relevance helps explain why (16), using the present perfect tense, is more appropriately used as a response to a question like 'Are you sure she knows about the exam?' rather than 'What did you do?' The latter would be more appropriate as a response to (17).

This can be further illustrated in (19) and (20). There are two verbs in example (19), which are both in the past tense: one simple past (*came*), the other past perfect (*had sent*). Example (20) is a paraphrase of (19):

(19) I <u>had sent</u> her an email about the exam before I came.

(20) I was in a state of having completed the action of sending her an email about the exam.

We can tell clearly that (17) is in the present tense, whereas (19) is in the past tense. Example (17) signifies the present state of the speaker, whereas (19) signifies the state of the speaker at a time in the past.

So what is the difference between (16) and (17)? Example (17) is a simple description of what the speaker did, as in the conversation in (21).

(21) Mary: What did you do on Sunday?
      Peter: I sent Susan an email about the exam.

It would be very unnatural for Peter to answer Mary's question in (21) with the response (16): 'I have sent Susan an email', because Mary was asking him about what he did in the past and not the relevance of that completed action (the sending of the email) to the present. The same explanation applies to (1) and (2) in the beginning of this chapter. Thus, (1) is a description of what 'I' did at a certain point in time in the past, and the action has little relevance to the present, whereas (2) is an expression to show the relevance of the completed action (i.e., doing homework) to the present (e.g., in a situation in which the boy asks his mother if he can play computer games).

Other aspect markers in Chinese

Although Chinese lacks tense markers, it has more aspect markers than English has. For instance, aspect markers in Mandarin Chinese include 過 (*guò*) (experiential) and 著 (*zhe*) (continuous). 過 (*guò*) is used to highlight the experience, as shown in (22) and (23).

(22) 大 雄 去 過 台 灣。
      Dàxióng   qù   guò   táiwān
      Daxiong   go   ASP   Taiwan
      'Daxiong has been to Taiwan.'

(23) 我 愛 過 他。
      Wǒ   ài   guò   tā
      I   love   ASP   he
      'I was once in love with him.'

過 (*guò*) is similar to 咗／了 (*zo2/le*), in that they both highlight the endpoint of an event. However, their meanings are completely different. Compare (24) and (25):

(24) 大 雄 去 了 台 灣。

     Dàxióng   *qù*   *le*   *táiwān*

     Daxiong   go   ASP   Taiwan

     'Daxiong went to Taiwan.'

(25) *我 愛 了 他。

     Wǒ   *ài*   *guò*   *tā*

     I   love   ASP   he

     'I have loved him.'

It is unacceptable to say (22) if *Daxiong* is still in Taiwan (Li & Thompson, 1981). It is only acceptable when *Daxiong* went to Taiwan and then came back. In (23) and (25), we can see that we can attach *guò* to 愛 (*ài*, 'love'), but *le* is not compatible with the same verb.

著 (*zhe*) (continuous aspect) is used with durative verbs. Durative verbs describe actions/events that have duration. For example, 等 (*děng*) 'wait' is a durative verb, unlike 爆炸 (*bào zhà* 'explode') and 畢業 (*bì yè* 'graduate'), verbs which are perceived as not having any internal time frame or duration (hence the oddity of *爆炸著 (**bào zhà zhe* 'exploding') and *畢著業 (**bì zhe yè* 'graduating'). 著 (*zhe*) in Mandarin Chinese or 住 (*zyu6*) in Cantonese, is very similar to 在 (*zài*) (Mandarin Chinese) or 緊 (*gan2*) (Cantonese) respectively. 在 (*zài*) and 緊 (*gan2*) are used to mark imperfective aspect, but 著 (*zhe*) and 在／緊 (*zài/gan2*) are used with different verb types. 在 (*zài*) can only be used with activity verbs (i.e., dynamic action verbs) (Li & Thompson, 1981). Other verb types, such as stative verbs, are not compatible with *zài*, as shown in (26)–(28):

(26) 李 四 在 跑 步。(activity verb)

     Lǐsì   *zài*   *pǎobù*

     Lisi   ASP   run

     'Lisi is running.'

(27) *李 四 在 愛 他 的 妻 子。(stative verb)

     Lǐsì   *zài*   *ài*   *tā*   *de*   *qīzi*

     Lisi   ASP   love   he   NOM   wife

     'Lisi is loving his wife.'

(28) *李 四 在 門 口 在 站。(verb of posture)

     Lǐsì   *zài*   *ménkǒu*   *zài*   *zhàn*

     Lisi   at   door   ASP   stand

     'Lisi is standing at the door.'

Zhe (著), on the other hand is compatible with most verb types, as shown in (29)–(31).

(29) 李 四 跑 著 步。

    Lǐsì   pǎo   zhe   bù

    Lisi   run   ASP   step

    'Lisi is running.'

(30) 李 四 愛 著 他 的 妻 子。

    Lǐsì   ài   zhe   tā   de5   qīzi

    Lisi   love   ASP   he   NOM   wife

    'Lisi is in love with his wife.'

(31) 李 四 在 門 口 站 著。

    Lǐsì   zài   ménkǒu   zhàn   zhe

    Lisi   at   door   stand   ASP

    'Lisi is standing at the door.'

However, you may notice that there is a slight difference between (26) and (29). Whereas (26) can occur on its own, (29) would sound better if it is attached to another clause, as in (32).

(32) 李 四 跑 著 步 去 學 校。

    Lǐsì   pǎo   zhe   bù   qù   xuéxiào

    Lisi   run   ASP   step   go   school

    'Lisi is running to school.'

In (32), 跑著步 (*pǎo zhe bù*, 'running') functions as a means for 去學校 (*qù xuéxiào*, 'going to school'). Thus 著 (*zhe*) fulfils a function of backgrounding a clause (Li & Bowerman, 1998).

There are also verbs to which both 在 (*zài*) and 著 (*zhe*) can be attached, but they produce different meanings. Consider (33) and (34):

(33) 她 在 穿 和 服。

    Tā   zài   chuān   héfú

    she   ASP   wear   kimono

    'She is putting on a kimono.'

(34) 她 穿 著 和 服。

    Tā   chuān   zhe   héfú

    she   wear   ASP   kimono

    'She is wearing a kimono. / She is in a kimono.'

While (33) and (34) may both be translated as 'She is wearing a kimono' in English, (33) describes an action of putting on traditional Japanese attire, whereas (34) describes a state in which the girl is in traditional Japanese attire. These examples clearly distinguish the different functions of the two aspect markers: *zài* is a progressive aspect marker, whereas *zhe* is a continuous aspect marker.

Misuse of English tense and aspect among Chinese EAL learners

Many L2 learners of English do not think that past tense is particularly difficult, because they started learning the function of past tense at a young age, and by and large they are able to produce past tense forms, including the irregular forms that they have memorized. The difficulty, however, does not lie in whether a learner knows if a verb is regular or not or is able to produce the correct form, but to supply past tense marking in appropriate contexts.

Indeed, past tense marking is often omitted by Chinese learners of English, especially when speaking. One reason is related to processing. Our cognitive resources are limited, and speaking a second language usually requires more effort than does speaking our first language. Research has shown that L2 learners tend to be less sensitive to morphological marking in the target language than are native speakers (Clahsen, Felser, Neubauer, Sato, & Silva, 2010). Learners tend to compromise inflections, because they tend not to severely affect the meaning of a sentence. They are not used to paying attention to inflections, especially when their first language lacks them. In the case of past tense marking, because Chinese does not require any tense marking and the time of the event is often conveyed through the use of time adverbials (e.g., *yesterday*, *last Sunday*), Chinese EAL learners of English tend to neglect English tense marking when making sense of English input or producing English output.

The second reason is related to a tendency to dissociate past tense with events that lack an endpoint (i.e., atelic events), especially stative verbs. This is one of the predictions of the Aspect Hypothesis (Andersen, 1991; Robison, 1990; Shirai, 1991). Even if learners have sufficient time to think (e.g., when they write in English), they sometimes make the wrong judgement about which tense should be used. The supply of past tense is usually easier when the event being described has an endpoint, such as the one in (35):

(35)   She left the room a few minutes ago.

Example (35) is a clear case of past tense: The act of leaving started and ended a few minutes ago. But in (36), many learners may have difficulty deciding what tense is more appropriate:

(36)   I saw a movie yesterday, and it <u>was</u> about the Second World War.

Be is a stative verb. That is, we tend to perceive that the property of being about the Second World War continues without an endpoint. Therefore, it is relatively difficult for us to decide whether past tense should be used in (36). But the use of past tense here only indicates the speaker's recalling of the movie. The speaker is viewing a past event from the present time, as illustrated in Figure 5.2. In short, it is perfectly acceptable to use present tense in reference to the Second World War, as in (37), but the meaning is slightly different. The speaker, instead of recalling what the movie was about, simply expresses the content of the movie.

(37) I saw a movie yesterday, and it <u>is</u> about the Second World War.

This tendency to dissociate past tense marking and atelic verbs may come from two sources. First, it may be natural to do so due to a distributional bias (Li & Shirai, 2000). That is, in the linguistic input past tense marking is more frequently used with telic verbs than with atelic verbs. This also affects native English-speaking children in their language development. Second, it may be due to L1 influence. Native speakers of Chinese, which does not have tense markers, tend not to rely on tense markers to signal the time of the event, especially when the event is a state and the state holds true even at the time of speech.

Questions and activities

1. Go to the EMCJ Multimodal Parallel Corpus at http://corpus.eduhk.hk/EMCJ/index.php. Search for the verb *called* in the movie *He's Just Not That Into You*. Look at the results. How many of them were actually translated with 了 (*le*) in Chinese?

2. Search for 在 in the movie '失戀 33 天' in the EMCJ Multimodal Parallel Corpus. Look for instances of '在 + verb'. What are the verbs that are used with 在?

3. You might want to work with a partner on this task. Take note of a Cantonese/Chinese conversation of about 100 words long that occurs around you (e.g., when you are at a restaurant, on the school bus). Analyse the conversation according to the following:
    (a) The event being referred to in the conversation: When did it happen?
    (b) Were there any aspect markers used? If so, what are they, and what verbs were used?
    (c) Translate the conversation into English. What tense/aspect markers would you use?

4. Past tense is sometimes not used even when describing events that happened in the past. This is called 'historical present'. Have you observed any instances of historical present? When is it usually used? What effect does historical present have in meaning? (Hint: Make use of the notion of how an event is perceived when past tense is used as shown in Figures 5.1 and 5.2.)

5. Both *the door is unlocked* and *the door was unlocked* are grammatical sentences, but they have subtle differences. What grammatical aspect is used in each sentence? (Hint: You can say *the door was unlocked by the owner*, but not *the door is unlocked by the owner*.)

Further reading

For readers who want to have a more in-depth understanding of the semantics of English aspect, Langacker (1982) will be a good choice. For a discussion of the actual use of aspect marking in Mandarin Chinese, readers can refer to Xiao and McEnery (2004). The study also briefly discusses the differences in aspect marking in Chinese and English.

6
Determiners
Articles and Demonstratives

Misuse of articles

The grammatical subsystem of articles is one of the most difficult areas for Chinese EAL learners of English in general (Luk & Shirai, 2009). The sentences in (1)–(3) are utterances produced by Chinese-L1 learners of English, and each of them has an error related to the misuse of articles or determiners.

(1)   *I graduated from EMI school.
(2)   *Apple is my favourite fruit.
(3)   *Learning language at young age is good.

In (1), there should be an indefinite article *an* in front of *EMI school*. In (2), it should be *The apple is my favourite fruit* or *Apples are my favourite fruit*. The sentence in (3) should be *Learning a language at a young age is good*. Although *language* can be countable or uncountable, countable should be used here because the sentence is about learning a modern language such as English, Japanese, Korean, etc. In this chapter, we describe the functions of articles in English and distinguish them from demonstratives in English and Chinese. We also attempt to provide Chinese learners of English with a way to systematically identify errors related to the misuse of articles.

Articles in English: Definiteness

The definite article: The

Most Cantonese-speaking learners of English in Hong Kong come across the functions of the articles *a/an* and *the* in primary school. They are often taught that *a/an* is used when something is mentioned for the first time, and *the* is used for things that have been mentioned previously.

This explanation is related to what is called 'hearer's knowledge' or definiteness. If the speaker mentions something which he or she believes that the hearer also knows about, the definite article should be used; on the other hand, if the speaker talks about something that he or she believes the hearer does not know about, an indefinite article should be used. The 'indefinite' and 'definite' cases are illustrated in (4) and (5) respectively.

(4)   (Background: Mary is talking to Peter about her experience at a French restaurant. Peter has not mentioned to Mary that he knows any French restaurants.)
       Mary: I went to a French restaurant in Tsim Sha Tsui, and it was so good.
       Peter: Where is it? I'd like to give it a try.

(5)   (Background: Mary is talking to Peter about her experience at a French restaurant. Peter has recommended a French restaurant in Tsim Sha Tsui to Mary.)
       Mary: I went to the French restaurant in Tsim Sha Tsui, and it was so good.
       Peter: I knew you'd love it.

In (4), Mary used the indefinite article *a* because Peter had never mentioned anything about French restaurants and she did not expect Peter to know about the restaurant. In contrast, in (5), Mary knew that Peter was aware of the restaurant, because he recommended it to her, and therefore she used the definite article *the*. The conversation would be very awkward if Mary used *the* in (4), as shown in (6).

(6)   (Background: Mary talked to Peter about her experience at a French restaurant. Peter has not mentioned to Mary that he knows any French restaurants.)
       Mary: I went to the French restaurant in Tsim Sha Tsui, and it was so good.[1]
       Peter: What restaurant?

While the explanation of mentioning for the first time or not is not incorrect, it fails to characterize many other usages of the definite and indefinite articles. In the following, we attempt to give a more detailed account of how the definite article *the* in English is used.

Unobvious cases of definiteness

The above examples illustrate probably the most common usages of *a/an* and *the*. Advanced learners of English in general have little problem with them. However, if we read an authentic English text, such as a newspaper article or a novel, we would

---

1. This sentence would be correct if there is only one French restaurant in Tsim Sha Tsui. However, this is not the case.

notice that most of the cases of *the* are different. Consider the excerpt in (7), which is adapted from the very beginning of the novel *Harry Potter and the Sorcerer's Stone*:

(7)   Mr. and Mrs. Dursley, of number four, Privet Drive, were proud to say that they were perfectly normal, thank you very much. They were (a) the last people you'd expect to be involved in anything strange or mysterious, because they just didn't hold with such nonsense.

Mr. Dursley was (b) the director of a firm called Grunnings, which made drills. He was a big, beefy man with hardly any neck, although he did have a very large mustache. Mrs. Dursley was thin and blonde and had nearly twice (c) the usual amount of neck, which came in very useful as she spent so much of her time craning over garden fences, spying on (d) the neighbors. The Dursleys had a small son called Dudley and in their opinion there was no finer boy anywhere. (Rowling, 1999, p. 1)

There are four instances of *the* in this excerpt. In (a), *the* is used with *last people*. In (b), *the* is used in front of *director of a firm called Grunnings*. *The* in (c) is used with *usual amount of neck*, and finally *the* in (d) is used with *neighbors*. None of these noun phrases has been mentioned before their appearance in the excerpt. For example, there is no mention of the word *director* before (b), nor is there any mention of *neighbors* before (d).

These usages of *the* in (7) are quite different from that in (5). The question is thus why *the* is used when these noun phrases are mentioned for the first time. In fact, these usages are also cases of hearer's (or reader's, in this case) knowledge (i.e., definite). That is, the author assumes the reader of the novel has knowledge about these noun phrases. Take *the director* as an example. It is probably common knowledge that there is a director, or a boss, in a company. Readers, therefore, do not feel particularly confused when we read *the director of a firm called Grunnings*. This explanation can also be applied to instances (c) and (d): In (c), part of our world knowledge includes knowing how long people's necks usually are, so that we have this common perception of the usual/typical length of people's necks; in (d), our world knowledge tells us that people usually live in a community where other people live, and therefore it is common that we have neighbours. That is, we can 'infer' the existence of a director when talking about a firm, and the existence of neighbours when talking about a home or family (Birner & Ward, 1994; Lyons, 1999).

The use of *the* in (a) can be explained by uniqueness (Birner & Ward, 1994). There is only one person or group of people (that are perceived as acting as one unit, as in this case) that comes last. This is the same as *the first, the second, the third, the second last*, etc.

Marking uniqueness is another sufficient condition for being definite. When something is unique, there is no ambiguity and it is identifiable by the hearer (Hawkins,

1991). Uniqueness can account for many uses of *the*, such as *The Queen of England* and *The Prime Minister of Japan*.

The fact that *the* is used with unique reference may explain why some proper names incorporate the definite article. Examples are *The White House, The Eiffel Tower*, and *The Louvre*. Incorporating the definite article makes these buildings sound unique.

The notion of uniqueness also helps explain the use of *the* + noun (in general, *the* + NP) to bear a generic sense. An expression is said to be generic when it refers to the type and not a specific entity in the world. Consider the sentence in (8), which has two readings.

(8)   The lion eats everything.

In the first reading, *the lion* refers to a lion that is known to the hearer. The speaker uses *the* to direct the hearer's attention to that lion, as opposed to any other lions. This is illustrated in Figure 6.1.

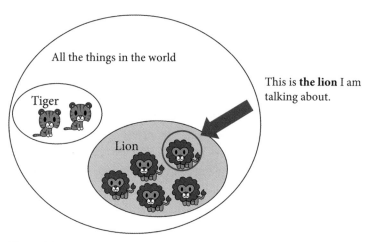

Figure 6.1
Using *the lion* to refer to a lion that is known to the hearer

In the second reading, *the lion* has a generic sense,[2] meaning that *the lion* here does not refer to one lion that exists in this world but to all the lions in the world, or as representative of lions in general. This is illustrated in Figure 6.2.

---

2.   It should be noted that indefinite singular (e.g., *a lion*) and indefinite plural (e.g., *lions*) can also be used for generic use. For details, see Lyons (1999).

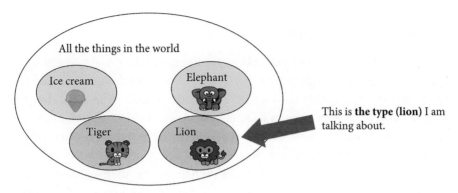

Figure 6.2
Using *the lion* to refer to a type of thing

In this case, the contrast is not made among individual lions; instead, the contrast is made among different types: the lion versus the tiger, the lion versus the elephant, the lion versus ice cream, and so forth.

But how can uniqueness explain the use of *the* to express a generic sense? When we are making a contrast between types (of people, things, etc.), we view all the lions in the world as one group, all the tigers as one group, all the ice cream as one group, etc., and each of these groups is unique (Lyons, 1999; Roberts, 2003). Since we are referring to the group, and not a member in the group, the definite article is used.

To summarize, the definite article *the* is used in the following cases:

(a)   Referring to persons or things that have been mentioned;

(b)   Referring to persons or things that can be inferred from persons or things that have been mentioned (e.g., *the director of a firm*); and

(c)   Referring to persons or things that are unique (e.g., *The White House*, generic sense of *the apple*).

Demonstratives in English: Pointing (deictic)

In the previous section, we discussed the functions of English articles. Articles belong to a larger group of function words called 'determiners'. In this section, we will talk about another category in English under determiners: 'demonstratives'.

Demonstratives refer to words such as *this*, *that*, *these*, and *those*. These words are often understood by Chinese learners of English to have similar functions as the English articles, especially the definite article *the*. Although there is some overlap in meaning and functions between demonstratives and articles, they are not identical. We will first explain the most basic functions of demonstratives.

Demonstratives are used to refer to things by pointing. Consider (9) and (10):

(9)   I saw that man in the café last night.

(10)   I saw the man in the café last night.

When reading (9), readers probably have an image in their mind, in which the speaker is pointing at a man who is not in the proximity of the speaker. However, the feeling of relative distance disappears when *the* is used, as in (10). Now the interpretation of *the man* relies on whether he has been mentioned previously in the conversation or whether there is a known person shared by the interlocutors who is identifiable given the context. The most basic function of demonstratives is thus to give some indication of the distance between the referent (e.g., the man being referred to) and the speaker. The use of *that* and *this* is therefore not related to the hearer's knowledge, or definiteness, but the actual physical context (i.e., deictic). Deictic expressions are 'those linguistic elements whose interpretation in simple sentences makes essential reference to properties of the extralinguistic context of the utterance in which they occur' (Anderson & Keenan, 1985, p. 259).

In colloquial speech, demonstratives in English are also used to 'point at' referents mentioned in conversation (Radden, 2007). For example:

(11)   I looked out of the window, and there was this woman, and she was going to back up the car, and forgot to open the gate, and . . . (Radden, 2007, p. 95)

According to Radden, *this* in this case is used to highlight the woman. It also creates a sense of 'greater immediacy and vividness' (Radden, 2007, p. 95), inviting the hearer to visualize 'this woman' while the speaker is saying something about her.

Demonstratives in Chinese

Unlike English, Chinese does not have articles (i.e., words that encode definiteness), but it has demonstratives. Consider the sentences in (12) and (13):

(12) （望 出 窗 外）你 看 到 那 幢 大 廈 嗎？張 三 就 住 在 那 裡。
      (wàng   chū   chuāng   wài)   nǐ   kàn   dào   nà zhuàng
      Look   out   window   outside   you   see   that   CL
      dàshà   ma?   zhāngsān   jiù   zhù   zài   nàlǐ
      building   Q   Zhangsan   then   live   in   there
      '(Looking out of the window) Do you see that building? Zhangsan lives there.'

(13) (在 電 器 店 內) 這 台 電 視 機 是 最 新 型 號，還 在 打 折。
     (zài   diànqì   diàn   nèi)   zhè   tái   diànshìjī   shì
     In   electronics   store   inside   this   CL   TV set   is
     zuì   xīn   xínghào   hái   zài   dǎzhé
     most   new   model   and   is   on sale
     '(Inside an electronics store) This TV set is the latest model, and it's on sale.'

In (12) and (13), the speakers are pointing at a building and a TV set, respectively. The speakers do not assume that the hearers know about the existence of the building or the TV set before the sentences are uttered. The existence of these entities can be made known to the hearer at the time of the utterance. Recall that definiteness has to do with the hearer's knowledge: If the speaker believes something is known to the hearer before the utterance is made, the entity is definite; otherwise, it is indefinite. Therefore, we can conclude that the usages of 那 (*nà*) and 這 (*zhè*), as in (12) and (13), illustrate the typical function of demonstratives rather than of articles.

Another difference between demonstratives and articles is that articles in English are obligatory, whereas in Chinese, demonstratives are not. In English, *a/an* is used with indefinite singular referents, and *the* is used with definite referents (singular, plural, or uncountable). Only indefinite plural or uncountable referents have 'zero article' (i.e., no article precedes the noun phrase, e.g., *we are university students*). However, demonstratives in Chinese are not obligatory even if the referent is definite. Consider the excerpt in (14), which is taken from a Chinese novel called *xīn nián* 'New Year' (衛斯理, 1997, p. 2):

(14) 所有人都繁忙，王其英是例外，他斜靠在鐵欄上，鐵欄在人行隧
     道的出口處，各種各樣的人，像潮水一樣湧出去，只有他懶洋洋
     地靠着鐵欄，甚至還有空打上幾個呵欠。
     Suǒyǒu   rén   dōu   fánmáng,   Wángqíyīng   shì   lìwài,
     All   people   also   busy   Wang Qiying   is   exception
     tā   xiékào   zài   tiě   lán   Shàng,
     he   lean   at   iron   railing   on
     tiě   lán   zài   rénxíng   suìdào   de   chūkǒu   chu,
     iron   railing   at   pedestrian   subway   NOM   exit   place
     gè   zhǒng   gè   yang   de   rén,
     every   kind   every   type   NOM   people
     xiàng   cháoshuǐ   yī   yang   yǒng   chū   qù,
     like   tide   one   face   rush   out   go
     zhǐ   yǒu   tā   lǎnyángyángdì   kào   zhe   tiě   lán,
     only   have   he   lazily   lean   against   iron   railing
     shènzhì   hái   yǒu   kòng   dǎ   shàng   jī   gè   hēqiàn。
     even   also   have   time   hit   complete   some   CL   yawn

We can see that 鐵欄 (*tiě lán*) 'metal railing' has been mentioned three times, and all of them refer to the same entity: the railings against which Wang leant. The reader should have known to which railing the second and third mention of the term *tiě lán* 'railing' refers. In other words, the referent (i.e., the railing) is definite. Despite this, no determiners (i.e., articles or demonstratives) are used in the second and third mention of the railing. This shows that it is not obligatory to mark definiteness in Chinese. In contrast, if it is in English, a definite article is needed, as shown in (15).

(15)   Wang leant against <u>a</u> railing, which was located at the entrance of the subway. While everybody was rushing out of the subway like flowing water, he was lazily leaning against <u>the</u> railing. He even had the time to yawn a few times.

Although we have said that demonstratives in Chinese are different from articles in English, it has been observed that cases in which demonstratives in Chinese are used for definite referents are increasing (Li & Thompson, 2009). Consider the use of 那 (*nà*) in Example (16):

(16)   你 上 次 跟 我 說 你 多 了 兩 張 演 唱 會 的 門 票。<u>那</u> 兩 張 門
       票 你 給 了 誰 ？
       Nǐ   shàng   cì   gēn   wǒ   shuō   nǐ   duō   le
       you   last   time   with   I   say   you   more   ASP
       liǎng   zhāng   yǎnchànghuì   de   ménpiào
       two   CL   concert   NOM   ticket
       nà   liǎng   zhāng   ménpiào   nǐ   gěi   le   shéi
       that   two   CL   ticket   you   give   ASP   who
       'You told me last time that you had two extra tickets for the concert. Whom did you give the tickets to?'

Apart from demonstratives, definiteness can be signalled by word order (Lyons, 1999). For example, noun phrases in the pre-verbal position are often definite (17a) and those in the post-verbal positions are often indefinite (17b).

(17)   *Mandarin* (Li & Thompson, 1981)
       a.   人 來 了。
            Rén   lái   le
            people come   ASP
            'The person has come.'
       b.   來 人 了。
            Lái   rén   le
            Come   people ASP
            'A person has come.'

(18) *Cantonese* (Matthews & Yip, 1994)

    a.   隻 貓 走 咗 入 黎。

        zek3 *maau1* *zau2* *zo2*   *yap6* *lai4*

        CL   cat   go   ASP   enter come

        'The cat came in.'

    b.   走 咗 隻 貓 入 黎。

        zau2 *zo2* *zek3* *maau1* *yap6* *lai4*

        go   ASP   CL   cat   enter come

        'A/The cat came in.'

Cases where *the* cannot be translated into *nà* (那)

We have seen that the definite article in English can be used in the following three cases:

Case 1   Referring to persons or things that have been mentioned

Case 2   Referring to persons or things that can be inferred from persons or things that have been mentioned (e.g., *the director of a firm*)

Case 3   Referring to persons or things that are unique (e.g., *The White House*, generic sense of *the apple*)

We have also explained that, in Chinese, demonstratives are sometimes used like definite articles. However, the use of demonstratives as definite articles may not be applicable to Cases 2 and 3. Consider the sentences in (19) and (20):

(19) He is *the* CEO of Apple.

(20) 他 是 蘋 果 公 司 的 總 裁。

     Tā *shì* *píngguǒ* *gōngsī*   *de*   *zǒngcái*

     He   is   apple   company NOM   CEO

     'He is the CEO of Apple.'

What Example (19) illustrates is the use of *the* to refer to an entity that can be inferred (i.e., Case 2). When the sentence is translated into Chinese, as in (20), we do not find any demonstratives before the term 總裁 (*zǒngcái*, 'CEO').

Now consider (21)–(23):

(21) The lion eats everything.

(22) 獅 子 什 麼 都 吃。

     Shīzi *shénme* *dōu*   *chī*

     Lion   what   also   eat

     'Lions eat everything.'

(23) 那 頭 獅 子 什 麼 都 吃。

Nà	tóu	shīzi	shénme	dōu	chī
That	CL	lion	what	also	eat

'That/the lion eats everything.'

We have said that (21) has two readings: a specific lion, and the lion as a type of animal. When we translate it into Chinese, these two readings may be rendered into two rather different sentences. Example (22) refers to the type of animal (i.e., generic sense), and the speaker's intended meaning is that this type of animal eats everything. On the other hand, (23) refers to a specific lion (i.e., the speaker assumes the hearer knows which one is referred to). We can see that, when *the* is used in the generic sense, no demonstratives are needed in the Chinese version.

Using articles correctly

We have seen some of the differences in the way referents are referred to in Chinese and English. These differences often lead Chinese students to misuse articles when speaking or writing in English. We have seen some of these errors at the beginning of this chapter. Articles are notoriously hard for L2 learners of English whose native language does not have a comparable system (DeKeyser, 2005; Luk & Shirai, 2009). To improve the accuracy of using articles, it may be helpful to understand how English noun phrases are formed. Consider the sentence in (24):

(24) *Boy kissed girl.

It should be obvious that (24) is ungrammatical. There should be *something* preceding the noun phrases *boy* and *girl*, as in (25).

(25) That boy kissed that girl.

By adding the words *that*, the hearer knows where to locate the referent. Articles have the same function. For example, the definite article suggests to the hearer that the speaker is talking about something that the hearer knows about; in contrast, an indefinite article suggests to the hearer that what the speaker is talking about is new to the hearer.

In English, it is necessary to use some linguistic forms (i.e., words) to make explicit the connection between a noun phrase and its referent. Therefore, it is necessary that noun phrases with a countable noun as the head normally be used with a determiner[3] so that they become referential (Stowell, 1991). This is further illustrated in Figure 6.3.

---

3. There are exceptions, though. Some idiomatic patterns may bear no determiners (e.g., *I now pronounce you husband and wife*; *I go to school by bus*).

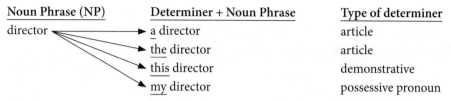

Noun Phrase (NP)	Determiner + Noun Phrase	Type of determiner
director	a director	article
	the director	article
	this director	demonstrative
	my director	possessive pronoun

Figure 6.3
Transformation from a noun phrase to a noun phrase with different determiners

However, sometimes we do see noun phrases without any determiners, as in (26).

(26)   Dogs are not allowed in restaurants.

The reason is that *dogs* and *restaurants* are indefinite and plural. In English, articles or demonstratives are not used with indefinite plural noun phrases.

Another case has to do with uncountable nouns, as shown in (27):

(27)   I don't like cheese.

Here, *cheese* is uncountable, and it is indefinite. We cannot say *a cheese*, because *a* is reserved for indefinite, countable, and singular noun phrases.

To summarize, EVERY noun phrase in English should have a determiner UNLESS the noun phrase is (a) countable, plural, and indefinite, or (b) uncountable and indefinite. Table 6.1 is a summary of the normative usage of *a* and *the*.

Table 6.1
A summary of the normative usage of *a* and *the*

	Definite	Indefinite
Countable and singular	the	a
Countable and plural/uncountable	the	zero (i.e., no article)

We will demonstrate this with example (28):

(28)   *We live in village.

We have two noun phrases in (28), *we* and *village*. *We* by itself is a determiner of some sort, because it is clear who the speaker is referring to (i.e., referential): to himself/herself and some other people. *Village* is a countable noun. We said that only plural or uncountable noun phrases can stand on their own without any determiners. *Village*, being a countable noun, is neither. So, a determiner is needed. Technically speaking, it is possible to avoid using any determiners by making it plural. The sentence would then become *we live in villages*, in which *villages* is plural and indefinite.

So, let us assume the people represented by *we* live in one single village. In fact, any determiner will make the sentence grammatical. Which is the best sentence depends on the intended meaning. Look at the sentences in (29)–(32):

(29) We live in a village.
(30) We live in the village.
(31) We live in that village.
(32) We live in his village.

Sentence (29) is used if the speaker wants to indicate that a village where he or she lives is unknown to the hearer (i.e., indefinite); (30) if he or she wishes to indicate that it is the village that the speaker believes is known to the hearer, or wants to distinguish 'the village' as opposed to 'the city' or 'the suburbs'; (31) if the speaker is physically pointing at the village, or has been talking about a village and wants to put emphasis on the village; and (32) if the village belongs to a man whom both the speaker and the hearer know.

To summarize, below are the steps one should take to ensure the correct use of articles:

Step 1:   Identify the noun phrase(s) in a sentence.
Step 2:   Determine whether the noun phrase(s) is (are) definite or indefinite.
Step 3:   Determine whether the noun phrase(s) is (are) singular, plural, or uncountable.
Step 4:   If a noun phrase is (i) indefinite and plural or (ii) indefinite and uncountable, no determiners are needed. If a noun phrase is indefinite and singular, use *a*. If a noun phrase is definite, use *the*.

(It should be noted that it is also acceptable to provide other determiners such as possessive pronouns or demonstratives, but each of these would change the intended meaning.)

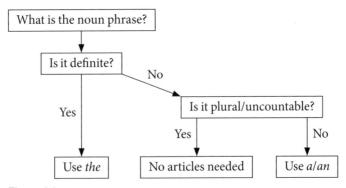

Figure 6.4
A flowchart or decision tree for ensuring the correct use of articles

Questions and activities

1. Read the following text. Look for instances of *the*. Which case does *the* belong to?

   Case 1: Referring to persons or things that have been mentioned.

   Case 2: Referring to persons or things that can be inferred from persons or things that have been mentioned (e.g., *the director of a firm*).

   Case 3: Referring to persons or things that are unique (e.g., *The White House*, eneric sense of *the apple, the lion*)

   The young woman in this photograph is me when I was writing *The House on Mango Street*. She's in her office, a room that had probably been a child's bedroom when families lived in this apartment. It has no door and is only slightly wider than the walk-in pantry. But it has great light and sits above the hallway door downstairs, so she can hear her neighbors come and go. She posed as if she's just looked up from her work for a moment, but in real life she never writes in this office. She writes in the kitchen, the only room with a heater. (Adapted from *The House on Mango Street*, Cisnero, 2013.)

2. Read the excerpt in Exercise 1 again. Now look for instances of *a*. Can you explain why *a* is used for each of these instances?

3. Read the excerpt Exercise 1 again. Now look for instances in which the noun phrase has no determiners. In each of these instances, explain why. Also, look for determiners other than *the* and *a*.

4. Read the excerpt below.

   一九六一年的春天，我們村子裡的小學校裡拉來了一車亮晶晶的煤塊，我們孤陋寡聞，不知道這是什麼東西。一個聰明的孩子拿起一塊煤，咯嘣咯嘣地吃起來。看他吃的香甜樣子，味道肯定很好，於是我們一擁而上，每人搶一塊煤，咯嘣咯嘣地吃起來了。我感到那煤塊越嚼越香，味道的確是好極了。看到我吃得香甜，村子裡的大人們也撲上來吃，學校裡的校長出來阻止，於是人們就開始哄搶。
   (莫言，《蒼蠅·門牙》, 2005, p. 5)

   Find *two* instances in which the noun phrases are definite (to the reader).
   Find *two* instances in which the noun phrases are indefinite.

Further reading

Classifiers sometimes are said to have a definite meaning in Chinese. Wu and Bodomo (2009) provide a comparison between classifiers in Chinese and a definite article, and argue that Chinese classifiers do not function as definite articles. Lyons (1999) provides an in-depth but reader-friendly discussion on definite/indefinite articles and other related concepts.

7
Subject-Prominence and Topic-Prominence

Introduction

In this chapter, we compare Chinese and English according to how information is organized in a sentence, or how information is structured at the sentence level (Lambrecht, 1994). In Chinese, many sentences are structurally similar to (1)–(3) below.

(1) 昆明有個圓通寺。寺後就是圓通山。從前是一座荒山，現在是一個公園，就叫圓通公園。(李廣田，《花潮》)

Kūnmíng	*yǒu*	*gè*	*yuántōng*	*sì*	*sì*	*hòu*	*jiù*
Kunming	has	CL	yuantong	temple	temple	behind	then

shì	*yuántōng*	*shān*
is	yuantong	mountain

Cóngqián	*shì*	*yī*	*zuò*	*huāng*	*shān*	*xiànzài*	*shì*
before	is	one	CL	deserted	mountain	now	is

yī	*gè*	*gōngyuán*	*jiù*	*jiào*	*yuántōng*	*gōngyuán*
one	CL	park	then	call	yuantong	park

(2) 到南京時，有朋友約去遊逛，勾留了一日；第二日上午便須渡江到浦口……(朱自清，《背影》)

Dào	*nánjīng*	*shí*	*yǒu*	*péngyǒu*	*yuē*	*qù*	*yóuguàng*
arrive	Nanjing	moment	has	friend	ask	go	travel

gōuliú	*le*	*yī*	*rì*	*dièr*	*rì*	*shàngwǔ*	*biàn*	*xū*
stay	ASP	one	day	next	day	morning	then	must

dù	*jiāng*	*dào*	*pǔkǒu*
cross	river	to	Pukou

(3) 像貓這種動物，咱們中間誰沒有認清？(葉紹鈞，《以畫為喻》)

Xiàng	*māo*	*zhè*	*zhǒng*	*dòngwù*	*zánmen*	*zhōngjiān*	*shéi*
like	cat	this	type	animal	we	within	who

méi	*yǒu*	*rènqīng*
not	have	recognize

Look at the underlined parts, which are placed at the beginning of the sentences. Are they 'subjects' in these sentences? Sentences in (4)–(6) are meant to be free/idiomatic (as opposed to literal or word-for-word) translations of (1)–(3) respectively.

(4) In Kunming, there is a temple called Yuan Tong Temple. Behind the temple is Yuan Tong Mountain. It <u>used to</u> be a deserted mountain, but <u>now</u> it is a park, and it is called Yuan Tong Park.

(5) . . . I needed to cross the river and be at Pukou <u>the next morning</u> . . .

(6) Who wouldn't recognize <u>an animal like a cat</u>?

In (4), 從前 (*cóngqián*, 'before') is translated into the verb phrase *used to*. The subject is *It*, which refers to Yuan Tong Mountain. In (5), the underlined phrase 第二日上午 is translated into a determiner phrase *the next morning* (i.e., determiner + noun phrase), but it is located at the end of the sentence, and the subject is *I*. In (6), the underlined phrase 像貓這種動物 is an object in the English version. By word order, therefore, the Chinese sentences are very different from the corresponding English sentences. The question that arises is: What is a subject in Chinese?

Subject in English

Before turning to the answer to this question, it is necessary for us to be clear about what a subject is in English. In English, a subject is typically a noun or noun phrase that (i) appears before the finite[1] verb[2] and (ii) agrees with the verb in number and person. In Standard English, an *-s* is added to the verb when the sentence is in the present tense and the singular subject is a noun (phrase) with a singular meaning or a third-person pronoun: *he/she/it*. The adding of the *-s* is what is called subject-verb agreement. Conversely, the presence of *-s* in the verb suggests that the subject is singular. In fact, in some languages such as Spanish, one can omit the subject and simply say the verb with the appropriate agreement, and the hearer will know who the subject is, as shown in (7) and (8).

(7) habl-o
    '(I) speak'

(8) habl-as
    '(you) speak'

Although we said that a subject agrees with the verb, not all noun phrases can occupy the subject position. Recall, in the chapter on transitivity (Chapter 3), that verbs select specific semantic roles to be the subject. For example, *eat* selects an

---

1. Finite verbs are verb forms that carry tense information. For example, *ate* is finite because it is a past tense form, while *eating* is not because *-ing* only indicates aspect and does not tell us what tense *eating* carries.

2. There are exceptions. For example, the subject of the construction *Here comes X* appears after the verb.

Actor/Agent (i.e., a person or an animal that intentionally puts food into his/her/its mouth, chews it and swallows it) to be the subject, whereas the intransitive *break* selects a Patient to be its subject. Therefore, for *eat*, only a person or an animal can appear right before the finite verb. This is illustrated in (9) and (10):

(9)   The cow ate all the grass.

(10)   *All the grass ate the cow. (To mean: 'the cow ate all the grass')

Another feature regarding subject in English is that it is compulsory. For example, *it* in (11) does not refer to any entity, whereas in (12) *it* refers to an object, although from this simple sentence we do not know what it refers to. We call the subject in (11) a 'dummy subject' or an 'expletive'.

(11)   <u>It</u> rained.

(12)   <u>It</u> broke.

We therefore call English a 'subject-prominent language', because in English a subject must be present and is often the first element to appear in a sentence.

'Subject' in Chinese

The notion of a subject, as shown above, is not applicable to Chinese. This is partly evidenced by the fact that there is no subject-verb agreement in Chinese. Example (13) compares French and Chinese.

(13)	Je	<u>parles</u>	我説	(*wǒ shuō*)
	Nous	<u>parlons</u>	我們説	(*wǒmen shuō*)
	Il	<u>parle</u>	他説	(*tā shuō*)
	Ils	<u>parlent</u>	他們説	(*tāmen shuō*)
	Vous	<u>parlez</u>	你們説	(*nǐ(men) shuō*)

We can see that, in French, the verb forms (e.g., of the verb *parler*, 'to speak') vary depending on the subjects, but the equivalent verb in Chinese 説 (*shuō*, 'speak') does not. Not only does Chinese have no requirement for subject-verb agreement, but Chinese also allows nouns phrases of different thematic roles to be placed before the verb, as illustrated in (1)–(3) at the beginning of this chapter.

Because there is no linguistic form (i.e., agreement, position of a noun phrase, etc.) that would suggest that a noun phrase is a subject, a different term is needed to characterize the linguistic unit that appears in the sentence-initial position in Chinese, which is called 主語 (*zhǔ yǔ*).

The Chinese term 主語 (*zhǔ yǔ*) is generally used to translate and is often held to be functionally equivalent to the Western grammatical concept of subject. Strictly speaking, however, *zhǔ yǔ* is closer to what is called a 'topic' in linguistics (LaPolla, 2009). Consider the sentences in (14)–(16):

(14) <u>那 些 舊 衣 服</u> 已 經 扔 掉 了。
       Nàxiē   jiù   yīfú   yǐjīng   rēng   diào   le
       those   old   clothes   already   throw   away   ASP
       'Those old clothes, (I) have thrown them away already.'

(15) <u>那 些 舊 衣 服</u> 我 已 經 扔 掉 了。
       Nàxiē   jiù   yīfú   wǒ   yǐjīng   rēng   diào   le
       those   old   clothes   I   already   throw   away   ASP
       'Those old clothes, I have thrown them away already.'

(16) <u>下 個 星 期</u> 才 去 吧。
       Xià   gè   xīngqī   cái   qù   ba
       next   CL   week   then   go   SFP
       '(Let's) go next week.'

Using the notion of *zhǔ yǔ*, we can analyse (14)–(16) in the following way.

主語 (topic)	謂語 (comment)
14a. 那些舊衣服	已經扔掉了
15a. 那些舊衣服	我已經扔掉了
	主語　謂語
16a. 下個星期	才去吧

We thus call Chinese a 'topic-prominent language', because a topic is often the first element to appear in the sentence.

Subject = Topic?

Are the terms Subject and Topic different names for the same thing? The answer is no. A subject in English is always a participant required by the verb. For example, *steal* normally requires at least two participants, one who does the act of stealing, and another, usually an object, which is the thing taken away by the first participant (see Chapter 3). Of course we can add a time to the sentence to indicate when the stealing happens or happened, but this is not a participant required by the verb. Therefore, the time of stealing can never be a subject of a sentence with *steal* as the main verb, as shown in (17):

(17) *Yesterday stole an orange. (to mean 'I stole an orange yesterday')

In English, the subject is not limited to the Actor/Agent/Doer. A Patient can also be the subject. This again depends on the verb, as shown in (18) (see Chapter 3 for details):

(18)   My ice cream is melting!

A topic, in contrast, accommodates a much larger range of semantic roles. A topic is not something that is required by the verb but something the speaker wants to focus on and wants 'joint attention' with the hearer (Tomasello, 1995). Matthews and Yip (1994) explained that the effect of a topic is comparable to that of the English construction 'as for' or 'as far as . . . is concerned'. Consider an example like the verb 偷 (*tōu*, 'steal'): A noun phrase expressing time can be the topic, and not the person who steals, as shown in (19):

(19)   前 天 偷 了 一 個 橙，昨 天 偷 了 一 個 西 瓜。
Qiántiān		*tōu*	*le*	*yī*	*gè*	*chéng*
the.day.before.yesterday		steal	ASP	one	CL	orange
zuótiān		*tōu*	*le*	*yī*	*gè*	*xīguā*
yesterday		steal	ASP	one	CL	watermelon

'The day before yesterday, (I) stole an orange. Yesterday, (I) stole a watermelon.'

On the other hand, in subject-prominent languages like English, a subject is necessary even if the verb does not require one. We have seen that in (11). In topic-prominent languages such as Chinese, however, a subject is not obligatory; for example, (20):

(20)   下 雨 啦。
Xià	*yǔ*	*la*
go.down	rain	SFP

'It's raining.'

In (20), there is only the verb 下雨 (*xià yǔ*, 'rain'); there is, however, no need to insert a dummy subject like 'it', as in the corresponding sentence *it is raining*.

Topicalization in English

We have seen that the topic-comment structure is a fundamental word order principle when composing Chinese sentences. English also allows for topicalization, but to a lesser degree than Chinese does. Green (1991) gave (21) and (22) as examples (p. 56):

(21)   <u>With regard to education</u>, Tony likes Smith's ideas.
(22)   <u>As for Tony</u>, he likes Smith's ideas on education.

Sometimes the subject is also the topic, as shown in (23):

(23) **Tony** likes Smith's ideas on education.

Although topicalization is acceptable in English, Green (1991) noted that these structures are 'marked', meaning that they are unusual. That is to say, they are only used when the reader/writer really wants to draw the reader's or listener's attention to a particular entity.

Chinese EAL learners' problems with topicalization in English

The difference between English and Chinese/Cantonese—subject-prominence as opposed to topic-prominence—often misleads learners into producing ungrammatical or unnatural utterances. Less proficient EAL learners may produce sentences like the one in (24) to mean 'I am the responsible person regarding that matter/issue':

(24) *That matter I am responsible person (Green, 1991, p. 53)

More advanced learners may not produce ungrammatical sentences, but the sentences they produce may sometimes sound clumsy and unnatural. Green (1991) and Yip (1995) showed that Hong Kong students tend to produce sentences like (25) and (26):

(25) According to research evidence, it shows that more Asian couples are getting divorced nowadays. (Green, 1991, p. 58)
(26) For Julia, she was a troop leader in the spies. (Yip & Matthews, 1995, cited in Yip, 1995)

Yip (1995) argues that, while (26) is marginally grammatical, it is highly unnatural. Green (1991, p. 58) points out that (25) can be rewritten in at least three ways, as in (27)–(29), which would sound more natural to native speakers.

(27) According to my research, more Asian couples are getting divorced.
(28) More Asian couples are getting divorced nowadays, according to my research.
(29) My research shows that more Asian couples are getting divorced nowadays.

Example (30) is another example given by Green (1991, p. 60):

(30) For the Western women's concept of freedom, it can allow them to make their own decisions who to marry.

Yip and Matthews (1995) described the underlined structure in (30) as a periphrastic construction (cf. Kwan, Chan, & Li, 2003), which is not preferred in Standard

English given that the topicalized phrase is the subject of what is *reported*. The preferred version is shown in (31).

> (31) The Western concept of freedom allows women to make their own deci-
>   sions [about] whom to marry.

How to form grammatical sentences and avoid over-topicalization

To deal with these problems when writing in English, learners of English can try the
following steps:

> Step 1: Determine what the verb takes as its argument(s).

As discussed in Chapter 3 and earlier in this chapter, what may be inserted in
the subject position depends on the argument structure of the verb. Many verbs in
English take an Agent/Actor (Doer) as the subject, but there are other semantic roles
that a verb can take. Look at Examples (32)–(36):

> (32) **The cup** broke.   [Patient]
> (33) **Mary** fears dogs.   [Experiencer]
> (34) **The dog** frightened Mary.   [Percept]
> (35) **John** angered his father.   [Percept]
> (36) **The ball** rolled into the river.   [Theme]

One should always bear in mind that the subject role depends on the verb. Even
if one wants to focus on *his father* in (35), it is ungrammatical to say **his father John
angered* or **his father angered*. In this case, either the passive or another word (verb or
adjective) should be used (e.g., *his father was angered by John; his father was angry*).

> Step 2: Always ask whether using a non-subject phrase to start a sentence is
>   necessary.

We have seen that (25) and (30) are considered unnatural by native English
speakers. Look at (30) again. Try rephrasing it in different ways. Following the para-
phrases in (27)–(29), (30) may similarly be paraphrased, as in (37)–(39):

> (37) In the Western concept of freedom, women can make their own deci-
>   sions on whom to marry.
> (38) Western women can make their own decisions on whom to marry in
>   their concept of freedom.
> (39) The Western women's concept of freedom allows them to make their own
>   decisions on whom to marry.

These sentences no longer have a prepositional phrase (PP = P + NP) co-referenced with *it* in the same sentence, as in (40):

(40) <u>In the second paragraph</u>, <u>it</u> reported that the three-day conference pre-ceded a large-scale education fair on study in the US. (Kwan et al., 2003, p. 92)

Kwan et al. (2003, pp. 89–91) also propose a set of procedures for teachers to help learners overcome the problem of overusing the topic-comment structure in English. The steps are outlined below.

Step 1   Assess learners' awareness of the problem.

Step 2   Illustrate and correct the problem by directing learners' attention to the source of the information and reminding them that the source of information should not be repeated.

Step 3   Reinforce learners' knowledge with an exercise that involves asking them to analyse the source of information and rewrite sentences in which the source of information is repeated.

Questions and activities

1.   Identify the subject in the following English sentences. Explain what agreement is used.

i.   I don't like English.

ii.   English is my favourite subject.

iii.   The house was owned by the heirs of the Royal Family.

iv.   Sam and Teresa were disappointed by their son's behaviour.

v.   Today Jennifer has one million followers on Twitter.

vi.   The dog quickly jumped into the water.

vii.   John F. Kennedy was supposedly assassinated by a man called Oswald.

2.   Read the following excerpt. Then, find cases in which 主語 (*zhǔ yǔ*, 'topic') is not a participant of the event described by the verb. What should the partici-pants be?

庭院無聲。枕簟生涼。溫暖的陽光，穿過葦簾，照在淡黃色的壁上。濃密的樹影，在微風中徐徐動搖。窗外不時的有好鳥飛鳴。這時世上一切，都已拋棄隔絕，一室便是宇宙，花影樹聲，都含妙理。是一年來最難得的光陰呵，可惜只有七天！黃昏時，弟弟歸來，音樂聲起，靜境便肅然破了。一塊暗綠色的綢子，蒙在燈上，屋裏一切都是幽涼的，好似悲劇的一幕。鏡中照見自己玲瓏的

白衣，竟悄然的覺得空靈神秘。當屋隅的四弦琴，顫動著，生澀
的，徐徐奏起。兩個歌喉，由不同的調子，漸漸合一。由悠揚，而
宛轉；由高吭，而沈緩的時候，怔忡的我，竟感到了無限的悵惘
與不寧。小孩子們真可愛，在我睡夢中，偷偷的來了，放下幾束
花，又走了。小弟弟拿來插在瓶裏，也在我睡夢中，偷偷的放在床
邊幾上。——開眼瞥見了，黃的和白的，不知名的小花，襯著淡綠
的短瓶。……原是不很香的，而每朵花裏，都包含著天真的友情。
（冰心，《閑情》）

3.   Translate the following excerpt into Chinese. Did you have any difficulty
      regarding topicalization?

> The last hour of Eddie's life was spent, like most of the others, at Ruby Pier,
> an amusement park by a great gray ocean. The park had the usual attrac-
> tions, a boardwalk, a Ferris wheel, roller coasters, bumper cars, a taffy
> stand, and an arcade where you could shoot streams of water into a clown's
> mouth. It also had a big new ride called Freddy's Free Fall, and this would
> be where Eddie would be killed, in an accident that would make news-
> papers around the state. (Albom, *The Five People You Meet in Heaven*, p. 1)
> (Ferris wheel: 摩天輪; taffy: 太妃糖)

Further reading

Data from other languages often help clarify linguistic concepts such as topic. Gundel
(1988) discusses the topic-comment structure in various languages from a typological perspective. Some linguists argue that topic and subject are diachronically related.
Readers who are interested in this issue may wish to read Shibatani (1991), who
argues that subject is a product of the grammaticalization of topic.

8

Europeanization

Influence of English on Chinese Grammar

Contact between Chinese and English: Historical background

Contact between English and Chinese speakers may be traced to the late seventeenth century, when British merchants and sailors, and later missionaries, came to China for commercial, trade-related, and religious reasons (see, e.g., Ansaldo, Matthews, & Smith, 2012; Bolton, 2003; Zhang, 2009). During the Qing dynasty (1644–1911), for practical purposes some Chinese merchants and interpreters learned and used English to communicate with the 'red-haired barbarians'. According to van Dyke (2005), there are historical records indicating 'that merchants in Canton [today's Guangzhou] were already using 'pidgin English' by about 1715' (p. 80) and 'by the 1730s, pidgin English appears to have gained a solid footing among both merchants and linguists [i.e., interpreters]' (p. 81). Similarly, Ansaldo (2009) observes that, while the presence of the British along the China coast was growing starting roughly from the last decades of the seventeenth century, they encountered great difficulties communicating with the local Chinese. In particular, 'the use of a mixture of English and Portuguese in the interactions with local Chinese was common until well into the middle of the eighteenth century' (Ansaldo, 2009, p. 189). The 'red-haired barbarians' were largely confined to the province of Guangdong and had limited freedom of travel. In addition, they were prohibited from learning the Chinese language, while few Chinese had heard of or were interested in learning their language, English. At the same time, since Chinese products such as silk, tea, and porcelain were greatly in demand in Europe, British traders and successive governments of the British Empire were displeased with unfavourable trading terms dictated to them. Backed by gunboats and advanced weaponry, the British decided to force open China's doors with their superior military strength. This was the background to the two Anglo-Chinese Wars (1839–1842 and 1860–1861), also known as the Opium Wars, which among other things led to the opening of 14 treaty ports on the China coast. The island of Hong Kong, a sleepy barren rock in southern China at the time, was also ceded to the British as a result of the unequal Treaty of Nanking (1842). By the early 20th century, contacts with Europeans and their languages were no longer rare. Apart from trading and commerce, the activities of British and American missionaries intensified; witness the opening of many colleges in different parts of China, where English was taught to local people (Adamson, 2002, 2004; Zhang, 2009).

Since the Opium Wars, Western ideas and products gradually became available in China, some involving alien practices that challenged the old social order and traditional values, including Confucian ethics (Lo Bianco, Orton, & Gao, 2009). During the reign of the emperor Guangxu (光緒), a movement was championed by the late Qing official Zhang Zhidong (張之洞, 1837–1909) and a few liberals. In 1898, Zhang Zhidong designed the curriculum of the Imperial Peking University by modelling it on the curricula of Tokyo and Kyoto Universities and incorporating the teaching of foreign languages at 同文館 (Tóngwén guǎn), which had been set up in 1862 for Chinese students to learn foreign languages from Western missionaries and to be trained as translators and interpreters (Kirkpatrick & Xu, 2012, p. 145). Zhang Zhidong further called for 'studying Chinese for its *essence*, while studying the West for its *practical usage*' (emphasis added).[1] The *tǐ–yòng* (體用) movement won the support of many intellectuals who were eager to bring about change and, for that reason, embraced Western progressive thinking. To them, it was the ultimate solution to the country's sociopolitical problems (humiliating unequal treaties dictated by Western powers, social instability, health hazards, unemployment, poverty, etc.). Some extremists even advocated total westernization,[2] including replacing logographic Chinese characters with an alphabetic script (Kirkpatrick & Xu, 2012; Li, 2017).

From the last decades leading to the demise of Imperial China and the beginning of the Republican era (1912), the Chinese language was also undergoing tremendous change. Traditionally, written Chinese followed a literary style known as *wényán wén* (文言文, hereafter *wenyan*), which is modelled on classical Chinese texts. This writing style was very different from the speech style, regardless of the speaker's dialect or local vernacular (compare, e.g., the first-person singular pronoun: 吾 (*wú/ng4*), vs. 我 (*wǒ/ngo5*). Many young critics, especially those who had the opportunity to learn one or more foreign languages, including Japanese, blamed the country's social woes and economic backwardness on a lack of alignment or correspondence between the ways one writes and speaks. To resolve this problem, it was widely believed that writing and speech should be aligned.[3] The intellectual at the forefront of the New Culture Movement[4] promoting vernacular Chinese (白話, *báihuà*, 'plain

---

1. 中學為體，西學為用 (*zhōng xué wéi tǐ, xī xué wéi yòng*, Lo Bianco et al., 2009).
2. 全盤西化 (*quán pán xīhuà/cyun4 pun4 sai1 faa3*, Lo Bianco et al., 2009).
3. 我手寫我口 (*wǒ shǒu xiě wǒ kǒu*, literally 'my-hand-write-my-mouth', or 'write as one speaks').
4. 新文化運動 (*xīn wénhuà yùndòng/san1 man4 faa3 wan6 dung6*).

speech') as the written medium of modern literary language was Hu Shi (胡適, 1891–1962), a returnee from the US who had earned a PhD at Columbia University. Later, in his official role as member of Imperial Peking University's Chinese Language and Literature Department, Hu Shi further championed the course of replacing *wenyan* with *baihua* as the educated discourse. This view was generally welcomed and soon proved to be very popular in society.

From the beginning of the 20th century onwards, therefore, written Chinese gradually became vernacularized as more and more writers chose to adhere to the norms of *baihua*. New ideas across a wide range of topics and genres written in foreign languages were introduced to Chinese readers via translation, for example, novels, short stories, poetry, essays, dramas, and literary theories. Aspiring young intellectuals took advantage of burgeoning newspapers and magazines as platforms to reach out to the general public. This encouraged the experimentation of literary writing in as well as translation into *baihua*. Many young writers who were hungry for and fascinated by Western ideas found inspiration in their reading of literature written by foreign writers. Educators, literary writers and critics, and leaders of social movements called for concerted efforts to breathe new life into the Chinese language which, they argued, had to change in order to keep up with the changing times. They saw the need for innovations in the Chinese language so that it could 'carry' or express novel ideas, in keeping with the spirit of and advances in the modern era. Thus various stakeholders in society, from literary writers and translators to educators and reform-minded intellectuals, were all eager to experiment with new vocabulary and morpho-syntactic features that were inspired by their reading and appreciation of original works written in various foreign languages, notably English.

It should be noted, however, that prior to the *baihua* movement, there was already a sizable body of literature written in a quasi-vernacular style, including the four literary classics.[5] In other words, vernacular-style writing was not entirely new before the May Fourth movement[6] in 1919, but there was general consensus among scholars that the language of the 'vernacular classics' was largely inadequate for giving expression to new ideas in modern times. This sentiment is clearly reflected in the following critique:

---

5.   四大名著 (*sì dà míng zhù*/*sei3 daai6 ming4 zyu3*): *The Romance of the Three Kingdoms* (《三國演義》, *Sān guó yǎn yì*/*Saam1 gwok3 jin2 ji6*), *Heroes of the Marshes/Outlaws of the Marshes/Water Margin* (《水滸傳》, *Shuǐ hǔ zhuàn*/*Seoi2 wu2 zyun2*), *Journey to the West/The Monkey King* (《西遊記》, *Xī yóu jì*/*Sai1 jau4 gei3*), and *The Dream of the Red Chamber* (《紅樓夢》, *Hóng lóu mèng*/*Hung4 lau4 mung6*). These works were all essentially based on Northern Mandarin (Wang, 1958b, p. 37).

6.   五四運動 (*Wǔ sì yùndòng*/*Ng5 sei3 wan6 dung6*).

翻譯——除出 [*sic*]能夠介紹原本的內容給中國讀者之外——還有一個很重
要的作用：就是幫助我們創造出新的中國現代言語。……

中國言語不精密，所以要使它更加精密；中國言語不清楚，所以要使
它更加清楚；中國言語不豐富，所以要使它更加豐富。[7] (瞿秋白, cited in
Tse, 1990, pp. 18–19)

In sum, at the dawn of the 20th century, the Chinese language was undergoing drastic
change. Norms of both speech and writing were being reshaped and redefined. Thanks
to the mass cultural awakening among writers of the New Literature Movement[8]
and the intelligentsia,[9] foreign languages which entered into contact with Chinese
were looked upon as models for refashioning the Chinese language of the future.
Of the foreign languages which had considerable impact on Chinese, English proved
to be the most influential. Such influences are generally referred to as Europeanization
(歐化, *ōu huà/aa1 faa3*), also known as Anglicization (英語化, *jīngyǔ huà/jing1
jyu5 faa3*) in recognition of English being the principal model for imitation. In the
process of experimenting with new words and structures from English, various outcomes were produced. In the rest of this chapter, we will critically examine different
types of Europeanized structure and assess the outcomes of transference at the lexical
and morpho-syntactic levels.

Europeanized features

Languages tend to influence one another when they enter into contact via their
speakers. In the case of contact between Chinese and European languages since the
turn of the 20th century, through translation and vernacular writing where lexical
and morpho-syntactic features of foreign languages were imitated, Europeanization
has left a clear imprint on Modern Chinese, standard or non-standard. One of the
clearest indicators of this trend is the creation and proliferation of new words of
foreign origin, typically via transliteration before being replaced by translation. For
instance, the word *grammar* was first transliterated as *gé lǎng mǎ* (葛朗瑪), before
being translated as *yǔfǎ* (語法) and *wénfǎ* (文法). Similarly, *sofa* was rendered as

---

7. 'Translation—apart from introducing the content of original works to Chinese readers—has another impor-
    tant function, namely, to help shape a new, modern Chinese language. . . . The Chinese language lacks preci-
    sion, so there is a need to make it more precise; the Chinese language lacks clarity, thus enhanced clarity
    is needed; the Chinese language is not so rich, hence the need to enrich it' (Qu Qiubai, cited in Tse, 1990,
    pp. 18–19; our translation).
8. 新文學運動 (*xīn wénxué yùndòng/san1 man4 hok6 wan6 dung6*).
9. Traditional vernacular writing was linguistically inadequate to express and carry new ideas. In contrast,
    Europeanized literature and essays received high praise and became increasingly popular. The following were
    among the most prominent thinkers and writers in the decade before and after the May Fourth movement
    (1919): Hu Shi (胡適), Lu Xun (魯迅), Zhou Zuoren (周作人), Xu Zhimo (徐志摩), Wen Yiduo (聞一多),
    Yu Dafu (郁達夫), Guo Moruo (郭沫若), Ba Jin (巴金), Lao She (老舍), Mao Dun (茅盾), Cao Yu (曹禺),
    and Qian Zhongshu (錢鍾書).

shāfā (沙發), *gallon* as *jiālún* (加侖), *logic* as *luójí* (邏輯) (see Tse, 1990, pp. 36–39). At the same time, existing monosyllabic Chinese verbs or adjectives were combined to designate new word meanings that were inspired by their corresponding English nouns; for instance, 約見 (*yuē jiàn*, literally 'arrange–see', meaning 'appointment') and 沉寂 (*chén jì*, 'deep–lonely', meaning 'stillness'):

取 消 了 他 的 約 見
qǔxiāo le tā de yuējiàn
cancel ASP his NOM appointment
'canceled his appointment' (Tse, 1990, p. 15)

他 終 於 打 破 了 沉 寂
tā zhōngyú dǎpò le chénjì
he finally broke ASP stillness
'He finally broke the stillness.' (Tse, 1990, p. 15)

Until the 1940s, as a result of extensive imitation and the publication of modern Chinese grammars,[10] some linguistic features that previously did not exist in Chinese gradually caught on and subsequently became widely accepted (Tse, 1990, 2001; Wang, 2012; see below). Other linguistic features, which already existed, were either made more precise or used more widely. Tse (1990) lists seven conducive features which, used judiciously, would help tighten up the structures and functions of modern Chinese, and so they were categorized as 'beneficial Europeanization' (良性歐化) (Tse, 1990, pp. 104–111).[11]

Beneficial Europeanization (良性歐化, *liáng xìng ōu huà*)

Creation of new affixes (bound morphemes)

Affixes like -者 (*-zhě*, e.g., 消費者, *xiāofèi zhě*, 'consumer'), -家 (*-jiā*, e.g., 銀行家, *yínháng-jiā*, 'banker'), -性 (*-xìng*, e.g., 可行性, *kěxíng-xìng*, 'feasibility'), -化

---

10. 馬建忠 [Ma Jianzhong] (1898), 《馬氏文通》 *Mǎshì wéntōng* [Basic principles for writing clearly and coherently by Mister Ma]; 黎錦熙 [Li Jinxi] (1924)《新著國語文法》 *Xīn zhù guóyǔ wénfǎ* [New Chinese grammar]; and 呂叔湘 [Lü Shuxiang] (1943)《中國文法要略》 *Zhōngguó wénfǎ yàolüè* [Essentials of Chinese grammar]. According to Tse (1990, p. 27), these grammars of modern Chinese were largely inspired by linguistic studies of Chinese phonology and grammar, for example: Bernhard Karlgren [高本漢] (1926), *Études sur la phonologie chinoise 1915–26* [Studies of Chinese phonology 1915–26], 趙元任、李方桂、羅常培譯,《中國音韻研究》(1948); Henri Maspero [馬百樂] (1934), *La langue chinoise* [The Chinese language], Conference de l'Institut de Linguistique de l'Université de Paris, 1933, Paris; and John Collinson Nesfield (1908), *Manual of English grammar and composition*, Macmillan.

11. Tse's (1990) preferred terminology is '善性歐化' (see Tse, 1990, pp. 104–111), which is opposed to 惡性歐化 (*é xìng ōu huà*, pp. 113–136). The terminology adopted in this book follows Wang's (2012) contrast between 良性歐化 (*liáng xìng ōu huà*, 'beneficial Europeanization') and 非良性歐化 (*fēi liáng xìng ōu huà*, 'adverse Europeanization').

(*-huà*, e.g., 現代化, *xiàndài-huà*, 'modernize'), 反- (*fǎn-*, e.g., 反傳統, *fǎn-chuántǒng*, 'anti-traditional') proliferated in translations and creative writing. Over time, words containing multiple bound morphemes became more and more popular. For instance:

<table>
<tr><td>

fǎn-fǎxīsī zhǔyì-zhě
anti-fascism-doctrine-*zhě*
'anti-fascist'

</td><td>反 法 西 斯 主 義 者</td></tr>
<tr><td>

fǎn-zīchǎn jiējí zìyóu-huà
anti-bourgeois-liberal-*huà*
'anti-bourgeois liberalization'

</td><td>反 資 產 階 級 自 由 化</td></tr>
</table>

Such a tendency was also extended to function words such as using the plural marker 們 (*-mén*) to express the meaning 'more than one', and using existing verbal suffixes or aspect markers 了／著／過 (*le/zhe/guo*) to mark perfective aspect, imperfective aspect, and experiential aspect, respectively (Tse, 1990, 2001; Wang, 2012). Compare:

1.   a.   她 穿 了 和 服
            tā chuān le héfú
            she wear ASP kimono
            'she has put on a kimono'

      b.   她 穿 著 和 服
            tā chuān zhe héfú
            she wear ASP kimono
            'she is wearing a kimono'

      c.   她 穿 過 和 服
            tā chuān guò héfú
            she wear ASP kimono
            'she has worn kimono [before]'

The plural marker and the aspect markers were already widely used in Mandarin-speaking areas. Exposure to European languages, mainly through literary writing and translation since the 1910s, facilitated their spread in the written vernacular or *baihua*. Similarly, under the influence of European languages, three discrete syntactic functions gradually evolved and were mapped onto the same character, pronounced almost identically as [*-de*] (examples below adapted from Tse, 1990, p. 47):[12]

---

12. In Modern Written Chinese, these three markers (*-de*) are often expressed by the same character 的. In Cantonese, however, their respective functions and exponents are distinct (Tang, 2015, pp. 9–10).

- 定語‘的’(*dìngyǔ -de*, 'nominalizer *-de*'):
  2. 他 必 須 規 規 矩 矩，才 能 對 得 起 將 來 **的** 老 婆
  tā bīxū guīguījǔjǔ   cái náng duì.de.qǐ jiānglái-de lǎopó
  he must well-behaved   so that not-let-down future-NOM wife
  'He must behave himself, so as not to let his future wife down.'
  [or: 'He must behave himself, so as to be worthy of his future wife.']
  (老舍，〈駱駝祥子〉)[13]

- 狀語‘地’(*zhuāngyǔ -de*, 'adverbial marker *-de*'):
  3. 梅 樹 確 是 不 少，密 密 **地**、低 低 **地** 整 列 著。
  méishù què shì bù shǎo   mìmì-de   dìdì-de zhěngliè zhe
  plum tree certainly be not few   densely   lowly line up ASP
  'Plum trees are certainly a lot, densely and lowly lining up.'
  (朱自清，〈看花〉)[14]

- 補語‘得’(*bǔyǔ -de*, post-verbal 'complementizer *-de*'):
  4. 這 深 紅 的 東 西，忽 然 生 了 奪 目 的 光 亮，
  zhè shēnhóng-de dōngxi   fūrán shēng-le duómù-de guāngliàng
  this deep red-NOM thing   suddenly emit-ASP dazzle-NOM lights
  射 **得** 人 眼 睛 發 痛。
  shè-de rén yǎnjīng fā tòng
  flash-COMP person eye get painful
  'This deep red thing suddenly emitted dazzling lights,
  making people's eyes hurt with pain.'
  (巴金，〈海上的日出〉)[15]

Induced use of clause-combining conjunctions

Traditionally, Chinese makes more use of parataxis (意合法, *yìhéfǎ*) than of hypotaxis (形合法, *xínghéfǎ*). The linking of clauses without using a connective is known as parataxis ('method of combination by *meaning*', Kirkpatrick & Xu, 2012, p. 119), for example, '*You jump. I jump*' (source: the film *Titanic*). Here, even though the logical relationship between the two clauses is not explicitly stated, in context, viewers of the film should have no problem arriving at a 'conditional' interpretation, as intended by the protagonist (i.e., 'If you jump, I'll jump', rather than, say, 'Because/Until you jump, I'll jump'). In a complex sentence involving a combination of main and subordinate clauses, the use of a connective or conjunction (e.g., *because, if, provided, as long as,*

---

13. *Luòtuó Xiángzǐ*, 'Camel Xiangzi', by Lao She.
14. *Kàn huā*, 'Watching flowers', by Zhu Ziqing.
15. *Hǎi shàng de rì chū*, 'Sunrise on the sea', by Ba Jin.

though, unless, until, whether) to mark the subordinate status of a clause is known as hypotaxis ('method of combination by *form*', Kirkpatrick & Xu, 2012, p. 119).

Prior to extensive contact with European languages, Chinese clauses tended to follow their logical or natural sequence without marking the logical relationship with a conjunction (連詞, *liáncí*). Consider the following examples adapted from Kirkpatrick and Xu (2012, p. 111), where the logical relationships—cause, concession, and condition—are deduced from the placement of the 'subordinate clause' before the 'main clause', respectively:

5.   a.   風 太 大，比 賽 改 期 了   (cause and effect)
        fēng tài dà   bǐsài gǎiqī le
        wind too big   match change time F.P.
        '(Because) the wind was too strong, the match was postponed.'

6.   a.   風 （是） 有 點 大，比 賽 不 能 改 期   (concession)
        fēng (shì) yǒu diǎn dà   bǐsài bùnáng gǎiqī
        wind (be) a little big   match cannot postpone
        '(Although) the wind is a little strong, the match cannot be postponed.'

7.   a.   強 風 停 息，比 賽 （就） 可 以 繼 續 進 行   (condition)
        qiáng fēng tíngxī   bǐsài (jiù) kěyǐ jìxù jinxing
        strong wind stop   match (then) can continue take place
        'The strong wind stops, the match can continue.'

In (5a), the first clause (風太大, *fēng tài dà*, 'too windy') is naturally understood as the cause for the effect stated in the second, main clause (比賽改期了, *bǐsài gǎiqī le*, 'the match was postponed'), despite the absence of a connective like 因為 (*yīnwèi*, 'because') that marks the causal relationship explicitly. Likewise, in (6a) and (7a), the first clause is naturally interpreted as a concession and condition, respectively, for the following (main) clause. In English, however, the hypotactic pattern is more common; the main-subordinate sequence (偏句後置, Tse, 2001, p. 18; see, e.g., 5b, 6b, and 7b) is more often encountered than the subordinate-main sequence (e.g., 5c, 6c, and 7c):

5.   b.   The match was postponed, because the wind was too strong.
      c.   Because the wind was too strong, the match was postponed.

6.   b.   The match cannot be postponed, although the wind is strong.
      c.   Although the wind is strong, the match cannot be postponed.

7.   b.   The match cannot continue, unless the strong wind stops.
      c.   Unless the strong wind stops, the match cannot continue.

As a result of extensive exposure to European languages, notably English, users of Modern Chinese tend to mark such logical relationships explicitly using conjunctions

like 因為 (*yīnwèi*, 'because'), 雖然 (*suīrán*, 'although'), and 除非 (*chúfēi*, 'unless').
Compare:

5.   d.   因 為 風 太 大，（所 以）比 賽 改 期 了
          yīnwèi fēng tài dà   (suǒyǐ) bǐsài gǎiqī le
          because wind too big,   (therefore) match change time F.P.
          'Because the wind was too strong, (so) the match was postponed.'

5.   e.   比 賽 改 期 了，因 為 風 太 大
          bǐsài gǎiqī le   yīnwèi fēng tài dà
          match postpone F.P.   because wind too strong
          'The match was postponed, because the wind was too strong.'

6.   d.   雖 然 風 有 點 大，（但 是）比 賽 不 能 改 期
          suīrán fēng yǒu diǎn dà   (dànshì) bǐsài bùnáng gǎiqī
          although wind a little big   (but) match cannot postpone
          'Although the wind is a little strong, the match cannot be postponed.'

6.   e.   比 賽 不 能 改 期，雖 然 風 有 點 大
          bǐsài bùnáng gǎiqī   suīrán fēng yǒu diǎn dà
          match cannot postpone   although wind a little big
          'The match cannot be postponed, although the wind is a little strong.'

7.   d.   除 非 強 風 停 息，（否 則）比 賽 不 可 以 繼 續 進 行
          chúfēi qiáng fēng tíngxī   (fǒuzé) bǐsài bù kěyǐ jìxù jìnxíng
          unless strong wind stop   (otherwise) match cannot continue take
          place
          'Unless the strong wind stops, the match cannot continue.'

7.   e.   比 賽 不 可 以 繼 續 進 行，除 非 強 風 停 息
          bǐsài bù kěyǐ jìxù jìnxíng   chúfēi qiáng fēng tíngxī
          match cannot continue take place   unless strong wind stop
          'The match cannot continue, unless the strong wind stops.'

Traditionally, therefore, Chinese tends to prefer linking clauses by following the natural temporal sequence, or what James Tai (1985) calls the Principle of Temporal Sequencing (PTS), whereby 'the relative word order between two syntactic units is determined by the temporal order of the states they represent in the conceptual world' (Tai, 1985, p. 50). Thus, whereas 到圖書館拿書 (*dào túshūguǎn ná shū*) means 'going to the library to get a book', in 拿書到圖書館 (*ná shū dào túshūguǎn*), the sequence of actions would be reversed: 'taking a book to the library' (Kirkpatrick & Xu, 2012, p. 112). As Kirkpatrick and Xu (2012) have shown, Tai's PTS is compatible with other unmarked or preferred 'frame-main' sequences in Chinese, such as topic–comment, big–small (e.g., presenting details of a physical location or address), whole–part, modifier–modified, and subordinate–main (p. 141). This is why, according to the famous linguist Wang Li (王力) (Wang, 1958a), 'in Chinese conditional, concessive and cause-and-effect sentences, the subordinate clause traditionally came before the main clause' (Kirkpatrick & Xu, 2012, p. 112). For this reason, explicit connectives are usually unnecessary in paratactic sentences in Chinese.

By contrast, Wang (1958a) points out that the paratactic pattern in English (e.g., 'You jump. I jump.') is relatively uncommon. Instead, the logical relationship between clauses tends to be marked explicitly by using a connective, hence hypotaxis. Regarding sequence, Wang observes that 'the so-called "if" clauses, the "because" clauses, the "though" clauses and the "when" clauses can go before or after the main clause' (Kirkpatrick & Xu, 2012, p. 112). This is clearly borne out in our examples (5d)–(5e), (6d)–(6e), and (7d)–(7e) above. In general, however, English prefers the 'salient' sequence, whereby the main message stated in the main clause is foregrounded. For instance, while Standard English grammar allows for both the main–subordinate, as in (5d), (6d), and (7d), and subordinate–main structures, as in (5e), (6e), and (7e), it is the main–subordinate sequence which is preferred and more commonly used. This is why hypotaxis is the unmarked clause combining pattern in English (Kirkpatrick & Xu, 2012).

Traditionally, parataxis—a subordinate–main structure without a connective—used to be the preferred clause combining strategy in Chinese. Massive translation of written works from English and other Western languages since the early 1900s, however, has popularized the use of the hypotactic, main–subordinate pattern so prevalent in these languages. The use of the hypotactic pattern, known in Chinese as 偏正複句, is made possible by the explicit marking of the subordinate clause using a connective (e.g., (5d)–(7d), (5e)–(7e)). Many more examples cited from literary works during this period may be found in Tse (1990). Such an influence of Europeanization is characterized as 'beneficial' because the insertion of an explicit connective such as 因為 (*yīnwèi*, 'because'), 如果 (*rúguǒ*, 'if') / 若然 (*ruòrán*, 'if'), 要是 (*yàoshì*, 'provided'), 只要 (*zhǐyào*, 'as long as'), 雖然 (*suīrán*, 'although'), 除非 (*chúfēi*, 'unless') often helps to disambiguate intended speaker/writer meanings. Consider a paratactic sentence like 你辦事，我放心 (*nǐ bàn shì, wǒ fàngxīn*). While the unmarked paratactic subordinate–main structure seems to be clear, the exact logical relationship is ambiguous and compatible with at least three interpretations (8a)–(8c) depending on the context:

8. a.   如 果 你 辦 事 ， 我 就 放 心 (~ if)
         rúguǒ nǐ bàn shì   wǒ jiù fàngxīn
         if you do thing   I then be at ease
         'If you are handling things, I will be at ease.'
         (More idiomatically: 'I will have confidence if you are in charge.')

8. b. 要 是 你 辦 事，我 就 放 心 (~ provided)
   yàoshì nǐ bàn shì   wǒ jiù fàngxīn
   provided you do thing   I then be at ease
   'Provided you are handling things, I will be at ease.'
   (More idiomatically: 'I will have confidence provided you are in charge.')

8. c. 只 要 你 辦 事，我 就 放 心 (~ as long as)
   zhǐyào nǐ bàn shì   wǒ jiù fàngxīn
   as long as you do thing   I then be at ease
   'As long as you are handling things, I will be at ease.'
   (More idiomatically: 'I will have confidence as long as you—and not anyone else—are in charge.')

As shown in these examples, the use of an explicit connective such as 如果 (*rúguǒ*, 8a), 要是 (*yàoshì*, 8b), or 只要 (*zhǐyào*, 8c)—all marking a condition but differ in modal force, (8c) being the most strongly worded—has the advantage of making the intended speaker/writer meaning more precise. It also allows for an alternative main-subordinate word order, as in (8d)–(8f) (Kirkpatrick & Xu, 2012):

8. d. 我 放 心，如 果 是 你 辦 事 的 話
   wǒ fàngxīn   rúguǒ shì nǐ bàn shì de huà
   I be at ease   if be you do thing in case
   'I will be at ease, if you are in charge.'

8. e. 我 放 心，要 是 你 辦 事 的 話
   wǒ fàngxīn   yàoshì shì nǐ bàn shì de huà
   I be at ease   provided you do thing in case
   'I will be at ease, provided you are in charge.'

8. f. 我 放 心，只 要 是 你 辦 事 的 話
   wǒ fàngxīn   zhǐyào shì nǐ bàn shì de huà
   I be at ease   as long as you do thing in case
   'I will be at ease, as long as you—and you only—are in charge.'

The induced use of connectives to combine clauses in Chinese resulted in a shift from parataxis to hypotaxis as the unmarked clause combining pattern. As a correlate of this shift, the order of the clauses becomes less rigid, because there is no risk of semantic confusion postposing the subordinate clause after the main clause, as shown in (5e), (6e), (7e), and (8d)–(8f). Examples such as (9) also became more and more common:

9.   是 的，我 一 定 會 來，要 是 明 天 不 下 雨
      shì de wǒ yídìng huì lái yàoshì míngtiān bùxiàyǔ
      yes F.P. I certainly will come provided tomorrow not rain
      'Yes, I'll certainly come, provided it doesn't rain tomorrow.' (Tse, 1990,
      p. 15)

Creation of pronouns

There used to be only one all-purpose third-person singular pronoun *tā* (他). Other
homophonous pronouns were coined after the model of English: 他 (*he/him*), 她
(*she/her*), 牠 (*it*–animate), 它 (*it*–inanimate), and 祂 (*He* in reference to God) (Tse,
1990). In speech, these are all pronounced [*tā*]; in writing, however, thanks to these
distinctive pronoun forms after the European model (compare: *he*, *she*, and *it* in
English), referencing in SWC has become clearer. The same is true of the coinage of
他們 (*tāmen*, 'they'/'them'—male) and 她們 (*tāmen*, 'they'/'them'—female). Further,
two 'pointer' pronouns—前者 (*qiánze*) and 後者 (*hòuzě*)—were created after the
model in English: *the former* and *the latter*. With these newly created pronouns,
textual meanings in writing have become much clearer.[16]

At the same time, a new structure gradually became widespread: the use of a premodifying clause before a pronoun. For instance, the title of a recent, popular Korean
TV drama series is called 來自星星的你 (*lái zì xīngxīng de nǐ*), which is almost
directly translated from Korean 별에서온그대 (literally 'star-from-come-NOM-
you'). While the spread of this structure—using a clause to premodify a pronoun—
in Modern Chinese is generally attributed to Europeanization, it should be noted
that it is more commonly found in two East Asian languages, Japanese and Korean,
especially in writing. This structure may have become popular in written Chinese as
a result of extensive translation of Japanese literary works and academic texts into
Chinese since the end of the 19th century.

Inserted expressions (插語法, *chāyǔfǎ*)

This feature allows the writer to provide additional information parenthetically like
an aside. For instance:

---

16. According to Hsu (1994), under the influence of English, the use of a third-person pronoun *ta* is increasingly
    considered acceptable in Taiwanese Mandarin, as in: 在場的人都說，這是廣東來的月餅，只是看著不敢
    吃它。('People over there just looked at the moon cake, exclaiming "this is from Canton", without daring to
    eat it'. Hsu, 1994, p. 177.)

10. 恰 巧 有 輛 剛 打 好 的 車 —— 定 作 而 沒 錢 取 貨 的 —— 跟 所 期 望 的 車 差 不 甚 多。[17]

(老舍，〈駱駝祥子〉)

The types of inserted expression vary; the use of short phrases such as 特別 (*tèbié*, 'in particular'), 尤其是 (*yóuqí shì*, 'especially'), 首先 (*shǒuxiān*, 'firstly'), 至少 (*zhìshǎo*, 'at least') helps bring out the speaker's/writer's emphasis or contrast more clearly (Hsu, 1994).

Using two or more verb phrases (VPs) to govern the same object

Structures such as (11) and (12) used to be rare in Chinese (Tse, 1990, p. 108):

11. 過 去 是、現 在 是、將 來 仍 然 是 我 們 的 學 習 榜 樣
    guòqu shì xiànzài shì jiānglái réngrán shì wǒmen de xuéxí bǎngyàng
    past be now be future still be our learning model
    '[He] was our role model in the past, is our role model now, and will remain so in the future.'

12. 進 行 了 並 正 在 進 行 著 建 設
    jìnxíng le bìng zhèngzài jìnxíng zhe jiànshè
    carry out ASP and currently carry out ASP construction
    'Construction that has been and is being carried out.'

As there is no tense in Chinese, this structure helps make the temporal meaning more precise (see Chapter 5).

Induced use of de (的) to create pre-modifying NPs

English noun phrases may be premodified (e.g., *the full moon*) or postmodified (e.g., *the full moon that we saw*) by one or more constituents, and the structure can be rather complex. The induced use of the nominalizing function of *de* (的) in Chinese allows for the possibility of premodifying (but not postmodifying) subjects. For instance, from 賣東西 (*mài dōngxi*, 'sell things'), one can derive 賣的東西 (*mài de dōngxi*, 'things being sold') and 賣東西的人 (*mài dōngxi de rén*, 'person[s] selling things'). The expressive power of Chinese has thus been enhanced considerably.

---

17. *Qiàqiǎo yǒu liǎng gāng dǎhǎo de chē—dìng zuò ér méi qián qǔ huò de—gēn suǒ qīwàng de chē chà bú shèn duō*
('It so happened that there was a ready-made vehicle—down payment paid but no money to collect—not so different compared with what is expected'. *Luòtuó Xiangzi*, 'Camel Xiangzi', by Lao She; cited in Tse, 1990, p. 24; our translation.)

Induced use of expressions that help enhance preciseness and logicality

In English, it is customary for speakers/writers to use some expressions, typically adverbs or PPs, to project their views more objectively, logistically, and/or precisely (e.g., *one of the* NP, *under certain circumstances, as a matter of fact, to some extent, from a particular perspective, in comparison with* NP, *basically*). Under the influence of such expressions, Chinese writers have evolved corresponding expressions such as the following (Tse, 1990, p. 109):

Europeanized expressions (beneficial)		Meaning
……之一	*... zhī yī*	'one of the ...'
就若干情況而言	*jiù ruògān qíngkuàng ér yán*	'under certain circumstances'
在一定程度上説	*zài yídìng chéngdù shàng shuō*	'to a certain extent'
從某一個角度來看	*cóng mǒu yígè jiǎodù lái kàn*	'from a certain point of view'
事實上	*shìshí shàng*	'actually'
基本上	*jīběn shang*	'basically'
比較來説	*bǐjiào lái shuō*	'comparatively speaking'

The expressive power of Modern Chinese, in preciseness and logicality, has thus been enhanced considerably.

Adverse Europeanization (非良性歐化, *fēi liáng xìng ōu huà*)

Europeanization refers to the influence of European languages on local languages at the lexical and morpho-syntactic levels. The influence may be perceived as beneficial (良性歐化, *liáng xìng ōu huà*) or adverse (非良性歐化, *fēi fiáng xìng ōu huà*), depending on the extent to which the nature of the influence conflicts with syntactic and rhetorical terseness in Chinese (Tse, 1990). By design, Chinese shows a strong preference for parataxis. This is manifested in its paucity of grammatical redundancies or function words. Consider the following title of the editorial in the mid-1990s concerning a British-based company's withdrawal of capital from Hong Kong (*Next* magazine [1 April 1994]):

13. 怡 和 撤 退 —— 情 有 可 原　於 理 不 合
    Yíhé chètuì — qíng yǒu kě yuán　yú lǐ bù hé
    Jardines withdraw understandable　unreasonable
    'Jardines withdraws: understandable but unreasonable.'

The predicate following the topic (怡和撤退, *Yíhé chètuì*, 'Jardines withdraws') consists of two four-character idioms. Without reading further into the text, the reader should have no problem identifying the stance of the editor(s), which may be glossed as 'although it is understandable (情有可原), it is unreasonable (於理不合)'. In other words, the sequence of these two four-character idioms conforms to the frame-main structure (Kirkpatrick & Xu, 2012). Notice that the stance of the magazine would have been altered if their sequence was reversed: 於理不合 情有可原 (*yú lǐ bù hé qíng yǒu kě yuán*) would mean 'although it is unreasonable, it is understandable'. This example supports Wang's (1958a) analysis that, in the absence of a connective, the unmarked sequence of the clauses in a paratactic sentence is subordinate–main. No connectives are necessary. Regarding the terseness of the Chinese language, Lee and Tse (1994) point out that:

> 漢語的意合性，容許語言單位在語意能夠搭配的原則上互相結合，免受形態成分的約束，使語言表現形式富於彈性，語意細緻豐富。
>
> ……
>
> 省略和隱含表現了漢語的簡潔性。一般來說，在準確無誤的前提下，能用越少的言辭表達越多的信息，傳意的效率也就越高。漢語不注重語法形式的完整，只求辭達而已；漢語的簡潔性，便讓句子的各種成分，在不妨礙意義的理解下，能不用的便盡量省去不用。西洋語言雖然都出現省略和隱含，但不如漢語這般普遍。（李家樹、謝耀基，1994, pp. 12, 13–14）[18]

As illustrated above, if the Europeanized structure or linguistic feature fills a functional gap or extends the expressive power in Chinese, that influence tends to be perceived as beneficial. On the other hand, where the meaning expressed by a grammatical marker or function word is subsumed elsewhere in the linguistic and/or communication context, overt grammatical marking is typically dispreferred. This is why, to ensure healthy development of the Chinese language, Europeanized linguistic features should be carefully assessed, using syntactic redundancy as the yardstick to determine their desirability. Those morpho-syntactic features that are wordy and semantically redundant, leading to convoluted structures, should be discouraged through language education. Tse (1990, pp. 113–136) lists ten such morpho-syntactic features; we will briefly discuss and exemplify seven of those features below.

---

18. 'The paratactic nature of the Chinese language allows syntactic units to be connected in accordance with their collocation patterns. This frees the Chinese language from formal morpho-syntactic constraints, and makes its structures syntactically agile and variegated, and its expressions semantically rich and fine-grained. . . . The Chinese language is characterized by terseness, which is made possible by ellipsis and the avoidance of syntactically redundant expressions. Generally speaking, under the premise of semantic precision, the smaller the number of words used to optimize the highest information load, the greater the degree of communicative efficacy. In Chinese, the formalism of syntactic structures is valued less compared with the succinct expression of meaning. Thanks to the characteristic of terseness in Chinese, various syntactic units that may be omitted can safely be ellipted, provided meaning is not adversely affected. Similar features of ellipsis and the avoidance of redundant morpho-syntactic units may also be found in Western languages, but not as common as in Chinese' (Lee & Tse, 1994, pp. 12, 13–14; our translation).

Overuse of certain suffixes, e.g., -性 (-*xìng*) and -們 (-*men*)

14.   這 本 書 具 很 高 的 可 讀 性。

      zhè běn shū jù hěn gāo de kě dú xìng

      this CL book has very high NOM can read *xìng*

      'This book has a high degree of readability.' (Tse, 1990, pp. 116–117)

15.   犯 了 嚴 重 性 的 錯 誤

      fàn le yánzhòng xìng de cuòwù

      commit ASP serious *xìng* NOM mistake

      'committed a mistake of a serious nature' (Tse, 1990, pp. 116–117)

In (14), instead of using the Europeanized nominal structure (可讀性, *kě dú xìng*),[19] the same meaning may be more succinctly expressed by an adjective phrase: 很有味 (*hěn yǒu wèi*), literally 'very have taste', which sounds more idiomatic in Chinese. In (15), the use of -*xìng* is redundant and unnecessary. In some cases, the suffixation of -*xìng* to words like 傾向 (*qīngxiàng*, 'tend to/tendency to'), 影響 (*yǐngxiǎng*, 'influence'), 爭論 (*zhēnglùn*, 'dispute') is open to debate. In still other cases, where the use of *xìng* may lead to ambiguity, its use should arguably be avoided. For instance:

16.   一 次 性 經 驗

      yí cì -xìng jīngyàn

      one CL sex/*xìng* experience

      'one sexual experience'/'one-off experience'

No wonder in his work 《翻譯研究》 (A study of translation), Frederick Tsai (思果) remarks:

> 「性」是個極可怕的字。「積極性」、「消極性」、「高尚性」等，全不是中國話。中國人不很喜歡用「性」字，英國的 -*ty*, -*ity*, -*ness* 倒是無往而不宜的。[20] (Tsai, 1987, p. 165)

Traditionally, the use of -*men* (-們) to express the meaning 'more than one' was limited to nouns with the semantic feature [+ human]. For example:

---

19. According to Wang (1958b, p. 232), the proliferation of -性 as a suffix in Chinese may be traced to Japanese influence (e.g., the English nouns *possibility*, *importance*, and *impermeability* were first translated into Japanese (kanji) as 可能性, 重要性, and 不〔可〕滲透性 respectively, which were subsequently adopted in Chinese).

20. '*Xìng* is a terrible morpho-syllable. "*Jījí xìng*", "*xiāojí xìng*" and "*gāoshàng xìng*" do not sound like Chinese at all. Compared with *xìng*, which is dispreferred by Chinese speakers/writers, -*ty*, -*ity*, -*ness* are ubiquitous and sound very natural in English' (Tsai, 1987, p. 165; our translation).

我們	*wŏmen*	'we' / 'us'
你們	*nĭmen*	'you'
他們	*tāmen*	'they'
學生們	*xuésheng-men*	'students'
客人們	*kèrén-men*	'guests'

Under the influence of the obligatory marking of English plural countable nouns using the suffix *-s* or *-es*, 們 (*-men*) was extended to refer to nouns with non-human referents as well; for example, 鼠子們 (*shŭzĭ-men*, 'mice'), 雞們 (*jī-men*, 'chickens'), 蝦兒們 (*xiāér-men*, 'shrimps'), and 小動物們 (*xiăodòngwù-men*, 'little animals'). This is not a welcome trend and should be discouraged. But even in nouns referring to humans, the affixation of *-men* often results in a Europeanized structure, which should be avoided (17–19 are adapted from Yu [余光中], 2002, p. 62):

17. 女性們的服裝每年都有新的花樣。
    nǚxìng -men de fúzhuāng měinián dōu yŏu xīnde huāyàng
    women PL NOM fashion every year all have new NOM style
    'There's a new look in women's fashion every year.'

18. 童子軍們的座右銘是日行一善。
    tóngzĭjūn -men de zuòyòumíng shì rì xíng yí shàn
    scouts PL NOM motto be do a good deed every day
    'The Scouts' motto is "do a good deed every day".'

19. 醫生們一致認為他已經康復了。
    yīshēng -men yízhì rènwèi tā yĭjīng kāngfù le
    doctors PL unanimous regard he already recover ASP
    'The doctors are unanimous that he has already recovered.'

As Yu (2002) remarks, in all of these cases (17–19), *-men* is syntactically redundant[21] and should be left out. He further echoes Tsai's (1987) axioms of good translation practice as follows:

> 翻譯是譯句，不是譯字。句是活的，字是死的，字必須用在句中，有了上下文，才具生命。歐化分子的毛病是，第一，見字而不見句；第二，以為英文的任何字都可以在中文裏找到同義詞；第三，以為把英文句子的每一部分都譯過來後，就等於把那句子譯過來了。事實上，英文裏有很多字都沒有現成的中文可以對譯，而一句英文在譯成中文時，往往需要刪去徒亂文意的虛字冗詞，填滿文法或語氣上的漏洞，甚至需要大動手術，調整文詞的次序。所謂"勿增、勿刪、勿改"的戒條，應該是指文意，而不是

---

21. That is, the meaning 'more than one' is subsumed or expressed in some other word(s) in the sentence, e.g., the collective noun 童子軍 (*tóngzĭjūn*), and the adverbs 都 (*dōu*) and 一致 (*yízhì*).

指文詞。文詞上的直譯、硬譯、死譯，是假精確，不是真精確。(Yu, 2002, p. 61; cf. Tsai [思果], 1987)[22]

Similarly, suffixing 著 (-*zhe*) to mental verbs like 愛 (*ài*, 'love'), 恨 (*hèn*, 'hate'), 害怕 (*hàipà*, 'fear'), 相信 (*xiāngxìn*, 'believe'), and 需要 (*xūyào*, 'need') would result in syntactic redundancy, so it should be avoided. Many examples of such a Europeanized usage may be found in Tse (1990, pp. 118–119). To render the equivalent of English -*ly*, the adverb marker *de/di* 地 was similarly overused after adverbs like 忽然 (*hūrán*) and 突然 (*tūrán*), both meaning 'suddenly'; reduplicated adverbs such as 剛剛 (*gānggāng*, just), 漸漸 (*jiànjiàn*, gradually), 慢慢 (*mànmàn*, slowly), and 悄悄 (*qiāoqiāo*, quietly). This trend was also extended to adverbial phrases ending with 然 (*rán*), 樣 (*yàng*), and 般 (*bān*), such as 依然 (*yīrán*), 照樣 (*zhàoyàng*), 一般 (*yībān*). In all of these adverbs or adverbial phrases, the affixation of *de/di* 地 adds nothing to the meaning. Being syntactically redundant, it should be avoided.

Overuse of personal and possessive pronouns

Where the meaning is contextually clear, personal and possessive pronouns are preferably not used. Under the influence of English and other foreign languages, however, many writers felt that they should be used, resulting in convoluted structures that violated the terseness of Chinese. For example:

20. **他** 不 管 有 多 傷 心，**他** 都 會 生 活 下 去。
    tā bùguǎn yǒu duō shāngxīn, tā dōu huì shēnghuó xiàqù
    3sg no matter have much upset 3sg also will live on
    'No matter how upset he is, <u>he</u> will live on.' (Tse, 1990, p. 129)

21. 快 把 **你 的** 槍 放 下。
    kuài bǎ nǐ de qiāng fàngxià
    quick DISP your gun put down
    'Put down your gun quickly.' (Tse, 1990, p. 129)

---

22. 'To translate is to translate sentences, not words. Sentences are full of life, but not words, which must be used to form sentences. Words come alive when their meanings are articulated with those of other words embedded in sentences. The main problem with those under the spell of Europeanization is threefold. First, they see words but not sentences. Second, they are under the false impression that for every English word, there is a synonym in Chinese. Third, they wrongly believe that as long as every part of an English sentence is given a translation, then that sentence has been translated. In fact, there are plenty of English words for which there is no ready-made Chinese equivalent; when an English sentence is rendered into Chinese, more often than not there is a need to purge superfluous function words and syntactic redundancies that interfere with a good translation. To fill those gaps manifested in the grammar or the tone of the writer, sometimes a major operation like word order alteration is required. The widely known axiomatic advice, "don't add, don't delete, and don't alter" should bear on textual meaning, not on words. Direct, stilted or rigid translation of words may appear to be precise, but such a "precision" would be far off the mark' (Yu, 2002, p. 61; our translation).

As shown in the English translation of (20), the use of the highlighted pronoun 'he' in the main clause is a grammatical requirement, without which the sentence would be ungrammatical. The same cannot be said of its Chinese counterpart, where the insertion of 他 (*tā*) in the second clause is grammatically unacceptable. In (21), strictly speaking the Chinese sentence is grammatically well formed. However, in those contexts where there is only one gun, and the meaning of 'your' is contextually understood (i.e., the interlocutor being the obvious 'gun bearer'), it is better to omit the possessive pronoun 你的 (*nǐ de*). In extreme cases, it may be misleading, as a different meaning is produced. Compare the following (Tse, 1990, pp. 121–122):

22. 瑪 莉 說 她 將 會 結 婚。
     mǎlì shuō tā jiāng huì jiéhūn
     Mary said she will get married
     (a) 'Mary said she would get married.' ('she' = Mary)
     (b) 'Mary said she would get married.' ('she' = another person)

23. 約 翰 回 家 後，他 立 刻 就 睡 覺。
     yuēhàn huíjiā hòu, tā lìkè jiù shuìjiào
     John return home after he immediately then sleep
     (a) 'John went to bed as soon as he came home.' ('he' = John)
     (b) 'John went to bed as soon as he came home.' ('he' = another person)

In English, it would be ungrammatical to leave out the pronoun (see Chapter 7). In Chinese, however, if the referent is the same as the subject in the first clause, the pronoun should not be used. The reason is that, as shown above, using a pronoun in the second clause (她／他, *tā*) would suggest another person is getting married (22) or going to bed (23). As Tse (1990) has rightly pointed out:

> 依照漢語習慣，主語和所有格代詞本可因承說而省去，但歐化文章並不如此；這樣，往往就容易破壞了語言的經濟性。[23]

Likewise, Cheung (2011) echoes Frederick Tsai's (1987) viewpoint and comments that:

> 中文的習慣是，可省則省。如果大家都知道一句話所指的人是誰，就不用重複。……中文不用代名詞，從頭到尾都用同一個名字也沒有問題。如果不重複名字的話，中文裏便常常用關係或身分來代替，如「叔」、「伯」等。[24] (Cheung, 2011, p. 29)

---

23. 'According to syntactic conventions in Chinese, subject pronouns and possessive pronouns in context may be ellipted, but not so in Europeanized Chinese texts. Such a Europeanized feature tends to spread at the expense of the terseness of the language' (Tse, 1990, p. 129; our translation).

24. 'In Chinese, what can be ellipted is conventionally ellipted. If the referent of a given expression is known or identifiable, then there is no need to repeat it. . . . It is normal if no pronouns are used; adhering to the same name from beginning to end is also fine. Where no names are repeated, often words denoting relationships or identities are used instead, e.g., "uncle"' (Cheung, 2011, p. 29; our translation).

Overuse of coordinating conjunctions (連詞, *liáncí*)

Unlike in English, which tends to use coordinating conjunctions to link words of the same word class (e.g., *husband and wife*; *rich but unhappy*; *sing and dance*; *slowly but surely*), in Chinese, coordinating conjunctions are often unnecessary, especially in chunks which appear as set phrases or idioms such as the following (Tse, 1990, p. 123):

男女老幼	*nán nǚ lǎo yòu*	'men and women, old and young'
士農工商	*shì nóng gōng shāng*	'scholars, farmers, artisans, and merchants'
禮義廉恥	*lǐ yì lián chǐ*	'sense of propriety, justice, integrity, and honour'
詩詞歌賦	*shī cí gē fù*	'verses, ditties, odes, and songs'

Or, different coordinating conjunctions are used depending on the units being linked together:

與	*yǔ*	linking nouns and pronouns
及	*jí*	linking nouns, but units different in status
並	*bìng*	linking verbs
而	*ér*	linking adjectives
以及	*yǐjí*	linking nouns, verbs, phrases, sentences (Tse, 1990, p. 123)

One consequence of Europeanization is that 和 (*hé*) was overused, while other coordinating conjunctions or linking devices were neglected. For example:

24. 爸爸和媽媽都很高興。
    bàba hé māma dōu hěn gāoxìng
    father and mother both very happy
    'Father and mother are both very happy.'

25. 做善事無分貧與富，亦無分你和我。
    zuò shànshì wú fēn pín yǔ fù, yì wú fēn nǐ hé wǒ
    do good deeds irrespective rich and poor also irrespective you and me
    'Good deeds should be done irrespective of the doer being rich and poor, you and me.'

In both (24) and (25), however, all the coordinating conjunctions (和, *hé* and 與, *yǔ*) are better left out, without affecting the grammaticality of the two sentences. The three coordinated units—爸爸媽媽，無分貧富，無分你我—are all established four-syllable idioms, whose syntactic integrity would be lost if a conjunction was added between the noun phrases. Regarding this trend, the famous writer, poet, and literary critic Yu (1987) points out that:

目前的不良趨勢，是原來不用連接詞的地方，在 and 意識的教唆下，都裝
上了連接詞；而所謂連接詞都由「和」、「與」、「及」、「以及」包辦，
可是靈活而宛轉的「而」、「並」、「而且」等詞，幾乎要絕跡了。(Yu,
1987, p. 6)[25]

Overuse of 一個 (*yígè*) and 一種 (*yìzhòng*)

When reference to a noun or NP is indefinite, European languages require the use
of an indefinite article (e.g., English *a/an*; French *un/une*; German *ein/eine*). Largely
as a result of translation, the obligatory marking of indefinite reference in Western
languages has led to the overuse of 一個 (*yígè*) and 一種 (*yìzhòng*). For instance,
Yu (1987) points out that a convoluted title of a student composition like (26)

26. 關 於 一 個 河 堤 孩 子 的 成 長 故 事
    guānyú yígè hédī háizi de chéngzhǎng gùshì
    about a CL riverbank child NOM grow up story
    'a story about a riverbank child's coming of age'

may be simplified by removing three disyllabic words—關於 (*guānyú*), 一個 (*yígè*),
and 故事 (*gùshì*). Yu's point is that there is minimal risk of confusion in a more
succinct title like 河堤孩子的成長, for, by reading into the story, the reader will
discover whether it is about one riverbank child or more than one. Below are some
more examples of the redundant use of 一個 (*yígè*) and 一種 (*yìzhòng*) (Tse, 1990,
p. 58, 124):

27. 我 像 是 **一 個** 溺 在 水 裡 的 兒 童 。
    wǒ xiàng shì yígè nì zài shuǐ lǐ de értóng
    I seem be a CL drown in water NOM child
    'I seem like a child drowning in water.'

28. 北 京 是 華 北 的 **一 個** 重 要 城 市 。
    běijīng shì huáběi de yígè zhòngyào chéngshì
    Beijing be northern China NOM a CL important city
    'Beijing is an important city in northern China.'

29. 這 是 **一 種** 不 怕 風 險 積 極 進 取 的 精 神 的 表 現 。
    zhè shì yìzhòng búpà fēngxiǎn jījí jìnqǔ de jīngshén de biǎoxiàn
    this be a CL dauntless aggressive NOM spirit NOM behaviour
    'This behaviour reflects a dauntless, aggressive spirit.'

---

25. 'Currently, under the adverse influence of [English] "and", there is a trend to insert a conjunction where no
conjunction is needed. The so-called conjunctions consist of only 和 (*hé*), 與 (*yǔ*), 及 (*jí*), and 以及 (*yǐjí*),
while their semantically more nuanced counterparts such as *ér* (而), *bìng* (並), *érqiě* (而且) are hardly visible'
(Yu, 1987, p. 6; our translation).

Even worse, sometimes 一個 (*yígè*) is used like the determiner of a noun with plural meaning (e.g., 人民, *rénmín*, 'people', 群眾, *qúnzhòng*, 'the masses'). Such a collocation is semantically odd and should be avoided.

Overuse of prepositions (介詞, *jiècí*)

English, like other European languages, makes more use of PPs than does Chinese. Under Western influence, English prepositions were rendered into Chinese, often resulting in convoluted structures. For instance, 'at 16 (years of age)' was rendered as a PP using 當, which was also typically used to translate 'as' and 'when':

30. a. 當 她 十 六 歲 的 時 候，就 從 鄉 下 到 了 上 海
          dāng tā shíliùsuì de shíhou, jiù cóng xiāngxia dào le shànghǎi
          when she 16 years old NOM time then from countryside reach ASP
          Shanghai
          'At age 16/When she was 16 years old, she went from the country-
          side to Shanghai.'

This was rightly criticized as syntactically clumsy, and may be simplified as:

30. b. 她 十 六 歲 就 從 鄉 下 到 了 上 海
          tā shíliùsuì jiù cóng xiāngxia dào le shànghǎi
          she 16 years old then from countryside reach ASP Shanghai
          'When she was 16 years old, she went from the countryside to
          Shanghai.'

These two contrastive examples[26] show clearly that the version without the discontinuous structure 當……的時候 (*dāng . . . de shíhòu*) (30b) sounds much better than does the Europeanized version (30a).[27]

Another problem with this discontinuous structure 當……的時候 (*dāng . . . de shíhòu*) is that the elements embedded within this structure are sometimes very long, making the sentence difficult to parse. Tse (1990, pp. 127–128) cites an example from the May Fourth writer Ba Jin (巴金), in which the clause structure embedded between 當……的時候 (*dāng . . . de shíhòu*) contains 37 characters.[28] Still another problem is that the second part of this discontinuous structure is sometimes dropped or accidentally omitted, leaving 當 (*dāng*) dangling in the first part of a complex sentence.

---

26. These two examples were adapted from Lü Shuxiang and Zhu Dexi's (1952) 'Notes on syntax and rhetoric' (呂淑湘、朱德熙，〈語法修辭講話〉, cited in Tse, 1990, p. 127).

27. Regarding this trend, Yu (1984) made the following criticism:「公式化的翻譯體，既然見 'when' 就當，五步一當，十步一當，當當之聲，遂不絕於耳了。」(Yu, 1984, cited in Tse, 1990, p. 127).

28.「當他們站在鐵板上面，機器旁邊，一面管理機器，一面望白茫茫的江面，看見輪船慢慢駛近岸邊的時候，他們心裡的感覺，如有人能夠真實地寫出來，一定是一首好詩。」(巴金，〈機器的詩〉, cited in Tse, 1990, pp. 127–128).

Similarly, the need to translate PPs involving *concerning, with regard to, regarding, with respect to, about*, etc. led to the overuse of 有關 (*yǒuguān*) and 關於 (*guānyú*). For example:

31.   今 天 我 們 討 論 有 關 臺 灣 交 通 的 問 題。
      jīntiān wǒmen tǎolùn yǒuguān táiwān jiāotōng de wèntí
      today we discuss about Taiwan traffic NOM problem
      'Today, we discuss Taiwan's traffic problems.' (Yu, 1987, p. 6)

32.   關 於 他 的 申 請，你 看 過 了 沒 有？
      guānyú tā de shēnqǐng, nǐ kàn guò le méiyǒu
      about his NOM application you see ASP not
      'About his application, have you seen it?' (Yu, 1987, p. 6)

In both (31) and (32), leaving out 有關 (*yǒuguān*) and 關於 (*guānyú*), respectively, would make the two sentences syntactically terser, while meaning is completely unaffected.

Overuse of the passive (被動句, *bèidòngjù*)

In Chinese, traditionally verb phrases with passive meaning tended to express something unfavourable to the person or thing affected (Chapter 4). For instance:

33.   他 忠 而 被 謗   (word with passive meaning: 被, *bèi*)
      tā zhōng ér bèi bàng
      he loyal yet PSV defame
      'He was loyal but was defamed by slander.'

34.   農 田 受 風 雨 侵 襲   (word with passive meaning: 受, *shòu*)
      nóngtián shòu fēngyǔ qīnxí
      farmland receive wind-rain batter
      'The farmland was battered by (strong) wind and (heavy) rain.'

35.   做 事 要 小 心，否 則 就 要 捱 罵 (word with passive meaning: 捱, *ái*)
      zuò shì yào xiǎoxīn, fǒuzé jiù yào ái mà
      do things must careful otherwise then will get scold
      'Be cautious when doing things, or [you] will receive a scolding.'

36.   他 出 身 寒 微，遭 人 譏 諷   (word with passive meaning: 遭, *zāo*)
      tā chūshēn hánwēi, zāo rén jīfěng
      he family background modest suffer ridicule mock
      'His modest family background was ridiculed and mocked by others.'

To a certain extent, this adverse meaning continues to be found when *bèi* (被) collocates with verbs of perception such as *see* and *hear*. For instance, while the English sentence *She was seen playing in the garden* does not necessarily suggest that the act of being seen is considered something unpleasant to the subject 'she', such a meaning is strongly suggested in the Chinese translation (see also Chapter 4):

37.　她 被 人 看 見 在 花 園 裏 玩
　　　tā bèi rén kànjiàn zài huāyuan lǐ wán
　　　she PSV person see in garden inside play
　　　'She was seen playing in the garden.'

Nevertheless, as a result of Europeanization, the adverse interpretation associated with 被 (*bèi*) has been diluted since the 1920s.[29] Today, 被 is used freely to denote processes with clearly positive meanings, as in the following cases, among many others (cf. Wang, 2012, p. 34):

被讚賞	*bèi zànshǎng*	'be praised'
被提名為代表	*bèi tímíng wái dàibiǎo*	'be nominated' as representative'
被選為議員	*bèi xuǎn wái yìyuán*	'be elected as councillor'

There are two tendencies associated with the overuse of the passive that are considered undesirable and should be avoided. First, after 被 (*bèi*) has evolved as *the* overt passive marker in modern Chinese, the use of other function words with a similar passive meaning such as 叫 (*jiào*), 教 (*jiào*), 讓 (*ràng*), 給 (*gěi*), and the discontinuous structure 為……所 (*wèi . . . suǒ*) has been neglected, the last mentioned being historically attested since the Han dynasty (206 BCE–CE 220, Wang, 1958a, pp. 424–425). Where appropriate, these function words could break the stylistic monotony of 被 (*bèi*). Second, where the passive meaning is subsumed in the larger context, then the overt passive marker 被 (*bèi*) need not and should not be used. For instance:

38.　犯 人 已 被 押 到
　　　fànrén yǐ bèi yā dào
　　　convict already PSV escort arrive
　　　'The convict has been escorted here.' (Tse, 1990, p. 133)

39.　你 們 都 該 被 罰
　　　nǐmen dōu gāi bèi fá
　　　you all should PSV punish
　　　'You should all be punished.' (Tse, 1990, p. 133)

In both (38) and (39), the passive meaning is contextually clear without using the passive marker 被 (*bèi*), making it syntactically redundant. In accordance with the characteristic of terseness in Chinese, it is better left out. The following example, adapted from Yu (1979),[30] is strongly suggestive of such an unwelcome trend:

---

29. Compare, e.g., 水被喝乾了；文件被放在抽屜裡；錢包被丟了 (Tse, 1990, p. 133).
30. Source:〈從西而不化到西而化之〉, Yu (1979, cited in Tse, 1990, p. 132).

40.　這 本 新 書 正 被 千 千 萬 萬 的 讀 者 搶 購 著。[31]
　　　zhè běn xīn shū zhèng bèi qiānqiānwànwàn de dúzhě qiǎnggòu zhe
　　　this CL book currently PSV thousands and thousands NOM reader panic buying ASP
　　　'This book is currently the target of panic buying by thousands and thousands of readers.'

Apart from checking whether an alternative function word or marker with passive meaning could be used, the redundant use of 被 (*bèi*) should be avoided (for contrastive differences between the English and the Chinese passive, see Chapter 4).

The overuse of 是 (*shì*)

Practically all European languages have the equivalent of the verb 'to be' (also known as the copula; e.g., French *être*, German *sein*). In modern Chinese, the function word which is closest in meaning to the verb to be is 是 (*shì*). Over time, a discontinuous structure 是……的 (*shì . . . de*) evolved, which is characterized by Chinese linguists as 描寫句 ('descriptive sentence') or 判斷句 ('judgement/opinion sentence'). In other words, this discontinuous structure is used typically to describe something or state the writer's opinion about a certain issue. For instance, in his critique of the overuse of Europeanized linguistic features, Wang (1958a) said that:

> 西洋語法所要求的形式，並不一定是中國語所要求的。所以描寫句用繫詞
> 在西洋是合語法的，在中國卻是不合語法的。……若以為西洋語法比中國
> 語法更合理，這種錯誤的觀念仍是必須矯正的。（王力, 1958a, cited in Tse,
> 1990, p. 134）[32]

It is interesting that in four of the six clauses in Wang's (1958a) critique cited here, he found it useful or even necessary to use the 是……的 (*shì . . . de*) structure. The main problem is that, if such a structure is repeated many times in a sequence, the text would sound stilted and monotonous. One such sample text collected during the May Fourth era may be found in Tse (1990).[33] Another problem is that some

---

31. For an alternative, more idiomatic way to express the target meaning in (40), consider: 這本新書非常受歡迎，千千萬萬的讀者正在瘋狂搶購著。

32. 'What is needed in the grammars of Western languages may not be needed in Chinese. Hence in the West using the copula in descriptive sentences is grammatical, but not in Chinese. . . . The belief that Western syntactic structures are more rational than their Chinese counterparts is mistaken and must be rectified' (Wang, 1958a, cited in Tse, 1990, p. 134; our translation).

33. 「自然是要親近的，人生是要觀察的，生活是要經驗的，同時書也是要讀的，雖然不一定要至少讀破多少卷。許多的天才是不用讀甚麼書的，可是更多的天才是博覽群書的。許多的天才是沒有經過學習時期的，可是更多的天才是花了多少年的心血才逐漸成熟的。況且天才向來是鳳毛麟角少見的，大多數以天才自負，或是被朋友以天才見許的人也許不過是野雞毛鹿角之類吧。」（陳西瀅，〈再論線裝書〉, cited in Tse, 1990, pp. 134–135).

authors would omit the second part . . . *de* (……的), as illustrated by the following examples (cited in Tse, 1990, pp. 133–135):

41. 轟 炸 機 頭 上 有 兩 三 個 發 動 機，
     hōngzhàjī tóu shàng yǒu liǎng sān gè fādòngjī
     bomber head on have two three engine
     發 出 來 的 聲 音 是 很 沉 重。
     fā chūlái de shēngyīn shì hěn chénzhòng
     emit NOM sound be very heavy
     'On top of the bomber were two to three engines; the sound they pro-
     duced was very heavy.' (Source: newspaper; cited in Tse, 1990, p. 134)

Owing to frequent and extensive translation into Chinese, therefore, there was a tendency to overuse 是 (*shì*). This is another unwelcome trend to guard against. In his
treatise of the history and types of Europeanization of modern Chinese, Tse (1990)
reminds us that we cannot copy European language features blindly rather than select
those that suit our needs. This is crucial for maintaining the strengths of the Chinese
language. In sum, when the Europeanized feature adds nothing to the meaning of the
original structure and is thus semantically and syntactically redundant, it is generally
regarded as an unwanted, adverse development that should be avoided.

Questions and activities

1. To render foreign concepts from English into Chinese, what linguistic means
    were used? Can you work out the corresponding English words of the following
    Chinese words (examples based on Tse, 1990, pp. 36–39)?
    Group 1:
    i.   瓦特 (*wǎ tè*), 馬達 (*mǎ dá*), 歐姆 (*ōu mǔ*), 伏特 (*fú tè*)
    ii. 吉普 (*jí pǔ*), 尼古丁 (*ní gǔ dīng*), 凡士林 (*fán shì lín*), 歇斯底里 (*xiē sī dǐ lǐ*)
    iii. 開末拉 (*kāi mò lā*), 煙士披里純 (*yān shì pī lǐ chún*), 懷娥鈴 (*huái é líng*), 基達爾 (*jī dá ěr*)
    Group 2:
    iv. 馬克思主義 (*mǎ kè sī zhǔ yì*), 浪漫主義 (*làng màn zhǔ yì*), 芒果 (*máng guǒ*), 酒吧 (*jiǔ bā*), 啤酒 (*pí jiǔ*)
    v.   沙丁魚 (*shā dīng yú*), 吉普車 (*jí pǔ chē*), 維他命 (*wéi tā mìng*), 幽默 (*yōu mò*), 模特兒 (*mó tèr*)
    vi. 咖啡粉 (*kā fēi fěn*), 坦克車 (*tǎn kè chē*), 沙發 (*shā fā*), 奧林匹克村 (*Ào lín pǐ kè cūn*)
2. Between transliteration and translation, which method is preferred? Why?
    Justify your answer with the help of the following examples (Tse, 1990, p. 36).

Group 3:

vii.   麥克風 (*mài kè fēng*)   擴音器 (*kuòyīnqì*)

viii. 愛康諾米 (*ài kāng nuò mǐ*)   經濟 (*jīng jì*)

ix.   德律維雄 (*dé lǜ wéi xióng*)   電視 (*diàn shì*)

x.   德謨克拉西 (*dé mó kè lā xī*)   民主 (*mín zhǔ*)

3. In Chinese, which noun suffixes denoting 'a person who . . .' are particularly productive (e.g., English *-ist*, as in *artist*, 藝術家 [*yì shù jiā*]; *pianist*, 鋼琴家 [*gāng qín jiā*]; *scientist*, 科學家 [*kē xué jiā*])? Use the following English words to help you.

-er   farmer, lawyer, messenger, newcomer, passer-by, reader, teacher, traveller, worker, writer . . .

-or   actor, sailor . . .

-ant   accountant, protestant . . .

-ian   magician, musician . . .

-eer   engineer, auctioneer . . .

4. There are other English nouns which denote 'person' but which are not derived from a related verb or noun (see below). How are they rendered into Chinese? Which Chinese suffix is used to render that meaning?

> *actuary, architect, author, bachelor, doctor, gourmet, martyr, master, member, passenger, priest, revolutionary, samurai, staff*

Can you think of others?

5. Can you simplify the following Europeanized structures while keeping the meaning more or less constant? In each case, which function word is semantically redundant and better left out?[34]

(a) 各位女士先生們，總理和各與會代表們

(b) 他們已把他們的心事告訴給神明，他們已把一年來的罪過在神前取得了寬恕。於是他們像修完了一勝業，他們的臉上帶著微笑，他們的心裡更非常輕鬆。(李廣田，〈山之子〉, cited in Tse, 1990, p. 129)

(c) 我們漸漸沒有這種受欺的度量，但我們也很欣快沒有這種奴隸的根性；我們正有我們自己的工作在，我們的手段與目的是一致的！(顧頡剛，〈古史辨自序〉, cited in Tse, 1990, p. 129)

(d) 如要停車，乃可在此 (see Tse, 1990, p. 130)

(e) 在春節期間

(f) 關於這個問題，我們下次再談

---

34. Some of the items below are adapted from Chan (1993).

(g)　對於她的決定，我們都很關注
(h)　我有一個問題，想跟你談談
(i)　日本是一個島國
(j)　應不應被浪費掉，應被提出來討論
(k)　那本書被我喜歡
(l)　你被我愛
(m)　紅樓夢被我讀
(n)　當然地不能算數
(o)　我完全地明白了
(p)　我們是已註冊了的團體
(q)　這有著很多優點
(r)　她從來沒有承認過

Further reading

Tse (1990) is a highly readable and comprehensive introduction to various language contact phenomena that we have been referring to as 'Europeanization'. A concise summary of that (1990) monograph may be found in Tse (2001). The two articles and monograph by Yu Guangzhong (1979, 1987, 2002) are also highly recommended. Frederick Tsai, better known in Chinese as 思果, has published several influential books on English–Chinese translation (Tsai 1982, 1987, 2002)—all highly readable and instructive regarding ill-advised as well as good translation practices. For an overview and critique of Tsai's approach and contributions to the field of translation, see Cheung (2011). Liu (2006) is a well-conceived, comprehensive, and systematic contrast between Chinese and English structures. Pinkham (2000) provides plenty of useful examples of what she calls 'Chinglish', showing how texts authored by experienced Chinese translators working in such diverse fields as journalism, foreign affairs, business, tourism, and advertising may sometimes suffer from stylistic anomalies of one kind or another that may be traced to their first language, Chinese.

9
Being Chinese, Speaking English
Pragmatic Norms and Speaker Identity

Understanding context in the study of pragmatics

In this chapter, we will go beyond grammar proper to understand what sorts of communication problem EAL learners are likely to encounter when interacting with native speakers (NSs) of English or among themselves. To do this, we will look into some of the well-known findings in *pragmatics*, a research area within linguistics which is generally defined as the study of language in use.

Unlike the study of grammar, which is often decontextualized, a study in pragmatics requires the researcher(s) to specify the *context* of social interaction. The term context may not be easy to define, but there is a simple way to understand what a context consists of. In a seminal article devoted to this topic, the sociolinguist Joshua Fishman (1965) points out that the context of a given situation or speech event may be specified if we have the answer to a general question:

'Who speaks what language to whom and when?'

For instance, the context of a lecture in a particular course may be specified as that of a lecturer lecturing to students of that course where contextual details such as the level of the course (undergraduate or postgraduate), the time of the day, the day of the week, teaching venue, and language of instruction are known to both lecturer and students. The language use is usually formal. After the lecture, if students are to order something to drink at the university cafeteria, they will most likely be addressing the employees informally in the local vernacular, although the item(s) ordered may be in English. In Hong Kong, for example, students ordering food and drinks at their university cafeterias would typically be 'mixing' Cantonese with English (or, arguably, Italian), as follows:

(1)   唔 該 一 杯 cappuccino
      ng4 goi1 jat1 bui1 cappuccino
      please   one cup   cappuccino
      'One cappuccino please'

In the above contexts, formal versus informal, the speakers in question would know intuitively, if subconsciously, which language at what level of formality is considered appropriate by their interlocutors, or participants engaged in context-specific social interaction.

Another sociolinguist, Dell Hymes (1976), proposed using the acronym SPEAKING to capture all the information required for specifying the context of a conversation, as follows (see 'Further reading' for more details):

S	Situation	Scene and setting (e.g., lecture theatre, tea room, church, court, restaurant, supermarket)
P	Participants	People present, and the roles they play (e.g., teacher–student, peer–peer, salesperson–customer, father–son)
E	End	Goal of communication (e.g., to provide information or service, to maintain collegial relationship, to buy a bus ticket)
A	Act	**Speech acts (e.g., to explain, extend an invitation, make a compliment, request, apologize, and the like)**
K	Key	Tone of speech (e.g., friendly, harsh, ironic)
I	Instrumentality	Channel (e.g., face-to-face, by phone, WhatsApp, Skype)
N	Norms of communication	Rules of speaking (e.g., formal or informal? Is code-mixing appropriate? Is slang acceptable?)
G	Genre	Culturally defined speech event (e.g., lecture, prayer, debate, consultation, court trial, small talk)

Figure 9.1
Hymes's (1976) acronym, SPEAKING, used to capture all the essential information pertaining to the context of social interaction

Speech act

Our focus in this chapter is on speech acts, which are concerned with 'How to do things with words' (Austin, 1962). A speech act is defined as an act 'performed when producing an utterance, e.g., giving a warning or making a request, a promise, or a claim' (Paradis, 2004, p. 245). Austin (1962) shows that human language—English, Chinese, Japanese, Korean, or any other natural language—is used not only to refer to people or to talk about things. Rather, what is said sometimes amounts to a verbalized act or action, with fairly specific consequences to the interlocutor(s) or situation present, hence a speech act. One famous and widely cited example is the naming of a ship. At a formal ship-naming ceremony, when the guest of honour says 'I name this ship Queen Elizabeth', he or she performs much more than uttering these six words. As a direct consequence of these words uttered by the guest of honour at that formal ceremony, a new ship with the name *Queen Elizabeth* is added to the world of floating vessels.

Similarly, a wedding ceremony is not complete without the right person allowed by law to perform a marriage ceremony saying to the newlyweds 'I (hereby/now) declare you husband and wife' (or the equivalent in Chinese, or the local language of a community where weddings are regulated by law). As a result of these words, the status of the bride and bridegroom undergo a qualitative change: They are now recognized as a couple, with all attendant legally binding rights and obligations, including but not limited to their undertaking which was spelled out in their solemnly recited oath, typically in the presence of family members and close friends. For the intended result of a speech act to take effect in speech events such as a wedding and a ship-naming ceremony, Austin (1962) further reminds us that a set of 'felicity conditions' must be met. For instance, the person presiding over a wedding ceremony must have the right professional background and authority to utter those words; similarly, no new ship will be added to the fleet if the words are said during role-play (e.g., student activity of a language class).

Subsequent research shows that, in addition to ceremonial events, many verbs of saying perform a similar function (Searle, 1969, 1979). For example, when a speaker (S) says any of the following in conversation or writing: *I accept . . . , I admit . . . , I agree . . . , I apologize . . . , I conclude . . . , I condemn . . . , I criticize . . . , I deny . . . , I disagree . . . , I promise . . . , I query . . . , I refuse . . . , I request . . . , I repeat . . . , I take your point, I warn . . .* , and so forth, S performs an act verbally in accordance with the meaning of the verb. For example:

- Making a judgement or stance, e.g., *I agree, I disagree, I take your point*
- Expressing an attitude, e.g., *I admit, I apologize, I deny*
- Declaring an obligation or an intention, e.g., *I accept, I promise, I refuse*
- Stating verbal action, e.g., *I conclude, I condemn, I criticize, I query, I repeat, I request, I warn*

The examples in (2) below, adapted with slight modification from Oishi (2006), provide further illustrations of other performative speech acts:

(2)   a.   I baptize thee in the name of Father, the Son, and the Holy Spirit.
       b.   I reprimand you for your negligence.
       c.   I order you to release the prisoners.
       d.   I divorce you! I divorce you! I divorce you! (Oishi, 2006, pp. 7–8)

All of the examples above make use of the first-person singular pronoun 'I' and the present tense. Notice, however, that the force (technically called 'illocutionary force') is not as strong if the subject refers to the first-person plural pronoun (*we*), still less when referring to the second- (*you*) or third-person (singular *he* or *she*; plural *they*). This is largely because, according to Speech Act theory, a speech act is performed deictically ('here and now') by the speaker in a speech situation. The consequence of the speech act typically bears on the hearer(s), although it may also impact some other participant(s) implicated but not present in the speech situation (e.g., *I promise you he'll be punished*).

Linguistic failure vs. pragmatic failure

As we all know, errors are unavoidable in the language-learning process, be it a first, second, or foreign language. Just as an infant must stumble many times before he or she can walk, making errors in a target language is arguably an integral part of the learning process. Relative to standard language norms, language errors have been described as different manifestations of the learners' 'linguistic failure'. Most of the problems we have examined so far are due to one form of linguistic failure or another.

In this chapter, however, we will examine a few recurrent cases of 'pragmatic failure' (Thomas, 1983), which happens when the linguistic realization of a speech act in L2 does not conform to the way NSs of L2 would normally say, or write in the case of written communication. We will illustrate pragmatic failure with the help of examples of Chinese EAL users using English to realize two speech acts when interacting with NSs or NNSs: (a) making requests, and (b) responding to compliments. Speech acts such as these take place almost every day, in Chinese or in English, depending on the interlocutor and context at large.

When expressing either of these two speech acts (among many others) in English, should Chinese EAL users be guided by the social norms and cultural values of their mother tongue (Cantonese or Mandarin), or their target language, English? One way to answer this question is to ask: When interacting with a NS of English, are EAL users supposed to behave in the same way as when they interact with someone who speaks the same L1 as they do?

Before moving on to discuss interactional problems arising from the realization of these two speech acts, we will briefly examine two crucial concepts in the study of cross-cultural and intercultural communication: face and politeness.

Face and politeness

Regardless of the language(s) and culture(s) in a community, be it monolingual or multilingual, 'face' and 'politeness' are two crucial and closely related concepts for understanding why people engaged in social interaction tend to behave the way they do. For Chinese students, the concept of face as an area of study in sociology and, later, sociolinguistics should be fairly straightforward given its terminological origin and significance in Chinese culture (compare: 面子, *miànzi/min6 zi2*; and 臉, *liǎn/lim6*; Scollon & Scollon, 1983; Bond & Hwang, 1986). Building on Goffman's (1955) notion of 'face' and 'facework', Brown and Levinson (1987) characterize face as a speaker's right to his or her good public image in interpersonal communication. According to their distinction between 'positive face' and 'negative face', a hearer's positive face needs are best attended to by making the hearer feel that his or her self-esteem is valued and appreciated. By contrast, the best way to attend to the hearer's negative face needs is to minimize intrusion in the hearer's independence to act freely. For instance, when making a request for an appointment:

(a)   I'm only available tomorrow; can we meet at 3 p.m.?

(b)   I understand how busy you are; would you happen to be free sometime next week?

Compared with the requester in (a), who pays no attention to the interlocutor's negative face needs in terms of limited choice of meeting time (3 p.m. tomorrow) or even readiness and availability to meet, the requester in (b) sounds more cautious, taking care to allow the interlocutor a lot of freedom in deciding whether he or she wants to meet with the requester and, if so, providing ample choice of preferred meeting time. In addition, compared with (a), the way the question is phrased in (b) ('would you happen to be free . . . ') also helps preserve the interlocutor's positive face.

As Scollon and Scollon (1995) have observed, in interpersonal communication, a speaker often finds it necessary to attend to both types of face needs of the hearer. This is not easy at all, given the face-threatening nature of many speech acts. The need to attend to the hearer's face is one reason why communication even in one's native language can be rather stressful sometimes, not to mention in those situations where one is obliged to use a second or foreign language. To communicate interpersonally is to expose oneself to 'face loss' to different extents: Just as an offer to help risks being rejected, so an invitation may not be taken up. When that happens, both speaker and hearer 'lose face' to some extent. As Scollon and Scollon (1995) put it, there is no faceless communication. This is also why when a speaker attends to a person's face needs, he or she will need to select a socially appropriate 'politeness strategy', which has been conventionalized or encoded in their language (Lii-Shih, 1994). Politeness strategies are useful for minimizing the damage, potential or real, of a face-threatening act. For example, when exploring options of meeting up somewhere the following day, which of the following remarks in (3) would make the hearer feel more (un)comfortable? Why?

(3)   a.   You're always late. Let me pick you up at your place at 6.

       b.   Traffic is busy on Monday morning. Shall we go together by taxi?

       c.   We can't afford to be late. Do you want (us) to go together?

       d.   Arriving late will be a disaster. It'd be nice if you could give me a ride.

In many languages, politeness strategies are highly codified. Depending on the perceived status of the interlocutor(s) as deserving respect, typically older or more senior than the speaker, who would select the expressions used for marking ***deference*** (i.e., [+ deference]). This is an example of 'upward communication', which is characteristic of employee talking to employer, student talking to teacher, son or younger brother talking to father or elder brother, and the like. On the other hand, when the hearer is perceived as an equal or has a lower status compared with the speaker (e.g., reversing the speaker and hearer roles in the above dyads), then the hearer would normally select those expressions that are not marked for deference (i.e., [– deference]). In other words, language expressions that are not marked for deference may occur in situations involving horizontal or downward communication.[1]

In some languages, different degrees of politeness (e.g., deference vs. solidarity) are expressed through linguistic devices called honorifics. This is the case of two East Asian languages, Japanese and Korean. For instance, with regard to the same basic, denotative meaning (e.g., 'Are you going?', 'good morning'), a speaker of Japanese or Korean is expected to use different expressions depending on who he or she is talking to. Thus in Korean, to ask 'Are you going?', a Korean speaker would instinctively select expression (4a) [+ deference] or (4b) [– deference], depending on the speaker's perceived relationship with the interlocutor (Table 9.1). Similarly, in Japanese, an elaborate greeting expression like (5a) characterized by [+ deference] may be regarded as more suitable when the interlocutor(s) is(are) someone deserving respect. By contrast, when the interlocutor is perceived as either equal or lower in status, a shorter greeting expression like (5b) [– deference] is normally used (Table 9.1).

Table 9.1

Politeness strategies in Korean and Japanese, as reflected in the choice of different expressions depending on the perceived status of the interlocutor(s)

	Status of the interlocutor(s)	**Deference**
Korean: 'Are you going?'		
(4) a. 가 십 니 까 ? (ga sim ni kka?)	to people deserving respect; to older persons in general	[+ deference]
b. 가 ? (ga?)	to people perceived either as 'equals' or lower in status	[– deference]
Japanese: 'Good morning'		
(5) a. おはようございます。 (o ha yō go za i ma su)	to people deserving respect; to older persons in general	[+ deference]
b. おはよう。 (o ha yō)	to people perceived either as 'equals' or lower in status	[– deference]

---

1. According to Scollon, Scollon, and Jones (2012), a speech situation may be characterized as symmetrical or asymmetrical, depending on the interlocutors' relationship. Asymmetrical communication is typical of speech situations which are marked by unequal power (hence, [+P]), regardless of the social distance between the interlocutors (hence, [+D] or [–D]). On the other hand, in symmetrical speech situations, the role of power difference is minimal (hence [–P]), while social distance may or may not be marked (hence [+D] or [–D]).

Making requests in English

Making a request is inherently a face-threatening act to both the interlocutor and the requester. Research shows that, in intra-ethnic communication among Chinese, in general, a request—in speech or in writing—is often delayed and preceded by elaborate face work, focusing on the quality of the speaker's (usually good) relationship with the interlocutor or addressee. Thus, before a request is made to borrow money from one's interlocutor, the requester would typically begin by saying something that appears to be unrelated to the request itself, for example, inquiring about the interlocutor's personal well-being ('Do you manage to find time for sports?), or sharing information about a mutual friend ('Frank is getting married; did you hear?').

In addition, the weightier the imposition (compare, e.g., a request to borrow $500, as opposed to $50,000), the more careful the Chinese speaker/writer usually is to ensure the hearer/listener's face needs are satisfied and good mutual relationship is established before raising the request. Weight of imposition is thus an important additional factor in the study of the language of requests (see, e.g., Kirkpatrick, 1991, 1993; cf. Jia & Cheng, 2002; Kong, 1998a, 1998b, 2006). In general, research on information sequencing shows that Chinese speakers/writers tend to be more indirect as they proceed **inductively** when making requests in Chinese. For instance, after analysing 46 Chinese college students' English essays involving making a request, Jia and Cheng (2002) found that over two-thirds (67.4%, n=31) used the inductive approach. Commenting on this finding, Jia and Cheng state that:

> The use of indirectness in Chinese English writing is even not uncommon among professors, teachers and scholars of advanced level of English or those who have been using and learning English for years. In fact even those who have been staying in native-English countries and have been influenced for long by the Anglo-American deductive model are often found falling back on this approach from time to time—they would unconsciously cling to the traditional Chinese writing model, which they acquired in their early education. (Jia & Cheng, 2002, p. 70)

Significantly, Jia and Cheng (2002) are able to support this analysis with strong empirical evidence: Of the 500+ abstracts received from scholars for the Third International Symposium on ELT [English Language Teaching] in China in May, 2001, the absolute majority of the Chinese scholars followed the inductive style, while the abstracts written by Anglo-American scholars invariably followed the deductive style (p. 70).

Requests being inherently face-threatening acts, NSs of English are naturally also concerned about the need to mitigate the threat before making their request. In speech, this is typically done by stating the reason for their request, such as those in the following situation when the speaker requests assistance to carry a suitcase upstairs (cf. Beltrán, 2013):

(6) a. Could you help carry this suitcase upstairs please? It's too heavy for me.

   b. Sorry to bother you, but I was wondering if you could carry this suitcase for me. I've hurt my legs.

Similarly, the weightier the imposition is, the more elaborate the face work before the request is made verbally. In writing, however, research shows that NSs of English tend to proceed more **deductively** and are therefore more direct in making requests (Kong, 1998a). In particular, compared with Chinese writers, NSs of English are generally less concerned about such face work when writing request letters, hence the impression that their requests are more direct (Kirkpatrick, 1991, 1993; cf. Kong, 1998a).

One interesting question is: How would English-L2 writers sequence the information in a request letter written in English? Research in contrastive rhetoric has shown that, when writing request letters in English, Chinese writers tend to transfer the 'delayed request' strategy into English (Kirkpatrick, 1991, 1993). This is partly because many Chinese EAL writers, when writing a request letter in English, find it necessary to preface their request with elaborate face work and to appeal to (good) interpersonal relationship with the addressee.

Responding to compliments in English

Many Chinese EAL learners and users are unsure how to respond when praised by a native English-speaking friend for their English (e.g., 'Your English is really good!'). Why is that so? Before answering this question, let us consider the findings to one interesting study related to responding to compliments in English.

Chen (1993) collected contrastive questionnaire data from 50 English-speaking college students in the US (questionnaire in English), and 50 Mandarin Chinese-speaking college students in Xi'an, China (same questionnaire translated into Chinese). The questionnaire was designed to elicit the subjects' responses to compliments on one's appearance, possessions, and achievement (or ability). The findings show that the two groups preferred rather different strategies. Below is a summary of their preferred strategies and their subcategories, as stated in Chen (1993, p. 54, Appendix B):

American English speakers' strategies (in decreasing order of frequency):

Accepting:	• thanking, agreeing, expressing gladness, joking
Returning:	• returning compliments, offering object of compliment (e.g., *Wanna wear it?*)
	• encouraging (e.g., *Well, you can get one too.*)

Deflecting:	• explaining (e.g., *Thanks, I worked hard for this.*) • doubting (e.g., *You're kidding, right?*)
Rejecting:	• rejecting and denigrating (e.g., *No, it's an old sweater.*)

Chinese speakers' strategies (in decreasing order of frequency):

Rejecting:	• disagreeing and denigrating (e.g., *No, I'm older and uglier.*) • expressing embarrassment (e.g., *I don't do it well. I'm embarrassed.*) • explaining (e.g., *No, I'm older and my face is more wrinkled.*)
Thanking and denigrating:	• (e.g., *Thanks. But the watch is not what I really like.*)
Accepting:	• thanking only

On the basis of these findings, Chen (1993) concludes that the two groups of student subjects responded rather differently when praised: The American subjects tended to agree to the compliment by accepting it, while the Chinese subjects' responses seemed to be guided by the maxim of modesty or 'self-praise avoidance' in general.

Chen's (1993) findings suggest that, when using Mandarin Chinese, mainland Chinese students tend to adhere to the cultural value of modesty or avoiding self-praise, which, when collectively observed by everyone in their community, serves as a norm guiding socially appropriate or 'correct' behaviour. In the US, on the other hand, there seems to be nothing unusual about accepting a compliment at face value, probably because modesty or avoiding self-praise is not considered to be socially appropriate or desirable.[2]

Now the question is: What happens when Chinese students are interacting with their American counterparts in English? There are two norms: one proper to their L1 Chinese culture, the other guided by the target language, English. This is what Michael Agar (1991, p. 168) means by a 'culture two' that travels with the second language' (cf. Agar, 1994). Should Chinese speakers of English resist that culture two by adhering to their Chinese norm of modesty or avoiding self-praise, or should they embrace it by adopting the American norm as a result of crossing the language

---

2. As it has been pointed out to the authors, in social interaction between NSs of English, receiving a compliment graciously and considering the giver's face is no less important. It is not self-praise to do this but rather out of consideration of the face of the giver of the compliment.

boundary? Notice that there is no model answer to these questions. In earlier research on ILP, there was an assumption that learners of English should strive to behave like NSs of English. Such an assumption is increasingly challenged and no longer held to be valid (see, e.g., Li, 1998, 2002).

In the last section of this unit, we will examine another popular issue in pragmatics which is also intimately related to Chinese EAL users' identity, the use of first-name address when interacting with NSs of English and among themselves.

The use of first-name address

Research shows that bilingual, especially educated, Chinese Hongkongers tend to adopt an English or English-sounding name, which they use when interacting with NSs but also among themselves (Li, 1997). For instance, over half of the Chinese legislative councillors in Hong Kong (37 out of 70, or 52.85%) have adopted an English name (e.g., *Alan Leong, Jasper Tsang, Emily Lau, Cyd Ho*; see Appendix). The sequence follows the Western naming practice: first or given name, followed by last or family name (compare *Hilary Clinton, Angela Merkel, Jamie Oliver*). This is different from Chinese naming practice where the family name comes before the given name (e.g., 曾鈺成, Jasper Tsang Yok-Sing).

For linguistic resources, apart from biblical names (e.g., *John* and *Mary*) and popular English first names from *Aaron* to *Zoe*, Li (1997) found that many Chinese Hongkongers' Western names were inspired by various sources:

- common English words, e.g., *Game, Man's, Rainy, Saturday, Windy*
- low-frequency English vocabulary, e.g., *Lithium, Rumple, Waddle*
- famous brand names, e.g., *Mercedes, Rolex, Volvo*
- one or more syllables in their Chinese given name, resulting in English-sounding names, e.g., *Kit, Ling, Wan, Yung*
- initials based on the first letters of the romanized Chinese given name, e.g., *C. Y.* (Chun-Ying), *K. K.* (Kwok-Keung)

Based on the results of a small-scale questionnaire survey, Li (1997) also found that it was quite common for the adoption of an English or English-sounding name to take place during the first two years of lower secondary school. Many Hong Kong students who studied in English-medium schools reported being encouraged or required by their teachers to adopt one, mainly to facilitate teaching and learning. Another interesting finding is that name-change (i.e., abandoning an old English name and adopting a new one) was rather common. Among the reasons were: difficult pronunciation, the old English name being no longer fashionable, the new name sounding better, and so forth. Li (1997) regards this popular practice as a special kind of borrowing. As names are intimately related to a person's identity, Li (1997) characterizes the popular practice of adopting an English or English-sounding name as acquiring a 'borrowed identity'.

Names are basic not only for self-identification but more crucially when they are used as terms of address in social interaction. For instance, the chief secretary for administration of the Hong Kong government is Mrs Carrie Lam Cheng Yuet-Ngor, whose name consists of the following elements:

[title + English name + husband's surname + maiden name + given name]

It is understandable why such an elaborate form is seldom heard in public media; rather, in English news stories, our chief secretary is more commonly referred to as (Mrs) Carrie Lam. In local Chinese news reports, she is usually referred to as 林太 (lam4 taai2, 'Mrs Lam', ['title + husband's surname']) or 林鄭月娥 (lam4 zeng6 jyut6 ngo4, [husband's surname + maiden name + given name]. In informal, chatty columns, however, she is often referred to as 林鄭 (lam4 zeng6, that is, ['husband's surname + maiden name']). English-speaking journalists, on the other hand, would often just call her Carrie. What is interesting is that, when interacting with Cantonese speakers, including protesters and journalists, she is often addressed by her English name, Carrie, resulting in the use of 'mixed code'. For example:

(7)   Carrie, 你點睇呀?
       Carrie, nei5 dim2 tai2 aa3?
       'Carrie, what do you think?'

It is very common for Hong Kong Chinese to address one another by their English (sounding) names, a practice which mirrors a society-wide preference among Hong Kong Chinese bilinguals, namely, to address one another using an English first name. But why? According to Li (1997), the main reason is that the Chinese given name, pronounced in an Anglicized manner, cannot function like an English first name. The reason is that addressing someone by his or her Chinese given name (e.g., Chi-lam) may be heard as downward rather than horizontal communication. Consider a name like 鄭月娥 (Cheng Yuet-Ngor). As a term of address, 'Yuet-Ngor' sounds like a parent or a teacher talking down to the addressee (i.e., [+ P, ± D], Scollon & Scollon, 1995; Li, 1997, pp. 504–505). On the other hand, the English-based first-name address system (e.g., Carrie) sounds more egalitarian [– P] while conveying a sense of solidarity [– D], which is thus ideal for speeding up the pace of getting acquainted (Scollon & Scollon, 1995). Such a system is especially common in North America (Louie, 1998). It is sufficient for one side of the new acquaintances to initiate a ritual-like invitation, such as 'please call me John', which is usually accepted and reciprocated. As noted by Fasold (1990) in his discussion of Brown and Ford's (1961) empirical insights regarding Americans' choice between first name (FN) address and title with last name (TLN) address:

[T]he difference between the two relationships for Americans is very small. Five minutes' conversation is often enough to move from a TLN relationship to a FN one. In my own experience, even five minutes will not be allowed to elapse if some relatively permanent basis for solidarity is beginning. For example, when employees first meet their co-workers or when a person who has just moved into a neighborhood meets the new neighbors, mutual FN is commonly exchanged as soon as the introductions are over. (Fasold, 1990, p. 8)

Many educated Chinese Hongkongers find this first-name (FN) address system so useful that they have no hesitation using it with their new Chinese acquaintances.

One important implication of the use of names as terms of address in intercultural communication is that, when interacting with other speakers of English, care should be taken not to initiate the FN address without first checking whether this would create discomfort to the addressee (see Scollon & Scollon, 1995, pp. 122–125 for more details).

Questions and activities

1.   Think of a context, and provide as many details as you can according to the SPEAKING model (Hymes, 1976). Then, let your group-mates guess what context it is. How useful is the SPEAKING model for generating the required information for defining a context?

2.   Think of the end of a court trial involving a criminal case, when the judge is about to reveal the verdict. What is usually said in English or Chinese (Cantonese or Mandarin)? What sorts of condition must be met for the pronouncement of the verdict to have its intended legal consequence? And, what does this example tell us about the 'felicity conditions' of a speech act?

3.   The Western concept of face was inspired by concerns for face in Chinese societies. Which Chinese expressions can you think of which are related to the (Western) concept of face? Can you work out their English 'equivalents'?

4.   Consider Brown and Levinson's (1987) distinction between 'positive face' and 'negative face'. Can you think of politeness strategies that may be used to attend to a person's (a) positive face needs, and (b) negative face needs? Illustrate your response with examples in each of the following scenarios:
     (i)   A friend of yours asks you to lend her/him $5,000 urgently.
     (ii)   A peer from the UK, a native speaker of English, invites you to work on a project together, but you are unsure whether to accept that invitation.

5.   Imagine you wish to ask two new friends to do you a favour, one a local classmate bilingual in Cantonese and English, the other a non-local, English-speaking classmate who speaks very little Cantonese. The stakes are high, so you would be very upset if your request is declined. How would you go about making that

request (i) in Cantonese, and (ii) in English? In either case, do you find it necessary to preface your request with a lot of face work? When framing your request in English, is there evidence of transfer of L1 information-sequencing norms to L2? Script your request in about 4–5 turns, and see which strategy you seem to prefer in giving you the best chance for the request to be accepted: inductive or deductive.

6.   Referring to Chen's (1993) findings, and based on your experience and observation, do you think mainland Chinese speakers of English today would reject a compliment when interacting with others in English? Why or why not?

7.   Recall the last time you received praise from different people. Did you accept or reject it? Did the maxim of modesty or 'self-praise avoidance' play any role at all? Why or why not?

8.   Imagine you are to introduce yourself to new acquaintances who are
      (a)   NSs of English, and
      (b)   other Chinese from the same L1 background as yours.
      How would you identify yourself by name? What advice does Li (1997) give for initiating first-name address with new English-speaking acquaintances? Why?

Further reading

How do we do things with language? What is meant by a 'speech act'? Austin's (1962) and Searle's (1969, 1979) works are classic and still have high reference value for those who wish to better understand the background to the emergence of the academic discipline 'pragmatics', or the study of language in use. Schmidt and Richards (1980) offer instructive examples how specific speech acts may be incorporated into the EAL curriculum. Dell Hymes's (1976) book is a good starting point for understanding what we mean by a context (see 'Ethnography of Speaking' http://tiemcenter.org/wp-content/uploads/sites/6/2012/05/Dell-Hymes-SPEAKING.pdf). To gain a more in-depth understanding of how bilingual interaction is influenced dynamically by 'contextualization cues', see Gumperz (1992). Lii-Shih (1994) is a highly readable introduction into politeness strategies in conversation. Bond and Hwang (1986) introduce the persuasive notion of face in Chinese societies from the social psychology perspective. For a discourse approach to 'intercultural communication', see Scollon and Scollon (1995) and Scollon et al. (2012).

Appendix

Members of the Fifth Legislative Council, retrieved from http://www.legco.gov.hk/general/english/members/yr12-16/biographies.htm. Notice that 52.8%, or 37 of the 70 Legislative Councillors—all Chinese Hongkongers—have adopted an English name (two English names in one case). Those legislative councillors who are also known by an English name are italicized.

President:

1.   *Hon Jasper TSANG Yok-sing, GBS, JP*

Members:

2.   *Hon Albert HO Chun-yan*
3.   Hon LEE Cheuk-yan
4.   *Hon James TO Kun-sun*
5.   Hon CHAN Kam-lam, SBS, JP
6.   Hon LEUNG Yiu-chung
7.   Dr Hon LAU Wong-fat, GBM, GBS, JP
8.   *Hon Emily LAU Wai-hing, JP*
9.   Hon TAM Yiu-chung, GBS, JP
10. *Hon Abraham SHEK Lai-him, GBS, JP*
11. *Hon Tommy CHEUNG Yu-yan, SBS, JP*
12. *Hon Frederick FUNG Kin-kee, SBS, JP*
13. *Hon Vincent FANG Kang, SBS, JP*
14. Hon WONG Kwok-hing, BBS, MH
15. *Prof Hon Joseph LEE Kok-long, SBS, JP, PhD, RN*
16. *Hon Jeffrey LAM Kin-fung, GBS, JP*
17. *Hon Andrew LEUNG Kwan-yuen, GBS, JP*
18. Hon WONG Ting-kwong, SBS, JP
19. *Hon Ronny TONG Ka-wah, SC*
20. *Hon Cyd HO Sau-lan, JP*
21. *Hon Starry LEE Wai-king, JP*
22. Dr Hon LAM Tai-fai, SBS, JP
23. Hon CHAN Hak-kan, JP
24. Hon CHAN Kin-por, BBS, JP
25. *Dr Hon Priscilla LEUNG Mei-fun, SBS, JP*
26. Dr Hon LEUNG Ka-lau
27. Hon CHEUNG Kwok-che
28. Hon WONG Kwok-kin, SBS
29. Hon IP Kwok-him, GBS, JP
30. *Hon Mrs Regina IP LAU Suk-yee, GBS, JP*
31. *Hon Paul TSE Wai-chun, JP*
32. *Hon Alan LEONG Kah-kit, SC*
33. Hon LEUNG Kwok-hung
34. *Hon Albert CHAN Wai-yip*
35. Hon WONG Yuk-man

36. *Hon Claudia MO*
37. *Hon Michael TIEN Puk-sun, BBS, JP*
38. *Hon James TIEN Pei-chun, GBS, JP*
39. Hon NG Leung-sing, SBS, JP
40. *Hon Steven HO Chun-yin*
41. *Hon Frankie YICK Chi-ming*
42. Hon WU Chi-wai, MH
43. Hon YIU Si-wing
44. *Hon Gary FAN Kwok-wai*
45. Hon MA Fung-kwok, SBS, JP
46. *Hon Charles Peter MOK, JP*
47. Hon CHAN Chi-chuen
48. Hon CHAN Han-pan, JP
49. *Dr Hon Kenneth CHAN Ka-lok*
50. Hon CHAN Yuen-han, SBS, JP
51. Hon LEUNG Che-cheung, BBS, MH, JP
52. *Hon Kenneth LEUNG*
53. *Hon Alice MAK Mei-kuen, JP*
54. Dr Hon KWOK Ka-ki
55. Hon KWOK Wai-keung
56. *Hon Dennis KWOK*
57. *Hon Christopher CHEUNG Wah-fung, SBS, JP*
58. *Dr Hon Fernando CHEUNG Chiu-hung*
59. Hon SIN Chung-kai, SBS, JP
60. *Dr Hon Helena WONG Pik-wan*
61. Hon IP Kin-yuen
62. *Dr Hon Elizabeth QUAT, JP*
63. *Hon Martin LIAO Cheung-kong, SBS, JP*
64. Hon POON Siu-ping, BBS, MH
65. Hon TANG Ka-piu, JP
66. Dr Hon CHIANG Lai-wan, JP
67. Ir Dr Hon LO Wai-kwok, BBS, MH, JP
68. Hon CHUNG Kwok-pan
69. *Hon Christopher CHUNG Shu-kun, BBS, MH, JP*
70. *Hon Tony TSE Wai-chuen, BBS*

Suggested Answers to Questions and Activities

1. Conversation Analysis, Error Analysis, and Cross-Linguistic Influence

1. There are many Chinese varieties or dialects within Greater China (mainland China, Taiwan, Hong Kong SAR, and Macao SAR). Most of these varieties are unintelligible to one another. Speakers of different varieties may find it difficult to communicate in their respective dialects. There is thus a need for a standard variety. This role is usually assigned to or performed by a 'national language' which, apart from being an important symbol of national identity, facilitates effective communication within its borders. In mainland China, the national language is called Modern Standard Chinese (MSC). In speech, MSC may be further specified as Putonghua (also known as Mandarin outside of China, *Guoyu* in Taiwan, and *Huayu* in Singapore), while the written standard is called Standard Written Chinese (SWC).

    Similarly, traditional English-speaking nations like the UK and the US are also linguistically extremely diverse. There is thus a similar need for a standard variety (e.g., BrE and AmE). For instance, in the UK, the way English is spoken by people in the south-eastern part of England was selected to be the standard. The selection of a particular variety to be the national standard is largely a sociopolitical process. Compared with local varieties or dialects, the national language is widely seen as being more prestigious. The selection process is usually dominated by people who are politically influential, wealthy, and better educated. That was the case with British English. It is therefore no accident that the received pronunciation (taught in school and used in public media such as the BBC) is also known as the Queen's English.

2. Cantonese, a Yue dialect widely spoken in Guangdong and Guangxi, is generally recognized as a regional dialect. Despite being a dialect and therefore 'non-standard', it is among the most prestigious Chinese variety in China. Many native speakers of Cantonese are under the false impression that Cantonese has no grammar. This is not true. Anyone who has any doubt about this may refer to scholarly works on Cantonese grammar such as Matthews and Yip (1994)

and Tang (2015). For instance, like MSC, Cantonese has its own classifiers and aspect markers.

3.   For historical reasons, there is no doubt that British English predominates in Hong Kong. This is evidenced by the fact that many of the civil servants, lawyers, and educators speak English with a BrE accent, partly as a result of pursuing higher education in the UK. In addition, the Hong Kong SAR government documents and textbooks continue to follow British spelling (e.g., *programme* instead of *program*). In school, the pedagogical model, from accent to lexico-grammatical usage patterns, continues to be BrE. The domains of business and media are two exceptions, however, largely because many of the Hong Kong Chinese professionals working in these two domains are returnees from the US or Canada (and, to a lesser extent, Australia) after completing their training there. Also, as the world becomes increasingly globalized and interconnected, access to other varieties of English such as American, Australian, or Canadian English is very convenient, not to mention TV programmes and video clips via YouTube and other social media.

4.   When we learn a new language (L2, e.g., English), say from age six, after we have acquired our first language (L1, e.g., Cantonese), our L1 knowledge (structures, markers, etc.) tends to influence the way we produce L2 output. This is called 'mother-tongue influence'. 'Negative transfer' results if the outcome of such influence is negative (i.e., non-standard features are produced). On the other hand, if the outcome is positive, we will speak of 'positive transfer'. A more neutral term is 'cross-linguistic influence' (CLI). In the process of learning English as a second or foreign language, many examples of CLI may be found.

2. Cantonese-English Contrastive Phonology

1.   (i)   bilabial
      (ii)   velar
      (iii)   alveolar
      (iv)   interdental
      (v)   labio-dental
2.   (i)   fricative
      (ii)   nasal
      (iii)   approximant
      (iv)   stop
      (v)   affricate
3.   (i)   鵰 (*diu1*): voiceless unaspirated onset [t], diphthong [iu]
              deal: voiced unaspirated onset, monophthong [i:], [l] as the coda

(ii) 風 (*fung1*): monophthong [ɔ] + velar nasal

phone: diphthong [oʊ] + alveolar nasal

(iii) 先 (*sin1*): [i]

sin: [i] (a lower vowel than [i])

(iv) 鋪 (*pou1*): no coda

poll: [l] as coda

(v) 蒸 (*zing1*): voiceless unaspirated alveolar affricate [ts] as onset, [i]

糕 (*gou1*): voiceless unaspirated onset [k], diphthong [oʊ], no coda

jingle: voiced unaspirated post-alveolar affricate [dʒ], [ɪ]. Voiced onset [g], monophthong [ə], [l] as coda

4. (i) consonant cluster

(ii) diphthong + coda

(iii) diphthong + coda

(iv) [r] as coda

3. Transitivity and Syntactic Structures

1. (i) *Borrow*: transitive. Example: *I borrowed a book. *I borrowed.*

(ii) *Wash*: transitive. Example: *I washed the car. *I washed.*

(iii) *Walk*: intransitive and transitive. Example: *I've walked a lot. I've walked the dog.*

(iv) *Trust*: transitive and intransitive (but only used with a prepositional phrase). Example: *I trust myself. She trusted in the power of justice. I trust you had a great journey. *I trust.*

(v) *Melt*: transitive and intransitive. Example: *The sun melted the ice. The ice melted.*

(vi) *Hang*: transitive and intransitive. Example: *I hung the picture. The picture was hanging on the wall.*

(vii) *Smile*: intransitive. Example: *I smiled (at her). *I smiled her.*

(viii) *Escape*: intransitive and transitive. Example: *I escaped from that building. I escaped the fire.*

2. (i) 踢: transitive. Example: 他踢毽子。*他踢了。

(ii) 委託: transitive. Example: 他委託陳先生為他處理事務。

(iii) 進去: transitive. Example: 他進去那房間。*他進去。

(iv) 死: intransitive. Example: 他死了。

(v) 開始: intransitive and transitive. Example: 表演開始了。他開始他的演奏。

(vi) 微笑: intransitive. Example: 他微笑。*他微笑她。

3. It might be slightly strange to call 死 a transitive verb, despite the fact that it can appear in the sentence 他死了父親, because semantically the act of dying

involves only one person. Despite being located at the beginning of the sentence, '他' does not function as the 'subject' of the sentence; rather, the 'Affectee' (not introduced in this book) would seem to be a more appropriate semantic role.

4. (i)   location
    (ii)   theme
    (iii) percept/patient
    (iv)   location
    (v)   instrument/theme
    (vi)   percept

5. *Worry* as a transitive verb. In a sentence like *John worries me*, *John* is the percept and *me* is the experiencer; that is, *John* made me feel anxious. The verb *worry* is often associated with the Chinese verb 擔心, which takes an experiencer as the subject and a percept as the object (i.e., the opposite of the English verb *worry*).

4. Passive Voice

1. Verbs that can be passivized: *think* (*He was thought to be . . .*), *call*, *notice*, *give*, *slip* (transitive) (*The bill was slipped under the mat*), *give*, *walk* (transitive) (*I was walked to my room by the manager of the hotel; this road has been walked on by thousands of people*).

2. Verbs that take one argument: *vanish*
    Verbs that take two arguments: *suit*, *frighten*, *flatter*, *lack*

3. No suggested answer.

4. 世界衛生組織在週二建議各國應規管電子香煙並禁制室內使用，直至證實其釋放的氣體對人無害。世衞亦呼籲各國應禁止商舖售賣含尼古丁氣體產品給未成年青年，及禁止或減少相應產品的廣告、推廣及贊助。這個以日內瓦為基地的組織指，全球電子香煙市場值高達 30 億，當中包括 400 個以上的品牌，固必須有適當的管制。報告亦指，要確立使用電子香煙影響的科學基礎，確保相關研究得以進行，公眾健康獲得保障，並令公眾認識電子香煙的潛在風險及好處，管制是必須的。

5. No suggested answer.

5. Tense and Aspect

1–3. No suggested answer.

4. Historical present is often used when a person recounts an event. Its use is mainly motivated by some 'immediacy' effect, as if the events being described are happening in front of our eyes. The following example is taken from Wolfson (1979, p. 171):

> Two years ago we were in Mexico, at Acapulco, and I called Mexico City and I asked for Juan. Now I've got to go through operators and I make it person-to-person. And the maid tells the operator in Spanish, and the operator tells me, 'He's not there.' I said, 'When will he be back?', and the maid and the operator are having this great big conversation. I keep getting the same answer. And finally the operator says to me, 'He's dead. He died. That's-he's not here. He died.' Well, I tell you, I was so upset. I said, 'Thank you,' and I hung up. I must have made that person-to-person call three times before the maid and the operator got together to try to explain to a person-to-person call that he was not there because he wasn't. But I was so upset and I couldn't find Maria's phone number in the telephone book.

5. The word 'unlocked' in 'the door is unlocked' is an adjective, and it describes the 'state' (as opposed to an action). The sentence thus describes a state in the present time. The word 'unlocked' in 'the door was unlocked' is a verb, and the sentence describes an action that happened in the past (e.g., someone put a key into the keyhole and turned the key).

6. Determiners: Articles and Demonstratives

1. 'The [2] young woman in this photograph is me when I was writing *The House on Mango Street*. She's in her office, a room that had probably been a child's bedroom when families lived in this apartment. It has no door and is only slightly wider than the [2] walk-in pantry. But it has great light and sits above the [2] hallway door downstairs, so she can hear her neighbors come and go. She posed as if she's just looked up from her work for a moment, but in real life she never writes in this office. She writes in the [2] kitchen, the [3] only room with a heater.'

2. 'a room that had probably . . .' = indefinite, classification
   'a child's bedroom . . .' = indefinite, classification
   'a moment' = indefinite
   'a heater' = indefinite

3. Noun phrases with no determiners: door', 'great light', 'real life'
   Other determiners: *this, her*

4. Definite: . . . 〔學校〕裡的校長，〔村子〕裡的大人們
   Indefinite: . . . 一車亮晶晶的煤塊，一個聰明的孩子

7. Subject-Prominence and Topic-Prominence

1. i.   I
   ii. English
   iii. The house

     iv.   Sam and Teresa

     v.   Jennifer

     vi.   The dog

     vii.   John F. Kennedy

2.   Examples may include: 庭院, 窗外, 鏡中

3.   像其他人一樣，埃迪在露比碼頭，一個位於海洋旁邊的遊樂場，度過了他人生最後的時光。這個遊樂場有遊樂場一般都有的玩意，如木板路、摩天輪、過山車、碰碰車、太妃糖檔、和射水入小丑口中的遊戲。遊樂場也有一個叫「弗雷迪的自由落體」的大型機動遊戲，而這個機動遊戲就是埃迪身亡的地方。整個州的所有報紙都將會報導這宗意外。

8. Europeanization: Influence of English on Chinese Grammar

1.   **Group 1: Translation method = Phonetic**

     i.   Watt, motor, ohm, volt

     ii.   jeep, nicotine, Vaseline, hysteria

     iii.   camera, inspiration, violin, guitar

    Group 2: Translation method = Semantic + phonetic

     iv.   Marxism, romanticism, mango, bar, beer

     v.   Sardine, jeep, vitamin, humour, model

     vi.   coffee powder, tank, sofa, Olympic village

2.   **Group 3: Semantic translation** (on the right) is clearly preferred to phonetic translation (on the left).

vii.	microphone	麥克風 (*mài kè fēng*)	擴音器 (*kuòyīnqì*)
viii.	economy	愛康諾米 (*ài kāng nuò mǐ*)	經濟 (*jīng jì*)
ix.	television	德律維雄 (*dé lǜ wéi xióng*)	電視 (*diàn shì*)
x.	democracy	德謨克拉西 (*dé mó kè lā xī*)	民主 (*mín zhǔ*)

3.   In English, there are more nouns denoting 'a person who . . .' that are formed with the suffixes -*er* and -*or* than there are nouns formed with other suffixes. The least productive is -*eer* (e.g., *engineer*). You may wish to google a few websites to confirm (keywords: 'words that end with'). In Chinese, apart from -家 (*jiā*/*gaa1*), -師 (*shī*/*si1*) and -者 (*zhě*/*ze2*) are high-frequency suffixes to render that meaning into Chinese.

4.   -生, -士, and -員 are among the more commonly used suffixes in Chinese for the meaning 'a person who . . .', among others.

5.   (a)   各位女士先生，總理和各與會代表

     (b)   他們已把心事告訴給神明，把一年來的罪過在神前取得了寬恕。於是他們像修完了一勝業，臉上帶著微笑，心裡更非常輕鬆。

     (c)   我們漸漸沒有這種受欺的度量，但也很欣快沒有這種奴隸的根性；我們正有自己的工作在，手段與目的是一致的！

(d)　停車在此

(e)　春節期間

(f)　這個問題，我們下次再談

(g)　她的決定，我們都很關注

(h)　我有問題，想跟你談談

(i)　日本是島國

(j)　應不應浪費掉，應提出來討論

(k)　那本書我喜歡

(l)　你，我愛／我愛你

(m)　紅樓夢我在讀／我在讀紅樓夢

(n)　當然不能算數

(o)　我完全明白了

(p)　我們是已註冊的團體

(q)　這有很多優點

(r)　她從來沒有承認

9. Being Chinese, Speaking English: Pragmatic Norms and Speaker Identity

1.　No suggested answer.

2.　Here is a concrete example: According to the report of a real court case, after analysing the validity of various types of evidence, the judge (Williams) proclaimed: 'Based on the evidence presented, this court finds that the state has not met its burden to prove beyond a reasonable doubt all required elements of the crimes charged. Therefore, *the verdict for each count is not guilty*.'[1] The suspect (Nero) was thereupon acquitted. For this verdict to take its intended effect, one important felicity condition is that it must be proclaimed by a judge, who is vested with the authority to make that decision or judgment. In addition, the verdict must be delivered in court, as part of the court trial (rather than, for example, during a visit in prison).

3.　'Face' (面子, *miàn zi/min6 zi2*); 'give someone face' (給臉, *gěi liǎn*; 畀面, *bei2 min2*); 'lose face' (丟臉, *diū liǎn/diu1 lim5*); 'have no face' (冇面, *mou5 min2*; 沒面子, *méi miàn zi*), 'shameless' (不要臉, *bú yào liǎn*; 唔要面, *m4 jiu3 min2*, 'no concern for face'), etc.

4.　No suggested answer.

5.　In general, the higher the stakes of your request, the more likely you would find it necessary to preface your request with some 'face work' (i.e., inductively).

1.　Full transcript: Judge Williams' ruling acquitting Officer Nero in Freddie Gray case (23 May 2016). *The Baltimore Sun*, emphasis added. Retrieved from http://www.baltimoresun.com/news/maryland/freddie-gray/bs-md-ci-williams-nero-transcript-20160523-story.html.

Saying anything that would remind the listener of your solidarity or friendship will help prepare him or her for that high-stake request.

6. Unlike university students during the 1990s, today's young people in mainland China have many more opportunities and experience interacting with Westerners. For this reason, it is possible that the American pattern of responding to compliments may be considered acceptable by mainland Chinese college students in the 2010s.

7. No suggested answer.

8. When communicating with a new acquaintance, Li (1997) cautions against initiating first-name address, especially one based on a Chinese speaker's given name, without first checking whether the interlocutor is likely to be receptive to this practice. A Chinese given name (e.g., Chor-Shing), when used like the equivalent of an English first name (e.g., David), is likely to be heard as downward communication (see Scollon & Scollon, 1995).

References

Adamson, B. (2002). Barbarian as a foreign language: English in China's schools. *World Englishes, 21*(2), 231–243.

Adamson, B. (2004). *China's English: A history of English in Chinese education*. Hong Kong: Hong Kong University Press.

Agar, M. (1991). The bicultural in bilingual. *Language in Society, 10*, 167–181.

Agar, M. (1994). *Language shock: Understanding the culture of conversation*. New York: William Morrow & Co.

Albom, M. (1997). *Tuesdays with Morrie*. New York: Doubleday.

Albom, M. (2003). *The five people you meet in heaven*. New York: Hyperion.

Andersen, R. W. (1991). Developmental sequences: The emergence of aspect marking in second language acquisition. In T. Huebner & C. A. Ferguson (Eds.), *Crosscurrents in second language acquisition and linguistic theories* (pp. 305–324). Amsterdam: John Benjamins.

Anderson, S. R., & Keenan, E. L. (1985). Deixis. In T. Shopen (Ed.), *Language typology and syntactic description III: Grammatical categories and the lexicon* (pp. 259–308). Cambridge: Cambridge University Press.

Ansaldo, U. (2009). *Contact languages: Ecology and evolution in Asia*. Cambridge: Cambridge University Press.

Ansaldo, U., Matthews, S., & Smith, G. (2012). China Coast Pidgin. In U. Ansaldo (Ed.), *Pidgins and creoles in Asia* (pp. 59–90). Amsterdam: John Benjamins.

Austin, J. L. (1962). *How to do things with words*. Oxford: Clarendon Press.

Beltrán, E. V. (2013). Requesting in English as a lingua franca: Proficiency effects in stay abroad. *Estudios de Lingüística Inglesa Aplicada (ELIA), 13*, 113–147.

Birner, B., & Ward, G. (1994). Uniqueness, familiarity, and the definite article in English. *Proceedings of the Twentieth Annual Meeting of the Berkeley Linguistics Society: General Session Dedicated to the Contributions of Charles J. Fillmore*, 93–102.

Bolton, K. (2000). The sociolinguistics of English in Hong Kong. *World Englishes, 19*(3), 265–285.

Bolton, K. (2003). *Chinese Englishes: A sociolinguistic history*. Cambridge: Cambridge University Press.

Bond, M. H., & Hwang, K.-K. (1986). The social psychology of Chinese people. In M. H. Bond (Ed.), *The psychology of the Chinese people* (pp. 213–266). New York: Oxford University Press.

Brinton, L. J., & Brinton, D. (2010). *The linguistic structure of modern English*. Amsterdam: John Benjamins.

Brown, A. (2014). *Pronunciation and phonetics: A practical guide for English language teachers.* New York: Routledge.

Brown, P., & Levinson, S. C. (1987). *Politeness: Some universals in language usage.* Cambridge: Cambridge University Press.

Brown, R., & Ford, M. (1961). Address in American English. *Journal of Abnormal and Social Psychology, 62,* 454–462. Reprinted in D. Hymes (Ed.) (1964), *Language and culture in society* (pp. 234–244). New York: Harper and Row.

Bunton, D. (1989). *Common English errors in Hong Kong.* Hong Kong: Longman.

Carnie, A. (2006). *Syntax: A generative introduction* (2nd edn.). Oxford: Wiley Blackwell.

Chan, A. Y. W. (2004). Syntactic transfer: Evidence from the interlanguage of Hong Kong Chinese ESL learners. *The Modern Language Journal, 88,* 56–74.

Chan, A. Y. W. (2006a). Strategies used by Cantonese speakers in pronouncing English initial consonant clusters: Insights into the interlanguage phonology of Cantonese ESL learners in Hong Kong. *IRAL Proceedings, 44,* 331–355.

Chan, A. Y. W. (2006b). Cantonese ESL learners' pronunciation of English final consonants. *Language, Culture and Curriculum, 19*(3), 296–312.

Chan, A. Y. W. (2006c). An algorithmic approach to error correction: An empirical study. *Foreign Language Annals, 39*(1), 131–147.

Chan, A. Y. W. (2010). An investigation into Cantonese ESL learners' acquisition of English initial consonant clusters. *Linguistics, 48*(1), 99–141.

Chan, A. Y. W., Kwan, B. S. C., & Li, D. C. S. (2003). Tackling the 'Independent Clause as Subject' problem. *Asian Journal of English Language Teaching, 13,* 107–117.

Chan, A. Y. W., & Li, D. C. S. (2000). English and Cantonese phonology in contrast: Explaining Cantonese ESL learners' English pronunciation problems. *Language, Culture & Curriculum, 13*(1), 67–85.

Chan, Y. H. (1993). 英語語法對香港中文的影響 [The influence of English syntax on Chinese usage in Hong Kong]. *Working Papers in Languages and Linguistics, 5,* pp. 135–145. Department of Chinese, Translation, and Linguistics, City Polytechnic of Hong Kong.

Chen, H. C. (2013). Chinese learners' acquisition of English word stress and factors affecting stress assignment. *Linguistics and Education, 24*(4), 545–555.

Chen, H. C. (2015). Acoustic analyses and intelligibility assessments of timing patterns among Chinese English learners with different dialect backgrounds. *Journal of Psycholinguistic Research, 44*(6), 749–773.

Chen, P. (1999). *Modern Chinese: History and sociolinguistics.* Cambridge: Cambridge University Press.

Chen, R. (1993). Responding to compliments: A contrastive study of politeness strategies between American English and Chinese speakers. *Journal of Pragmatics, 20,* 49–75.

Cheung, Y. K. [張宇傑]. (2011). *A critical study of Frederick Tsai's approaches to translation* (unpublished master's thesis). The University of Hong Kong, Hong Kong.

Chomsky, N. (1981). *Lectures on government and binding.* Dordrecht: Foris.

Clahsen, H., Felser, C., Neubauer, K., Sato, M., & Silva, R. (2010). Morphological structure in native and nonnative language processing. *Language Learning, 60*(1), 21–43.

Comrie, B. (1976). *Aspect.* Cambridge: Cambridge University Press.

Crystal, D. (1997). *The Cambridge encyclopedia of language.* Cambridge: Cambridge University Press.

DeKeyser, R. M. (2005). What makes learning second-language grammar difficult? A review of issues. *Language Learning, 55*(S1), 1–25.

Diessel, H. (2006). Demonstratives, joint attention, and the emergence of grammar. *Cognitive Linguistics, 17*(4), 463–489.

Duanmu, S. (2007). *The phonology of Standard Chinese* (2nd ed.). Oxford: Oxford University Press.

Edge, J. (1989). *Mistakes and correction*. London: Longman.

Fasold, R. W. (1990). *The sociolinguistics of language*. Oxford: Blackwell.

Fishman, J. A. (1965). Who speaks what language to whom and when? *La Linguistique, 2*, 67–88. Reprinted in W. Li (Ed.) (2007), *The bilingualism reader* (2nd ed.) (pp. 55–70). London: Routledge.

Frawley, W. (1992). *Linguistic semantics*. Hillsdale, NJ: Lawrence Erlbaum.

Gass, S. M., & Selinker, L. (2008). *Second language acquisition: An introductory course* (3rd ed.). New York: Routledge.

Goffman, E. (1955). On facework: An analysis of ritual elements in social interaction. *Psychiatry, 18*, 213–231.

Green, C. (1991). Typological transfer, discourse accent and the Chinese writer of English. *Hongkong Papers in Linguistics and Language Teaching, 14*, 51–63.

Gumperz, J. J. (1992). Contextualization and understanding. In A. Duranti & C. Goodwin (Eds.), *Rethinking context* (pp. 229–252). Cambridge: Cambridge University Press.

Gundel, J. K. (1988). Universals of topic-comment structure. In M. Hammond, E. Moravcsik, & J. Wirth (Eds.), *Studies in syntactic typology* (pp. 209–239). Amsterdam: John Benjamins.

Hale, K., & Keyser, J. (2013). Some transitivity alternations in English. *Anuario del Seminario de Filología Vasca "Julio de Urquijo"* [International Journal of Basque Linguistics and Philology], *20*(3), 605–638.

Halle, M. (1973). Stress rules in English: A new version. *Linguistic Inquiry, 4*(4), 451–464.

Hartmann, R. R. K., & Stork, F. C. (1972). *Dictionary of language and linguistics*. London: Applied Science.

Haspelmath, M. (1990). The grammaticization of passive morphology. *Studies in Language, 14*(1), 25–72.

Hawkins, J. A. (1991). On (in)definite articles: Implicatures and (un)grammaticality prediction. *Journal of Linguistics, 27*(2), 405–442.

Hopper, P. J., & Thompson, S. A. (1980). Transitivity in grammar and discourse. *Language, 56*, 251–299.

Hou, W. [侯維瑞] (1992). 英國英語與美國英語 [British English and American English]. Shanghai: Shanghai Foreign Language Education Press.

Hsu, J.-L. (1994). Englishization and language change in modern Chinese in Taiwan. *World Englishes, 13*(2), 167–184.

Hung, T. (2002). Towards a phonology of Hong Kong English. In K. Bolton (Ed.), *Hong Kong English: Autonomy and creativity* (pp. 119–140). Hong Kong: Hong Kong University Press.

Hymes, D. (1976). *Foundations in sociolinguistics: An ethnographic approach* (8th ed.). Philadelphia: University of Pennsylvania Press.

International Phonetic Association. (2015). Retrieved from https://www.internationalphonetic association.org/.

Jackendoff, R. (1990). *Semantic structures*. Cambridge, MA: MIT Press.

James, C. (1980). *Contrastive analysis*. London: Longman.

James, C. (1998). *Errors in language learning and use: Exploring error analysis*. Harlow, UK: Pearson Education.

Jia, Y., & Cheng, C. (2002). Indirectness in Chinese English writing. *Asian Englishes, 5*(1), 64–74.

Kasper, G., & Rose, K. R. (2002). *Pragmatic development in a second language.* Malden, MA: Blackwell.

Kellerman, E. (1995). Crosslinguistic influence: Transfer to nowhere? *Annual Review of Applied Linguistics, 15,* 125–150.

Kirkpatrick, A. (1991). Information sequencing in Mandarin in letters of request. *Anthropological Linguistics, 33*(2), 1–20.

Kirkpatrick, A. (1993). Information sequencing in Modern Standard Chinese. *Australian Review of Applied Linguistics, 16*(2), 27–60.

Kirkpatrick, A., & Xu, Z. (2012). *Chinese rhetoric and writing: An introduction for language teachers.* Fort Collins, CO: The WAC Clearinghouse.

Kleiser, G. (2008). *Exploring English grammar.* New Delhi: A. P. H. Publishing.

Kong, K. C. C. (1998a). Are simple business request letters really simple? A comparison of Chinese and English business request letters. *Text & Talk, 18,* 103–141.

Kong, K. C. C. (1998b). Politeness of service encounters in Hong Kong. *Pragmatics, 8*(4), 555–575.

Kong, K. C. C. (2006). Accounts as a politeness strategy in the internal directive documents of a business firm in Hong Kong. *Journal of Asian Pacific Communication, 16*(1), 77–101.

Kwan, B. S. C., Chan, A. Y. W., & Li, D. C. S. (2003). 'According to the expert, he said . . .': A consciousness-raising approach to helping Cantonese speakers overcome problems in topic-comment structures. *Asia Pacific Journal of Language in Education, 5*(2), 87–94.

Lado, R. (1957). *Linguistics across cultures: Applied linguistics for language teachers.* Ann Arbor, MI: University of Michigan Press.

Ladefoged, P. (2001). *A course in phonetics* (4th ed.). Boston, MA: Heinle & Heinle.

Ladefoged, P. (2009). American English. *Handbook of the IPA.* Cambridge: Cambridge University Press.

Lambrecht, K. (1994). *Information structure and sentence form: Topic, focus and the mental representations of discourse referents.* Cambridge: Cambridge University Press.

Langacker, R. W. (1982). Remarks on English aspect. In P. J. Hopper (Ed.), *Tense-aspect: Between semantics & pragmatics* (pp. 265–304). Amsterdam: John Benjamins.

LaPolla, R. J. (2009). Chinese as a topic-comment (not topic-prominent and not SVO) language. In J. Xing (Ed.), *Studies of Chinese linguistics: Functional approaches* (pp. 9–22). Hong Kong: Hong Kong University Press.

Lee, K. S., & Tse, Y. K. [李家樹、謝耀基] (1994). 漢語的特性和運用 [The characteristics and use of Chinese]. Hong Kong: Hong Kong University Press.

Lee, S., & Li, D. C. S. (2013). Multilingualism in Greater China and the Chinese language diaspora. In T. K. Bhatia, & W. C. Ritchie (Eds.), *Wiley-Blackwell handbook of bilingualism and multilingualism* (pp. 813–842). Malden, MA: Blackwell.

Levin, B. (1993). *English verb classes and alternations: A preliminary investigation.* Chicago, IL: University of Chicago Press.

Levin, B., & Rappaport Hovav, M. (1995). *Unaccusativity: At the syntax–lexical semantics interface.* Cambridge, MA: The MIT Press.

Li, C. N., & Thompson, S. A. (2009). *Mandarin Chinese: A functional reference grammar.* Taipei: The Crane Publishing.

Li, D. C. S. (1997). Borrowed identity: Signaling involvement with a Western name. *Journal of Pragmatics, 28*, 489–513.

Li, D. C. S. (1998). Incorporating L1 pragmatic norms and cultural values in L2: Developing English language curriculum for EIL in the Asia-Pacific region. *Asian Englishes, 1*(1), 31–50.

Li, D. C. S. (2000). Hong Kong English: New variety of English or interlanguage? *English Australia Journal, 18*(1), 50–59.

Li, D. C. S. (2002). Pragmatic dissonance: The ecstasy and agony of speaking *like* a native speaker of English. In D. C. S. Li (Ed.), *Discourses in search of members: In honor of Ron Scollon* (pp. 559–593). New York: University Press of America.

Li, D. C. S. (2006). Chinese as a lingua franca in Greater China. *Annual Review of Applied Linguistics, 26*, 149–176.

Li, D. C. S. (2007). Researching and teaching China and Hong Kong English: Issues, problems and prospects. *English Today, 23*(3&4), 11–17.

Li, D. C. S. (2011). 'Perfective paradox': A cross-linguistic study of the aspectual functions of *-guo* in Mandarin Chinese. *Chinese Language and Discourse, 2*(1), 23–57.

Li, D. C. S. (2015). Lingua francas in Greater China. In W. S. Y. Wang & C. F. Sun (Eds.), *Oxford Handbook of Chinese Linguistics* (pp. 578–588). Oxford: Oxford University Press.

Li, D. C. S. (2017). *Multilingual Hong Kong: Languages, literacies and identities*. Cham, Switzerland: Springer.

Li, D. C. S., & Chan, A. Y. W. (1999). Helping teachers correct structural and lexical English errors. *Hong Kong Journal of Applied Linguistics, 4*(1), 79–101.

Li, D. C. S., & Chan, A. Y. W. (2001). Form-focused negative feedback: Correcting three common errors. *TESL Reporter, 34*, 22–34.

Li, D. C. S., Chan, A. Y. W., & Kwan, B. S. C. (2002). Common errors and their correction. http://personal.cityu.edu.hk/~encrproj/error_types.htm.

Li, D. C. S., Keung, S., Poon, H. F., & Xu, Z. (2016). Learning Cantonese as an additional language (CAL) or not: What the CAL learners say. *Global Chinese, 2*(1), 1–22.

Li, D. C. S., & Lee, S. (2004). Bilingualism in East Asia. In T. K. Bhatia & W. C. Ritchie (Eds.), *The handbook of bilingualism* (pp. 742–779). Malden, MA: Blackwell.

Li, P., & Bowerman, M. (1998). The acquisition of lexical and grammatical aspect in Chinese. *First Language, 18*(54), 311–350.

Li, P., & Shirai, Y. (2000). *The acquisition of lexical and grammatical aspect*. Berlin: Mouton de Gruyter.

Liberman, M. (2009). Language Log. 16 March. Retrieved from http://languagelog.ldc.upenn.edu/nll/?p=1242.

Lii-Shih, Y.-H. E. (1994). *Conversational politeness and foreign language teaching* [語言禮貌與外語教學]. Taipei: The Crane Publishing.

Littlewood, W. (1984). Foreign and second language learning: Language acquisition research and its implications for the classroom. Cambridge: Cambridge University Press.

Liu, M. [劉宓慶] (2006). 新編漢英對比與翻譯 [Chinese-English contrast and translation: A new edition]. Beijing: China Translation & Publishing Corporation.

Lo Bianco, J., Orton, J., & Gao, Y. (Eds.) (2009). *China and English: Globalization and the dilemmas of identity*. Bristol, UK: Multilingual Matters.

Lock, G. (1996). *Functional English grammar: An introduction for second language teachers*. Cambridge: Cambridge University Press.

Longman Dictionary of Contemporary English. (n.d.). Retrieved from http://www.ldoceonline. com/.

Louie, E. W. (1998). *Chinese American names: Tradition and transition.* Jefferson, NC: McFarland & Co.

Luk, Z. P. S., & Shirai, Y. (2009). Is the acquisition order of grammatical morphemes impervious to L1 knowledge? Evidence from the acquisition of plural *-s*, articles, and possessive *'s. Language Learning, 59*(4), 721–754.

Matthews S., & Yip, V. (1994). *Cantonese: A comprehensive grammar.* London: Routledge.

McBride, C. (2016). *Children's literacy development: A cross-cultural perspective on learning to read and write* (2nd ed.). Abingdon, Oxon: Routledge.

Newbrook, M. (1991). *Exploring English errors: Grammar, vocabulary, pronunciation* (Vols. 1 & 2). Hong Kong: Oxford University Press.

Norman, J. (1988). *Chinese.* New York: Cambridge University Press.

Norrish, J. (1983). *Language learners and their errors.* London: Macmillan Press.

Oishi, E. (2006). Austin's speech act theory and the speech situation. *Esercizi Filosofici, 1,* 1–14. Retrieved from http://www.univ.trieste.it/~eserfilo/art106/oishi106.pdf.

Paradis, M. (2004). *A neurolinguistic theory of bilingualism.* Amsterdam: John Benjamins.

Pinkham, J. (2000). *The translator's guide to Chinglish* [中式英語之鑒]. Beijing: Foreign Language Teaching and Research Press.

Pullum, G. (2011). Language Log. 24 January. Retrieved from http://languagelog.ldc.upenn. edu/nll/?p=2922.

Radden, G. (2007). *Cognitive English grammar.* Amsterdam: John Benjamins.

Ramsey, S. R. (1987). *The languages of China.* Princeton, NJ: Princeton University Press.

Richards, J. C. (1971). A non-contrastive approach to error analysis. *English Language Teaching Journal, 25,* 204–219.

Richards, J. C. (1973). Error analysis and second language strategies. In J. W. Oller & J. C. Richards (Eds.), *Focus on the learner: Pragmatic perspectives for the language teacher* (pp. 114–135). Rowley, MA: Newbury House.

Richards, J. C. (1974). *Error analysis: Perspectives on second language acquisition.* London: Longman.

Richards, J. C., Platt, J., & Weber, H. (1985). *Longman dictionary of applied linguistics.* Harlow, UK: Longman.

Ringbom, H. (1987). *The role of the first language in foreign language learning.* Clevedon, UK: Multilingual Matters.

Ringbom, H. (2007). *Cross-linguistic similarity in foreign language learning.* Clevedon, UK: Multilingual Matters.

Roberts, C. (2003). Uniqueness in definite noun phrases. *Linguistics and philosophy, 26*(3), 287–350.

Robins, R. H. (1964). *General linguistics: An introductory survey.* London: Longmans, Green and Co., Ltd.

Robison, R. E. (1990). The primacy of aspect. *Studies in Second Language Acquisition, 12*(3), 315–330.

Rogers, H. (2000). *The sounds of language: An introduction to phonetics.* Harlow, UK: Pearson.

Rowling, J. K. (1998). *Harry Potter and the sorcerer's stone.* New York: Scholastic.

Saeed, J. I. (2003). *Semantics* (2nd ed.). Malden, MA: Blackwell.

Sasse, H.-J. (2002). Recent activity in the theory of aspect: Accomplishments, achievements, or just non-progressive state? *Linguistic Typology, 6,* 199–271.

Schachter, J. (1974). An error in error analysis. *Language Learning, 24*(2), 205–214.

Schachter, J., & Celce-Murcia, M. (1977). Some reservations concerning error analysis. *TESOL Quarterly, 11*, 441–451.

Schmidt, R. W., & Richards, J. C. (1980). Speech acts and second language learning. *Applied Linguistics, 1*(2), 129–157.

Scollon, R., & Scollon, S. W. (1983). Face in interethnic communication. In J. C. Richards & R. W. Schmidt (Eds.), *Language and communication* (pp. 156–189). London: Longman.

Scollon, R., & Scollon, S. W. (1995). *Intercultural communication: A discourse approach*. Oxford, UK: Blackwell.

Scollon, R., Scollon, S. B. K., & Jones, R. H. (2012). *Intercultural communication: A discourse approach* (3rd ed.). Malden, MA: Wiley-Blackwell.

Seargeant, P. (2012). *Exploring World Englishes: Language in a global context*. Abingdon, Oxon; New York: Routledge.

Seargeant, P., & Swann, J. (Eds.). (2012). *English in the world: History, diversity, change*. Abingdon, Oxon: Routledge.

Searle, J. R. (1969). *Speech acts*. Cambridge: Cambridge University Press.

Searle, J. R. (1979). *Expression and meaning*. Cambridge: Cambridge University Press.

Selinker, L. (1972). Interlanguage. *International Review of Applied Linguistics, 10*(3), 209–241.

Shi, D. (1997). Issues on Chinese passive. *Journal of Chinese linguistics, 25*(1), 41–70.

Shibatani, M. (1991). Grammaticization of topic into subject. In E. C. Traugott & B. Heine (Eds.), *Approaches to grammaticalization (Vol. 2): Focus on types of grammatical markers* (pp. 93–133). Amsterdam: John Benjamins.

Shirai, Y. (1991). *Primacy of aspect in language acquisition: Simplified input and prototype* (unpublished doctoral dissertation). University of California, Los Angeles.

Stowell, T. (1991). Determiners in NP and DP. In K. Leffel & D. Bouchard (Eds.), *Views on phrase structure* (pp. 37–56). Netherlands: Springer.

Tai, J. H. Y. (1985). Temporal sequence and word order in Chinese. In J. Haiman (Ed.), *Iconicity in syntax* (pp. 49–72). Amsterdam: John Benjamins.

Tang, S.-W. [鄧思穎]. (2015). 粵語語法講義 [An outline of Cantonese grammar]. Hong Kong: Commercial Press.

Tang, S. W., Fan, K., Lee, H. T., Lun, S., Luke, K. K., Tung, C. S., & Cheung, K. H. [鄧思穎、范國、李行德、藺蓀、陸鏡光、童哲生、張群顯] (2002). 粵語拼音字表 [JyutPing romanized word list] (2nd ed.). Hong Kong: Linguistic Society of Hong Kong.

Thomas, J. (1983). Cross-cultural pragmatic failure. *Applied Linguistics, 4*(2), 91–112.

Thompson, S. A. (1987). The passive in English: A discourse perspective. In R. Channon (Ed.), *In honor of Ilse Lehiste* (pp. 497–512). Dordrecht, The Netherlands: Foris Publications.

Tomasello, M. (1995). Joint attention social cognition. In C. Moore & P. Dunham (Eds.), *Joint attention: Its origins and role in development* (pp. 103–130). New York: Psychology Press.

Trudgill, P., & Hannah, J. (1994). *International English: A guide to varieties of standard English*. London & New York: Edward Arnold.

Tsai, Frederic [思果] (1982). 翻譯新究 [New studies in translation]. Taipei: Vast Plain Publishing House.

Tsai, Frederic [思果] (1987). 翻譯研究 [A study of translation]. Taipei: Vast Plain Publishing House.

Tsai, Frederic [思果] (2002). 譯道探微 [Exploring the nuts and bolts of translation]. Beijing: China Translation & Publishing Corporation.

Tse, Y. K. [謝耀基] (1990). 現代漢語歐化語法概論 [Introduction to Europeanization in modern Chinese]. Hong Kong: Kwong Ming Bookstore.

Tse, Y. K. [謝耀基] (2001). 漢語語法歐化綜述 [Europeanization of Chinese grammar: A summary]. 語文研究 [Study of language], *78*(1), 17–22.

Tsunoda, T. (1985). Remarks on transitivity. *Journal of Linguistics, 21*, 385–396.

van Dijk, M. (2006). *Let us prey.* Bloomington, IN: AuthorHouse.

van Dyke, P. A. (2005). *The Canton trade: Life and enterprise on the China coast, 1700–1845.* Hong Kong: Hong Kong University Press.

Wang, J. [王菊泉] (2012). 漢語特點與歐化譯文的改造 [Characteristics of the Chinese language and the refashioning of Europeanized translations]. In W. Pan [潘文國] (Ed.), 英漢對比與翻譯 [Contrastive and translation studies of English and Chinese] (pp. 33–56). Shanghai: Shanghai Foreign Language Education Press.

Wang, L. [王力]. (1958a). 中國現代語法 [Modern Chinese grammar]. Beijing: Commercial Press.

Wang, L. [王力]. (1958b). 漢語史稿 [A historical introduction to Chinese]. Beijing: Kexue chubanshe.

Webster, M., & Lam, W. C. P. (1991). Further notes on the influence of Cantonese on the English of Hong Kong students. In D. Bunton, & D. Allison (Eds.), *Institute of Language in Education Journal, Special Issue No. 2: English usage in Hong Kong* (pp. 35–42). Hong Kong: Education Department.

Widdowson, H. G. (2003). *Defining issues in English language teaching.* Oxford: Oxford University Press.

Wolfson, N. (1979). The conversational historical present alternation. *Language, 55*(1), 168–182.

Wu, Y., & Bodomo, A. (2009). Classifiers ≠ determiners. *Linguistic Inquiry, 40*(3), 487–503.

Xiao, R., & McEnery, T. (2004). *Aspect in Mandarin Chinese: A corpus-based study.* Amsterdam: John Benjamins.

Yip, V. (1995). *Interlanguage and learnability: From Chinese to English.* Amsterdam: John Benjamins.

Yip, V., & Matthews, S. (1995). I-interlanguage and typology: The case of topic-prominence. In L. Selinker, M. S. Smith, & L. Eubank (Eds.), *Current state of interlanguage* (pp. 17–30). Amsterdam: John Benjamins.

Yip, V., & Matthews, S. (2007). *The bilingual child: Early development and language contact.* Cambridge: Cambridge University Press.

Yiu, H. (1992). 病句診症室 [Wrong sentences diagnosed]. Hong Kong: Joint Publishing.

Yu, G. [余光中]. (1979). 從西而不化到西而化之 [From odd Westernization to smooth Westernization]. *Ming Pao Monthly* [明報月刊], *8*(164).

Yu, G. [余光中]. (1987). 怎樣改進英式中文？—論中文的常態與變態 [How to improve Anglicized Chinese? On what is normal and abnormal in Chinese]. *Ming Pao Monthly* [明報月刊], October, pp. 1–12.

Yu, G. [余光中]. (2002). 余光中談翻譯 [Yu Guangzhong on translation]. Beijing: China Translation & Publishing Corporation.

Yuan, B. (1997). Asymmetry of null subjects and null objects in Chinese speakers' L2 English. *Studies in Second Language Acquisition, 19*, 467–497.

Zee, E. (2009). Chinese (Cantonese). *Handbook of the IPA.* Cambridge: Cambridge University Press.

Zhang, Z. [張振江]. (2009). *Language and society in early Hong Kong (1841–1884)* [早期香港的社會和語言：1841–1884]. Zhongshan: Zhongshan University Press.

Zhao, Y. [趙元任]. (1982). 國語語法——中國話的文法 [A grammar of spoken Chinese]. Taipei: Xuehai chubanshe.

Zobl, H. (1989). Canonical typological structures and ergativity in English L2 acquisition. In S. M. Gass & J. Schachter (Eds.), *Linguistic perspectives on second language acquisition* (pp. 203–221). Cambridge: Cambridge University Press.

冰心，《閑情》（1988）。取自應屆畢業生網站；http://wenxue.yjbys.com/bingxin/69559.html，2016 年 4 月 26 日。

李廣田。《花潮》。取自王朝網絡；http://tc.wangchao.net.cn/baike/detail_1112192.html，2016 年 4 月 26 日。

莫言，《蒼蠅·門牙》。台北：麥田出版，2005，頁 5。

衛斯理，《新年》。香港：明窗出版社，1997，頁 2。

葉紹鈞。《以畫為喻》。取自百度文庫；http://wenku.baidu.com/view/368ed7765901020207409ca7.html?re=view，2016年4月26日。

朱自清。《背影》。取自互動百科網站；http://www.baike.com/wiki/背影，2016 年 4 月 26 日。

About the Authors

David C. S. Li is a professor and head of the Department of Chinese and Bilingual Studies (CBS) at the Hong Kong Polytechnic University. He obtained his BA in English (Hong Kong), MA in applied linguistics (France), and PhD in linguistics (Germany). He has published in contrastive aspectology (tense and aspect), World Englishes, 'Hong Kong English', 'China English', bilingual interaction and code-switching (translanguaging), multilingualism in Greater China, Chinese learners' EFL learning difficulties and error-correction strategies, Cantonese as an additional language in Hong Kong, and South Asian Hongkongers' needs for written Chinese.

Zoe Pei-sui Luk is an assistant professor in the Department of Linguistics and Modern Language Studies at the Education University of Hong Kong. She obtained her BA in Japanese studies (the Chinese University of Hong Kong) and her MA and PhD in linguistics (University of Pittsburgh). She has published journal articles and book chapters on various topics in language acquisition, including the influence of a first language on second language acquisition, the development of tense-aspect marking in bilingual children, and typological differences between languages and their effect on language acquisition.

Index